GETTING THE WORD OUT

GETTING THE WORD OUT

How to Communicate the Gospel in Today's World

THEODORE BAEHR

1817

Harper & Row, Publishers, San Francisco

Cambridge, Hagerstown, New York, Philadelphia, Washington
London, Mexico City, São Paulo, Singapore, Sydney

FIRST EDITION

Library of Congress Cataloging-in-Publication Data

Baehr, Theodore.
    Getting the Word Out.

    1. Communication (Theology)   2. Mass media in
religion.   I. Title.
BV4319.B24   1986   260   86-45346
ISBN 0-06-060326-7

---

86 87 88 89 90 RRD 10 9 8 7 6 5 4 3 2 1

This book is dedicated to Jesus,
and to Lili, Bruce, and I. E. Theodore,
with love and great
thanksgiving.

Do your best to present yourself to God as one approved, a workman who does not need to be ashamed and who correctly handles the word of truth.

2 Timothy 2:15

Father in Heaven,

Thank you for giving us good news to proclaim—the news of new life available to each of us through your Son, Jesus the Christ. Thank you for your Holy Spirit, our Teacher. Bless all who read this book. Grant us, as your people, the ability to communicate your truth more effectively to the world through all the media. Help us to reveal your Word to those in need. Help us to lift up your Holy Name, Jesus, through the power of your Holy Spirit. Amen.

Contents

Acknowledgments

I want to thank: Roy, Victor, Peirce, James, John, Hagan, Jim, Philippa, Jane, Steve, Jack, Linda, Ken, Karen, Tish, Terry, Michael, Dottie, Dick, Carol, Grey, Fred, Bill, Larry, Chuck, Sonia, Randy, Denny, Ryner, Ralph, Jim, Jean, Loomis, Prof. Scott-Craig, Bob, Shorty, Charles, Kathy, Trudy, Tom, Joan, Ray, Gary, Audrey, Whitney, Alexis, Larry, Lou, Peter, Dick, Ralph, Thetis, Margaret Ann, Frank, George, Andre, Jay, Bill, Dave, Connie, Catherine, Rick, Hank, Kathy, directors, supporters, friends, and, most of all, Evelyn.

Introduction

What is your goal? Success? Good relationships? Obedience to God and his great commission? Whatever it is, you must be able to communicate effectively to achieve it.

In the summer of 1981, I was invited to Knoxville, Tennessee, by nine local churches, representing different denominations, to consult on the design of an exhibit that would communicate their presence and biblical views to the many people who would visit the 1982 World's Fair. About thirty consultants, media experts, and theologians from throughout the United States came to advise the Knoxville churches on their exhibit. The theme of the fair was energy, so the prevailing opinion of those present was that the exhibit should contain posters illustrating energy (e.g., a power plant, an engine, an atomic bomb), with biblical captions (e.g., "Blessed are the peacemakers," Matt. 5:9; "Blessed are the poor," Luke 6:20; and "The land is mine and you are but aliens and my tenants," Lev. 25:23).

This approach sounded very dull. As the meeting continued, I recalled the 1964 World's Fair in New York City, where almost all the exhibits had long waiting lines except the Protestant exhibit, which consisted of posters with biblical captions.* I reasoned that people come to a world's fair to be entertained by a visionary exhibit that captures their imagination. If the churches wanted to attract people to their exhibit, they should use the latest technology and the best creative talent to build the most exciting exhibit at the fair.

---

*Years later I found out that there was an excellent film at the Protestant exhibit, but at the time of the New York fair, the existence of that film was hidden from some of the visitors by the solemn atmosphere of the primary room, which was the first room a visitor entered.

The churches asked me to be executive producer of the exhibit, which we named "The Power." In prayer, God gave me a vision of an exciting Disneyland type exhibit that presented God as the Author of all energy—"The Power." A month of meetings with creative talent focused this vision: the audience would step into a time-rocket, blast off back to the beginning of time; find themselves plunged into total darkness; watch God create the heavens and the earth; land in paradise; get kicked out for disobedience; enter into the human world; become overwhelmed by the cacophony of voices competing for attention; cry out for help; meet Jesus; follow him though the cross into his Body (the Church), where they could be filled with his Spirit, to do his work; and finish by singing "The Lord's Prayer" together.

After months of hard work by a wide range of the top craftspeople from the electronic media and show business, "The Power" became a reality—the most technologically sophisticated exhibit at the fair, visited by over a million people and representing the combined statement of fifteen Christian denominations. Newspapers from all over the United States called "The Power" the most exciting exhibit at the fair, and children of all ages enjoyed this trip through time and space.

The churches, acting together as the communicator, made "The Power" possible by adhering to the basic principles of good communications. They *asked the right questions* to determine

What they wanted to communicate
What their forum and marketplace was
Who their audience was
What the appropriate genre (or format) was
What the appropriate medium was
What the grammar and language of the appropriate genre and medium were

In this process, they discovered that sometimes "hands on," do-it-yourself production (such as posters) is not as effective as "hands off" production, in which the communicator discerns what his or her talents and gifts are and brings on board the appropriate, professional talent to complement, or supplement, them.

The churches wanted to communicate their presence and their biblical views to the World's Fair visitors—that was their goal. They succeeded. Moreover, after the fair closed, "The Power" was purchased by the Media Ministry of the Missionary Oblates to be displayed permanently at the National Shrine of Our Lady of the Snows in Belleville, Illinois, just outside St. Louis, Missouri. Through this permanent display, the churches will continue to present their message to people for years to come.

This story has a happy ending; however, not all our communications succeed in doing what we want them to do. Sometimes they fail because of circumstances beyond our control. (As one of Murphy's laws reminds us, If you explain something so clearly that no one can misunderstand, someone will.) Often they fail because we have failed to ask the right questions—out of laziness, impatience, or fear. We are sometimes too much like the solipsist, incapable of knowing anything except ourselves, believing that we are all there is and everything else is a part of us.

God has given each of us, as human beings created in his Image, the ability to communicate, and we must work to develop that God-given ability. Most of us do it fairly well and take our ability for granted. However, "Jesus came . . . preaching" (Mark 1:14), and spent three years preparing his followers to preach "the gospel of the kingdom of God" (Mark 1:14). We must continually apply ourselves in humility to perfecting our ability to deliver his good news, confident that his Holy Spirit communicates through us.

Several years ago I was discussing the eternal academic question—how do we educate today's rebellious students?—with a graduate professor of business. He told me about an intelligent, attractive student of his who refused to speak English, preferring to use slang. Graduation was fast approaching, so the professor took the student aside and explained that one cannot succeed in the business world unless one learns to speak its language. Unfortunately, this is not an isolated incident. Recently, 80 percent of the entering class at one of the country's largest universities did not pass the basic reading and writing skills examinations. There is no reason for us to relive the story of Babel—without good communication it is impossible to build a society.*

For Christians, effective communication means much more than achieving one's goals, desires, and needs; it is at the heart of God's story, and we have been called to tell that story. His story begins: "In the beginning *was* the Word" (John 1:1, KJV). That Word of God is Jesus the Christ, the Son of God, the great communicator.

Ever since the Fall, his story continues, the Word of God has been in the business of rescuing people, created in his image, from death; and he has called us to help him. As Jesus says, "You will receive power when the Holy Spirit comes on you; and you *will be* my witnesses" (Acts 1:8).

We want to proclaim his gospel because we love him and because we love our neighbor so much that we want to save our neighbor from death. Our witnessing is a direct, natural, inevitable consequence of our becoming and being Christians. Filled with power, we will witness. However, how effective is our witness?

In this regard, God is primarily interested in our character so that we can witness in *word and deed* to his salvation. He is interested in us as individuals and our testimony to others. He is not interested in the survival of our civilizations or monuments or in our other achievements. (Note the story of Jonah and, for that matter, the story of the seven churches in chapters 2 and 3 of the Revelation of St. John the Divine.) You

---

*The story of Babel points out that, from God's perspective, as long as human beings had one language there was nothing they could not do. So God confounded their language. Confounding our language was all God had to do to stop the building of the tower of Babel. The story is really a superb example (either way) of the power of good communication.

did not choose him; he "chose you to go and bear fruit—fruit that will last" (John 15:16).

The good news is that "we are God's fellow workers" (1 Cor. 3:9), called to witness, yet it is he who witnesses through us. Unlike the Muslim, who must convert the non-Muslim any way possible, whether through argument, persuasion, bribery, or torture, we do not have to worry about converting anyone, for God's Holy Spirit converts. We are called merely to tell about Jesus and his salvation.

In preaching Jesus Christ, we must not compromise with the world system or forsake our zeal for him. Yet, since we love him and our audience, we need to translate what we are saying into the appropriate language and place it in the appropriate context so that our audience is able to hear and understand it. We should make ourselves "a slave to everyone, to win as many as possible" (1 Cor. 9:19).

It would be a great breakthrough if communicators would refrain from using the word *Christian* as an adjective and limit its use to the way in which the early church and the Romans used it, as a noun. In the Book of the Acts of the Apostles, a Christian is a person who confesses and follows Jesus Christ. Paul is a Christian who makes tents; however, the tents that Paul makes are not "Christian" tents.

If we restricted the use of *Christian*, we would no longer be confused by "Christian" art and media. Instead, we would have Christians who made a work of art, for example, or created a television program. The work of art or the television program that the Christian made may, or may not, communicate the Gospel of Jesus Christ. If we evaluated the art as art, the television program as a program, and the tent as a tent (including any Gospel messages woven into the fabric), we would be delivered from worshiping the thing as a sacred object set apart by the use of *Christian* as an adjective.

Setting the art, music, book, or whatever it is apart by calling it "Christian" permits attitudes that undermine the quality of a specific work. Blinded by the word *Christian*, we often take an indulgent attitude toward sloppy or bad workmanship, thereby perpetuating inferior communication and art. It is just as destructive to good workmanship when artists and communicators forsake excellence, knowing that the adjective *Christian* pinned to their work will cover up a multitude of imperfections. Quality is undermined by artists or communicators who decide not only to rest in the Lord but also to let the Lord do everything while they sleep—or socialize. These are individuals who are failing to exercise their talents, learn their craft, or invest time and effort in the work he has given them to do. We are not saved by works, but we are called to work with diligence and industry, knowing God will work in us, providing us with the strength to do his will.

It is clear that the use of *Christian* as an adjective will not be abandoned in the near future, by either pagans or Christians. However, as Christians, we must always do our best, evaluating our work honestly against the highest possible standards, because we love him, trust him, and want all that we do to glorify him. Furthermore, we must help each other to do our best work by refusing to settle for anything less.

A psychiatrist who was advising me on the production of a PBS television program on divorce prevention noted that he had been on a U.S. government commission to discover the reasons for chronic poverty in Appalachia. Before going into the field, the members assumed that the problem had to do with environment or lack of education. In the field, the committee found that they could move up a creek beyond so-called civilization and find a house and family that was falling apart, yet they could go farther up the creek and find a well-kept home and an industrious family. The difference was not isolation or lack of education; rather, the family that was doing well almost always had a relative nearby, or a neighbor, who cared enough to be demanding and interested in their welfare.

We must be interested in the welfare of the family of believers. "I don't care" and "Don't get involved" are negative, destructive phrases. Healthy criticism, which is loving, not judgmental, and sincere concern help all of us.

Often we do not have the time to love our neighbor; we are too busy worrying about money, since we really do not trust God to provide. The good news is that he will provide when we take the time to love him and our neighbor. Trusting God to provide takes time, and trusting him to the degree that we can be available for and responsive to our neighbor (our families, our friends, and our enemies) takes time and the power of his Spirit.

Sometimes we are just too concerned with our business to pay attention to others, but Jesus, the Communicator, was and is always available and calls us to be available. During a brief trip to Los Angeles to line up stars for a PBS television program, I had been asked to visit with an elderly friend of a friend. Time was short, and I found myself hoping that I could call up and cancel this unnecessary meeting. Somehow all my meetings went better and faster than I expected, and I had enough time to make the visit. The meeting was a great blessing—a chance to share and rejoice—and, in addition, this wonderful woman gave me a list (including connections and numbers) for people who would be interested in appearing on the program I was planning.

If we focus on him and his grace, we will be freed from fear and available to communicate his Gospel. For instance, four days before "The Power" exhibit was to open at the 1982 World's Fair, we were $150,000 short of funds. We were paid up to date (more than $1 million in goods and services and $600,000 in cash expenditures), but the crew was anticipating that we would not have the final $150,000 to pay them on Friday morning, the day before the grand opening.

The members of the crew were the best in the country, chosen because of their skills not their religious beliefs. Thus many of them were more committed to receiving their wages than proclaiming the Gospel. The churches had spent all the money they could and had no idea where they could find any more. One of my associates suggested that I should give up, stay in Atlanta, and not bother to go to Knoxville, but I knew that this was God's exhibit and he would finance it.

I flew to Knoxville late Tuesday afternoon. My director took me aside to tell me that the crew was going to walk off the job. I prayed. Around 9:00 P.M., a man stopped by the exhibit and asked me how things were going. I told him that we needed $150,000 in the bank in Atlanta by Thursday. He himself did not have a lot of money, but he felt that the exhibit was the responsibility of the people of Knoxville and invited me to a prayer meeting that the sponsoring churches were holding early the next morning. Thanks to God's grace, we had $175,000 in the bank by Thursday. The extra $25,000 was enough to pay for maintenance for the first few months of operation.

We should never worry about finances, time, or any of the other obstacles that seem to stand in the way of our fulfilling his call for us. Instead, we should concern ourselves with doing God's will so that we can trust in his provision. This is the assurance that we have in approaching God: that if we ask anything according to his will he hears us. And, if we know that he hears us—whatever we ask—we know that we have what we ask of him (1 John 5:14–15).

We learn God's will by studying his word, the Bible, and by allowing his Spirit to live in us. The good news is that he gives each of us our own unique combination of motivations, talents, and gifts, which, when discerned, will help each of us discover how we can best communicate what we want and what genre and medium is appropriate for us. All too often, we become frustrated by trying to use a medium that does not suit our unique motivational talents. Some of us are chosen to be writers, some executive producers, some directors, some art directors, and so on. Chapter 3 will help start you on the road to discovering your own unique God-given motivational talents.

When you discover your unique motivational talent and learn

the language and grammar of the medium you will be using, you will be able to access any channel of communication (network television, radio, newspaper, etc.), capture and motivate an audience, and communicate the Gospel in all its glory.

In 1981, as president of the Episcopal Radio-TV Foundation, I initiated and produced for the Protestant Radio-TV Center (a consortium of four denominations) for PBS television satellite distribution a series entitled "Perspectives." After a year on the PBS satellite, "Perspectives" was carried on 120 PBS stations and cable systems. Several programs in the series won important national awards. Moreover, every program I produced and hosted had a biblical perspective.

One evening at a benefit dinner, a renowned church organist opened a conversation with me by complaining that Christians could not place programs on PBS television because PBS would not carry anything with a religious message. A Christian who produced television programs had complained to my new friend that he could not convince PBS to carry his latest program. I mentioned "Perspectives" and suggested that the problem was not necessarily PBS; it might be the quality of the program in question or that it did not fit the PBS format. In fact, I was already aware of the program in question, and it was not directed or edited very well, although it had a great message. PBS does carry religious programming, and Christians should use PBS more often (although it is true that some member stations do not carry religious programming).

Of course, it could have been a problem with one of the PBS member stations or with specific personnel. However, all too often the problem is not the gatekeeper,* or "the other guy," but instead the design and quality of the program. This book will help you overcome those problems; we will examine the medium of television and how to place your program on the channel of your choice.

---

*In telecommunications, radio, and television, the gatekeeper is the individual or corporation who controls access to the use of the channel or medium of communication.

W. C. Fields proclaimed one of the most practical rules of effective communication, "Tell them what you are going to say; say it; and tell them what you said." With that principle in mind, let's look at the structure of this book.

I noted at the beginning of this introduction that the ability to communicate effectively is a key to achieving your goals, purposes, and desires. To do it, you must learn the basic principles of good communication, as well as the language and grammar of the genre and the medium you will be using. *Asking the right questions* is the key to applying these basic principles to a specific communication.

Part I examines the fundamental principles of powerful communication. Chapter 1 helps you to ask the right questions. Chapter 2 looks at the power behind your communication, which may be yourself, others, or God. Chapter 3 helps you to discern your motivational talents. Chapter 4 helps you to tune in to your audience. Chapter 5 helps you to design your presentation so that it is logical, clear, and powerful. Chapter 6 helps you to choose the appropriate genre, or format.

Part II shows you how to choose and use the appropriate medium. Chapter 7, on choosing the appropriate medium, introduces the four chapters immediately following it, each of which looks at a different kind of media by focusing in depth on a representative medium within each category. Chapter 8 looks at television as representative of audiovisual media. Chapter 9 looks at radio as representative of auditory media. Chapter 10 examines public speaking as representative of presentations before a live audience. Chapter 11 focuses on the newsletter as an example of written presentations. Chapters 3 to 11 have detailed exercises giving you step by step instructions. These are designated by ▬▬▬▬

The conclusion discusses briefly what God wants us to say as Christians who are communicators. This book is your manual to help you do it effectively.

I. THE FOUNDATIONS OF POWERFUL COMMUNICATION

1. How Do I Communicate?

No man is an Island.

JOHN DONNE

What do you want to communicate? Why do you want to communicate? To whom do you want to communicate? Communication is basic to our being human. It joins us together as a community by giving us the ability to exchange and hold in common thoughts, ideas, needs, and desires. Furthermore, it gives us the opportunity to be in communion with God. Our God is the God who communicates, who speaks forth creation and who is himself the Word, as John proclaims so eloquently: "In the beginning was the Word, and the Word was with God, and the Word was God" (John 1:1, KJV).

Babies come into the world trying to make known their desires, needs, and feelings. They become frustrated when they are not understood. They are happy about learning to talk, but in the interest of preserving their identity, they want their audience to understand their approach to language. All too often "the Child is father of the Man" with regard to our approach to communication, though not in the sense that Wordsworth intended.

Several years ago, people from around the country convened in Cincinnati to discuss the future of Episcopal communications. After a briefing by the conveners, we split into small groups to discern what word or words best described Episcopal communications in their present state. Several groups came back to report, in jest, that the most appropriate word was *smug*. All of us thought this was funny, and *smug* became a buzzword at the meeting.

In a more serious vein, we were well aware of the problems

of "smug" communications: pride, provincialism, and solipsism. In fact, these problems are common. The alternative is for us to stop before we communicate and take the time to ascertain the nature of our audience, our own talents, the nature of the medium we've chosen, and all the pertinent aspects of each presentation so that it will achieve the result we intend. Effective communication enables us to share our thoughts, achieve our goals, fulfill our desires—to survive in a fallen world teetering on the brink of destruction.

At the National Council of Churches' 1980 Consultation on the Electronic Church, many denominational representatives felt that the electronic church* posed "one of the most serious threats to the local congregation."[1] Four years later, a study on the electronic church conducted by the Annenberg School of Communications and the Gallup Organization showed that "watching religious television does not keep people from going to church or from contributing to their local congregations." In fact, according to Dean George Gerbner of the Annenberg School, "viewers of religious programs are by and large also the believers, the churchgoers, the contributors. . . . There must be other explanations if church attendance has declined and there is a lack of financial support."[2]

The task that confronts us is to strive to produce better, more effective communications that proclaim his gospel through every medium. The mainline churches have been producing excellent religious television programs for over forty years, programs like "The Lion, the Witch, and the Wardrobe," "Insight," and "Davey and Goliath." It is important for all Christian communicators to strive for excellence and avoid time-consuming sibling rivalries.

At the 1984 Continental Congress on the Christian World View, several speakers told of the influence that the movie *Chariots of Fire* had had on their lives. In particular, they noted

---

*The "electronic church" (sometimes, the "electric church") is the name that has been given to television and radio preachers, many of whom are evangelical, and their listening or viewing audiences.

that Eric Liddell's statement that his running gave God pleasure encouraged each of them to start exercising their God-
given talents rather than limiting themselves to so-called
Christian endeavors. When my turn came to speak, I noted
that the scriptwriter and the actor who played Liddell had
collaborated on the dialogue that proclaimed the Gospel so
clearly, yet neither of them was a Christian. In fact, Colin
Welland, the scriptwriter, says to this day that *Chariots* is about
a "couple of young fellows who put their fingers up to the
world."[3] Clearly, he has a very different perspective than most
Christians toward what *Chariots of Fire* is saying.

I also reported that most of the money for *Chariots* was put
up by a Muslim, Mohammed el Fayed. The only committed
Christian who was prominent in *Chariots* was the actor who
played Abrahams, the Jewish runner. *Chariots of Fire* shows
that God can and will raise up stones to witness to him
through the entertainment media, if Christians fail to do so.

As Johannes Heinrichs has pointed out, "Theologically
speaking Christianity can be wholly and completely interpreted as a religion of communication, both divine-human and
inter-human."[4] Therefore, as Christians, our ability to communicate effectively and successfully through every medium
is extremely important. It allows us to witness to the great
news of new life available in Christ and to minister to the
needs of our neighbors.

Our most basic communications question is:

*How do I communicate exactly what I need or want to
communicate to the person I want or need to reach, using the
appropriate genre and medium properly so that my audience
will understand and be convinced, motivated, educated, and/
or informed?*

The key to effective and successful communication is *asking
the right questions*—to ascertain exactly what I want to communicate; why I want to communicate it; whom I want to
reach; how I want to do it, what medium is appropriate with

respect to "I"; what my motivational talents are; and what impact or consequence I want my work to have.

Being effective always takes work. Communication is a conscious process involving two or more unique individuals. It is a bridge for thoughts, ideas, and information between those individuals. Before any bridge is built, it has to be designed properly, or it will collapse. Every detail is important.

As we have heard all our lives, the process of writing (for most of us) is 10 percent inspiration and 90 percent perspiration. The same is true for any medium: learn to ask the right questions and apply the answers, learn the right language and the right grammar, and the communication bridge will be 90 percent built.

Of course, no matter what the medium, the same way as a baby learns to talk, there will come a time when the right questions, the words, and the syntax are second nature to us. Once we become adept, we should not regress into baby talk unless it is a necessary, conscious, and effective part of a specific communication.

Let's look briefly at some of the right questions for us to ask if we want to improve our communications. These questions are grouped in categories chosen to clarify their purpose. In reality, these categories and questions are closely interrelated; however, to help focus our communications I have separated them and distinguished them from one another. Some of them will be treated in depth in the chapters that follow. Additional questions that relate to a specific medium or topic will also be treated throughout the book. You should adapt, add to, and subtract from these lists of questions to suit your own particular needs. Ask these questions before you begin to communicate:

Power:

Yours, O Lord, is the greatness and the power and the glory and the majesty and the splendor, for everything in heaven and earth is yours.

1 CHRONICLES 29:11

Are my communications powerful?

What empowers my communications?

Power is by definition the ability, the capacity, the strength, the authority, the energy, the force, and the right to do or accomplish something. As believers, we know that God is omnipotent; God the Father is the source of all power; Jesus has all authority in heaven and on earth; and the Holy Spirit gives us power to communicate His Gospel. Therefore, every power question begins and ends with God.

However, there are many levels of power in a communication. To understand what empowers a specific communication, the first question that each of us should ask ourselves is,

Why Do I Want to Communicate?

I raised you up for this very purpose, that I might display my power in you and that my name might be proclaimed in all the earth.

ROMANS 9:17

The essence of powerful and effective communication is self-knowledge, vulnerability, openness, and a clear understanding of "why I want to communicate." Whether you want to reach, teach, serve, proclaim, respond, sell, or ask, knowing what motivates you (self? others? God?) will help you to evaluate the driving power of your communication.

The question Why do I want to communicate? refers to the motivational level of power, what it is that prompts the communication in the first place and drives it to its destination, its ultimate reason for being. As demonstrated by the proclamations of the prophets, God's call will empower far more than self-interest will (the words of those whom the prophets addressed have long been forgotten, for the most part).

The motivational level can be compared to a race car driver. A timid or unmotivated driver will not have the will to win. A bad driver will not have the skill to win and may, in fact, be dangerous. A skilled, determined driver can win the race, just as powerful motivation can empower a communication to capture the hearts and minds of the audience.

The other critical power question we should ask is

What is My Premise?

The tongue has the power of life and death.

PROVERBS 18:21

The premise is the engine or motor. Just as a driver and an engine drive a car, so the motivation and the premise empower a communication.

By definition, a premise proposes the hypothesis that leads, necessarily and logically, to the conclusion through the process of proving the argument put forth in the premise. The premise is a succinct, summary statement of what the communication is going to prove. The measure of its success is whether it logically proves the stated or implied premise. Proving the premise dramatically and logically is what powers the communication.

For example, your premise might be "Good triumphs over evil."* The process of proving that particular premise will move your communication along through each logical step until the conclusion expressed in the premise is reached. You could prove that "good triumphs over evil" in any number of ways, but if any is to be successful, it must be both logical and faithful to that premise. You could prove that premise by telling the story of a hero who defeats an evil lord who had been exploiting the people, or you could tell the story of a son who reclaims the land that evil tenants had stolen from his father. Whatever way you choose, good must triumph over evil

---

*Note that your premise does not have to be a universal truth, but it must be true for your communication and you must prove it.

to prove your premise. The proof of your premise will drive your communication to a powerful, logical conclusion.

Your premise, your motivation, your genre or format, your chosen medium, your gifts, your talents, and your audience will determine what you are communicating, regardless of what it is you intend to communicate. Therefore, it is critical that you state your premise correctly and precisely and that you distinguish between what you want to communicate, or your idea, and what you are communicating, which depends to a large degree on your premise.

Wisdom:

The fear of the Lord is the beginning of wisdom.

PSALM 110:9

Just as important as power is wisdom, which should be exercised throughout the process. Wisdom is the ability to make sound judgments and to deal sagaciously with facts and with every other aspect of a communication. In our automotive metaphor, wisdom enables us to stay on the road by helping us make the many decisions involved in steering our car to its destination. "If any of you lacks wisdom, he should ask God, who gives generously to all without finding fault, and it will be given to him" (James 1:5).

Our "wisdom" question is

Who Am I?

He who trusts in himself is a fool, but he who walks in wisdom is kept safe.

PROVERBS 18:6

As Christians, we know that each of us is created by God, in his image, for a special purpose. Each of us has been given the gifts, talents, and desire to fulfill his purpose for us.

Too many of us do not know what God's purpose is for our lives or what our unique gifts and talents are. Therefore, when we try to communicate we are often ineffective because the genre or the medium we have chosen is not suited to our talents or the role we have chosen is not appropriate for us (for example, we may try to be an evangelist when we have been called to be a prophet).

This does not mean that some of us are exempt from testifying to the Gospel of Jesus Christ: *We are all commanded to proclaim the Gospel.* However, how we present it will depend on who we are and what God has given us. In our automotive metaphor, knowing who I am and what my gifts and talents are helps me to make sound judgments regarding how fast I can take a curve or, for that matter, what kind of car is best for me to drive in the first place.

The question Who am I? should be asked in conjunction with our other questions and should not be treated as pure speculation.

Call:

Then I heard the voice of the Lord saying, "Whom shall I send? And who will go for us?"

And I said, "Here I am. Send me!"

He said, "Go and tell this people."

ISAIAH 6:8–9A

We have been called by God out of darkness into the eternal glory of his kingdom to take our place in his body, to be His witnesses "in Jerusalem, and in all Judea and Sumaria, and to the ends of the earth." Responding to God's call requires power, wisdom, and understanding. We have asked the power and wisdom questions; shortly, we will consider understanding. Here we look at that aspect of our call which relates to those to whom and with whom we are called to communicate—our audience.

Who Is my Audience?

After Paul had seen the vision, we got ready at once to leave for Macedonia, concluding that God had called us to preach the gospel to them.

Acts 16:10

The question Who is my audience? is in fact a set of questions, including

> What are the physical, psychological, emotional, spiritual, racial, political, sexual, and other characteristics of the audience I am trying to reach?
> What do they want to hear?
> How well will they respond to the genre I have chosen?
> Where do they live?
> Will the medium I have chosen reach them?
> Who will, and who does, the medium I have chosen reach?
> Is there a more appropriate, or a more effective, or a less expensive medium I can use to reach my intended audience?

If we want to reach our intended audience and have maximum impact on that audience we must clearly define who they are.

If our intended audience is small, it would be foolish to buy prime time on broadcast television to reach them; however, broadcasting by satellite might be advisable if that small audience is spread out over a large, sparsely populated area such as Alaska or Minnesota.

Once we have chosen the appropriate medium for reaching our intended audience, we have to determine how we can best adapt and translate our message without compromising it, put it in a context our audience will understand and relate to. Just as Paul talked to the Epicurean and Stoic philosophers about the "unknown God," whom he proceeded to make known, so we should tailor our communications to our audience, being extremely careful not to lose our message in the process. Part of this process is choosing the appropriate genre or format, whether story, parable, interview, instruction, sermon, or some other format.

It is not uncommon for Christians to fall into the "make-believe mission" trap, either by choosing the wrong medium for the audience they intend to reach, by failing to speak to their audience in a language that audience can understand, by failing to address the audience from its own cultural perspective, or by all of the above. To say that we are reaching Afghanistan for Christ because we are sending an English-language television program over a satellite whose "footprint" covers that area of Asia is "make-believe mission" if almost no one in Afghanistan has a satellite dish and very few speak English or relate to the cultural context of our communication (as when we discuss the latest stock market quotes as an indicator of the timing of the Rapture*).

Whomever we are called to reach, we have to know who they are and where they are. In our automobile metaphor, knowing who our audience is and where they live gives us our destination—where we are going, where we have been called.

Understanding:

The Fear of the Lord—that is wisdom, and to shun evil is understanding.
JOB 28:28

Frequently in Scripture power, wisdom, knowledge, and understanding are mentioned together in discussing the attributes of God and of those individuals who seek, follow, and love God. By definition, understanding means to comprehend, or apprehend, the meaning of something. Understanding is the power to comprehend, judge, and render experience intelligible.

God considers understanding so important that he tells us to get it "though it cost all you have" (Prov. 4:7). We must understand our motivation, our premise, our chosen medium,

---

* The Rapture is the popular term for the taking up of living Christians upon Jesus Christ's return.

our gifts, talents, and resources, the truth, and our audience to communicate effectively. This may sound difficult; however, by asking the right questions and trusting in his grace, we can communicate powerfully, effectively, and in love.

Although understanding applies to all aspects of our communications, the question that directly involves understanding is

What Am I Communicating?

Understanding is a fountain of life to those who have it.

PROVERBS 16:22

The first step toward understanding what you are communicating is to set forth exactly what it is you want to communicate. It would be nice to say that you know exactly what that is, so if you do, say so. However, many people have the desire to communicate, the means to do so, the ability, but no clear idea of what they want to get across. Every year movies, television programs, and other big-budget presentations fail because the author did not know what he or she wanted to say. Anyone who has stared at a blank piece of paper or at an empty CRT monitor in the throes of "writer's block" knows that we do not always know what we want to say.

However, to be intelligible to your audience, that is precisely what you must know. Asking the right questions will help you to formulate your ideas. Setting forth your thoughts and ideas as briefly and succinctly as possible is an excellent way to get started.

Once you are clear about what you want to communicate, you must determine what format or genre you will use, and you need to understand the genre you choose and how it affects what you say. You must understand also the medium you will be using and how that particular medium affects your communication. You must adapt your message to the genre and medium you choose.

Furthermore, you must know your audience and how they

are likely to receive your presentation; as I have already noted, you must adapt your message to your audience. You must understand also what God wants you to communicate and how that affects your message. Finally, after you have made your presentation, you should seek feedback from your audience so that you can improve and perfect what you have done.

In our automotive metaphor, understanding what we are communicating is being able to deliver our message in an intelligible fashion when we arrive at our destination, the audience.

Truth:

Speak the truth to each other.

ZECHARIAH 8:16

We all know that truth is: truth is veracity, sincerity, genuineness, conformity to rule, exactness, and correctness. Truth is the opposite of falsehood. Truth is often defined as that which conforms to reality. As Christians, we know that truth conforms ultimately to the Word of God.

Truth is also necessary in the most imaginative fiction, for such fiction must be true to the rules established by the author or it will seem to its audience shallow, empty, and false. Christians can and should create great works of imagination in all the media, in the tradition of C. S. Lewis and Bach, realizing that truth demands not strict realism but an attention to detail that keeps it true to its own rules. Truth, like all the other factors we have considered, affects our communication at various levels.

The key truth question is

What Does God Want Me to Communicate?

Do not be quick with your mouth, do not be hasty in your heart to utter anything before God.

ECCLESIASTES 5:2.

God tells us to "make disciples . . . teaching them to obey everything I have commanded you" (Matt. 28:19, 20). God wants us to witness in word and deed to his Word, his salvation, and his good news. This is both a simple and a complex task; because, although the Gospel can be stated very briefly, the whole Gospel contains eternal, infinite truth that bursts forth from Scripture to fill every aspect of life and death, even touching the very threshold of eternity.

In his Word, we are told that "one day Samson went to Gaza, where he saw a prostitute. He went in to spend the night with her" (Judg. 16:1). The Word of God is true to life, the good and the bad, because God is interested in saving us from death. We create false visions of life when we deny the reality of evil and death; saccharine stories are not truthful. On the other hand, pagans often deny the reality of good and seldom touch upon the possibility of real life, eternal life. However, there are instances of nonbelievers clearly communicating his Truth, as in paintings of the crucifixion, or movies like *Chariots of Fire* and Pier Paolo Pasolini's *Gospel According to St. Matthew*, both of which were produced and written by nonbelievers. (Pasolini, the late well-known Italian film director who was a committed communist, did not give an ideological interpretation of the life of Christ in this film but adhered closely to the facts of the Gospel.)

Truth is the gasoline, the fuel on which our automobile runs. Water it down, and our car will run very poorly, eventually breaking down completely.

Stewardship:
Each one should use whatever gift he has received to serve others.
1 PETER 4:10

We have been appointed by God as stewards over everything that he created on earth, in the sea, and in the air. As stewards, we are to manage, supervise, harvest, protect, nourish, and care for that magnificent creation that has been entrusted to us. Being good stewards requires effective communication, and communicating effectively requires good stewardship of the resources available to us.

Everything about asking the right questions could be seen as a function of stewardship, since the key to good steward-ship is accurate ascertainment. In terms of our automobile metaphor, stewardship involves determining not only whether we have enough money, gas, oil, food, water, and other sup-plies, but also whether we have the motivation, the ability, the skill, the right car, and a destination—all of them necessary for our trip. To help focus and clarify our ascertainment ques-tions, however, our stewardship question is limited and does not include questions covered elsewhere.

Our stewardship question is

What Are My Resources?

Suppose one of you wants to build a tower. Will he not first sit down and estimate the cost to see if he has enough money to complete it? For if he lays the foundation and is not able to finish it, everyone who sees it will ridicule him.

LUKE 14:28–29

At some point in our lives, most of us have fallen into the predicament of not being able to finish a project because we did not have enough resources (money, time, supplies, energy, and/or assistance), because we mismanaged our resources, because we failed to recognize our resources, or because of all these. As Jesus noted, this is embarrassing and usually unnecessary, although there are occasions when unpredictable circumstances sabotage a project. Before we start, we should count the cost and ascertain what our resources are, then target our audience and choose our medium of communication based on the resources available to us.

Counting the cost and ascertaining our resources does not mean that we must forsake our call to communicate to a specific audience. It does mean that we take the time to pre-pare properly by finding out what we will have to secure through fund-raising and prayer or what steps we will have to take to adapt our plans to our limited resources.

It is very important to remind ourselves, when we ask this

question, that sometimes trying to do everything ourselves ("hands on" production) can be the most expensive approach in the long run. The excess cost of "hands on" production can show up either in the time it takes for us to learn new skills, or in a lack of quality in our final product that prevents it from reaching the intended audience with what we were trying to get across to them.

Once when I was teaching a workshop, a student told me that his church had been talked into purchasing a large amount of video equipment to tell their community about themselves. The church proceeded to use the equipment for this purpose. To their great surprise, the finished product looked like a home movie, and in their disappointment, they put their new equipment in a closet and forgot it. This is a classic case of video burnout.

They would not have burned out on the equipment if they had taken the time to learn about it before they bought it and to determine whether they had the resources, including the talent, to use this equipment for the production they had in mind. Only after ascertaining what the equipment could do and what their resources were should have decided whether or not to buy it. Whether or not they decided to buy the equipment, they should have considered hiring people with the right skills to produce what they wanted ("hands off" production). Note the mistakes inherent in their approach: they put their faith in the new technology to solve their communication problems (a state of mind that could be called videolatry); they did not ask themselves the questions that would help them determine how to say what they wanted to say; and they did not inventory their resources.

"Hands off" production should not become a shibboleth. There are many instances in which "hands on" production is appropriate, especially when the skills are available to effectively use the chosen medium, or when learning to use this medium is important in itself.

At a church in New York City, we involved a group of teenagers in producing their own television program, which aired on the local-access cable television channel, because the production process itself was an important thing for them to learn. Producing their own television program helped them to think about the nature of the medium, the nature of the Gospel, and how they could communicate the Gospel through that medium. Many of the teenagers discovered their motivational talents. Several of them came to know Jesus as Savior while producing that program.

In counting the cost of equipment, remember that the more sophisticated the equipment, usually the more it costs to maintain. When I was the director of the Television Center at the Brooklyn College, campus of the City University of New York, the chief engineer estimated that the annual maintenance cost for new equipment was equivalent to one third its purchase price.

Advances in technology have reduced these maintenance costs. Moreover, less sophisticated equipment and equipment meant for the general public cost much less to maintain. Nevertheless, it is important to count the cost of maintaining equipment and to be prepared to meet those costs before you purchase equipment; otherwise, you will find yourself with broken-down expensive equipment taking up precious space and reminding you of your folly.

You may have more resources available to you than you realize. In many cases, ascertaining what your resources are means becoming aware of what talent and what assets you have within your parish or church. Before you buy equipment, ask if anyone in your church has what you need, whether it is video, audio, film, or computer equipment. Sometimes what you need is available, even if only for a short-term loan. If no one in your local church has the equipment, then check with local businesses, community groups, and schools. Often the local television station, cable television system, or radio station will help you.

If you want broadcast access to the local cable system, television station, or radio station, you should find out who runs it, why they run it, and why they might be interested in your program. Most often, they run their station or system to make a profit, and they will be interested in what you want to do if it will help them to get more viewers or listeners. Your program may increase their audience directly, or it may improve their image with the community, thereby helping them to attract more viewers or listeners.

A few years ago, representatives of the Chinese community in New York City approached their local cable system about access to program time on the premier channel on the system. At first, the cable system said that no time was available. The community representatives countered by pointing out that not only would many Chinese subscribers be added to the customer roles of the cable system but also the appropriate New York City licensing board would look favorably on the system at license-renewal time if they were given the time they wanted. The cable system changed its corporate mind and gave the Chinese community three hours per week on the premier cable channel.

Locating talent may be the most important aspect of ascertaining your resources. Gifted individuals, motivated by God and working together in love, can do wonders with second-rate equipment. Many Emmy Award-winning television programs have been produced on nonprofessional equipment by dedicated people. The talent questions in Chapter 3 will help you to find the right people.

Try to be a good steward of the talent available. Skilled people must be given the freedom to exercise their professional judgment while they are guided toward the communication goal. If you do not have the ability to shepherd the talent necessary, find a producer who can. Respect is the key to working with skilled people.

As stated in the Introduction, God provides the resources for us to do what he has called us to do. If you count the cost and find yourself short of resources, pray. God answers.

Impact:

Nobody should seek his own good, but the good of others.

1 CORINTHIANS 10:24

Impact is the other side of power. It is the force with which our communication collides with the audience. Impact depends on our ability to address our audience where they need to be addressed. To ascertain how to communicate for maximum impact, we should ask this multilayered question:

What Needs to be Communicated to my Audience?

The poor and the needy search for water, but there is none; their tongues are parched with thirst. But I the Lord will answer them; I, the God of Israel, will not forsake them.

ISAIAH 41:17

The advertising industry is built on addressing people's needs so that they will buy products to meet those needs. Often the advertised product will not meet the need that the advertiser uses to motivate people to buy the product. For instance, to sell a product, a television advertiser may address the audience's social need for love, claiming that the product—toothpaste, for example—will give those in the audience more friends of the opposite sex. However, that product will not meet the audience's need for love, nor will it give them more friends of the opposite sex. Listening to the audience, through market research, tells an advertiser what "needs" must be addressed for maximum impact. There are several categories of needs:

- *Physical* needs, for food, clothing, shelter, procreation, or survival
- *Security* needs, for personal protection from danger, deprivation, or accidents
- *Social* needs, for love, community, or home
- *Self-esteem* needs, for respect, productiveness, or recognition

- *Self-fulfillment* needs, for success or accomplishment
And, most of all
- *Spiritual* need, which can manifest itself as the desire for
any or all of the above-mentioned needs but, in fact, is a
desire for communion with God—Father, Son and Holy
Spirit—for "man does not live by bread alone" (Matt. 4:4)

Needs are expressed by desires, but desires can be fanned
by temptation into all-consuming concupiscence. Hunger is
an essential desire that expresses the natural physical need
for food, but gluttony is hunger run amuck.

All of us are sinners, but as communicators who are also
Christians, we should not fan natural desires into sins just
so we can motivate our audience to buy our products—or
our ideas. The natural desires to procreate, to love, and to
be loved have often been fanned and forged into lust so that
an advertiser can sell a product like bluejeans. More often
than not, the desire that has been thus blown out of proportion will not be satisfied by the product in question—the
product can't deliver on the promises made for it in the
advertisement.

Communicators all too often resort to aggravating desires
to give impact to their message; they are too lazy, or rushed,
to ask themselves all the other questions that would help
them make their presentation effective. Addressing and aggravating desires become a quick fix, an easy way to have
impact on an audience, a substitute for building a truly
powerful, effective communication.

For us to have a powerful impact on our audience, we
must ascertain and address their needs, wants, and feelings
by listening to them. To do so, we should undertake the
appropriate market research. Furthermore, our communications will deliver on God's promises if we are communicating his Truth. If we discipline ourselves to ask the right
questions, apply the answers properly, and learn the language and grammar of our chosen medium, we will communicate powerfully and effectively.

Prophecy:

The Ninevites believed God. They declared a fast, and all of them from the greatest to the least, put on sackcloth.

JONAH 3:5

Jonah did not want to go to Nineveh to proclaim God's judgment because he knew that God would relent from sending destruction on Nineveh if the Ninevites repented. Jonah wanted sinful Nineveh destroyed. He wanted the prophecy God gave him to preach to be fulfilled. He preached destruction, and he wanted the destruction he preached to occur to prove that he was a prophet of the one true God. He was concerned with his image and his righteousness, not about the people of Nineveh. He did not want his prophesying to bring the Ninevites to active repentence, but it did.

To prophesy means to foretell, or tell forth, under divine inspiration. All our communications should be divinely inspired, because his Holy Spirit dwells in us; they should tell forth, and/or foretell, in that they proclaim the truth.

Prophesying relates to and affects all aspects of communication, so our prophesy question will be limited to a focus on the consequences of prophesying. The key question that relates to our call to prophesy is

Will my Communication Result in Action?

And so John came, baptizing in the desert region and preaching a baptism of repentance for the forgiveness of sins. The whole Judean countryside and all the people of Jerusalem went out to him. Confessing their sins, they were baptized by him in the Jordan River.

MARK 1:4, 5

Unlike Jonah, most of us want our message to result in action. In one sense, it always does, even if that action is only the internal decision to reject or ignore it. However, we are not concerned here with communications that are ignored or that are received and then forgotten. To prophesy is to demand a reaction, a movement of the heart, a conscious decision, a motivation to do or reject the necessary consequences of the message. If you have clearly stated your premise, which you will learn how to do if you don't already know, and you have answered all the pertinent ascertainment questions we have discussed, your communication will result in action.

To prophesy is to proclaim with such inherent power that our audience climbs into our car and drives with us into the kingdom of God.

Revelation:

For now we see through a glass darkly; but then face to face: now I know in part; but then shall I know even as I am known.

1 CORINTHIANS 13:12, KJV

From the first chapter of Paul's Letter to the Romans, we know that all of creation reveals God's eternal power and divine nature. God communicates himself and his will to us through revelation, and we reveal his revelation to others. Communication should make the unknown known to those to and with whom we are communicating. Therefore, our revelation question is

Did my Communication Succeed?

The Spirit searches all things, even the deep things of God.

1 CORINTHIANS 2:10

This question may be restated in several ways to help us evaluate our effectiveness:

Did my communication make the unknown known?
Did it communicate what I intended?
How did my audience react to it?

To find out how effective your communication has been you must have feedback, which simply means taking the time to listen to your audience afterwards (whether or not they joined us on our drive in the eternal kingdom of God).

There are many methods and devices for obtaining feedback from your audience, but regardless of technique, the important point is that we seek feedback from our audience and from God and that we heed that feedback. Feedback helps us to continually reevaluate our communications and improve them.

This does not mean that we compromise or dilute our message when we receive negative feedback. Instead, we use it improve our presentation of the revelation we have received from God so that we can help to bring more people into the kingdom. Feedback should bring us closer to God and to the joy (and cost) or communicating his good news. As Jesus said, "For I gave them the words that you gave me and they accepted them. They knew with certainty that I came from you, and they believed that you sent me" (John 17:8).

At the beginning of this chapter, we asked the most basic communication question:

How do I communicate exactly what I need or want to communicate to the person I want or need to reach, using the appropriate genre and medium properly so that my audience will understand, and be convinced, motivated, educated, and/ or informed?

The answer we have seen is threefold:

> *Ask and answer the right ascertainment questions* to arrive at exactly what I want to communicate; why I want to communicate it; whom I want to reach; how I want to do it, what genre and medium are appropriate with respect to what my motivational talents are, and what impact or consequence I want my work to have.
>
> *Learn* the language and grammar of the appropriate genre and the chosen medium.
>
> *Apply* the answers to the questions and the language and grammar of the chosen genre and medium.

To simplify our task in the future let us review the ascertainment questions posed in this chapter, keeping in mind that there are questions we may add to this list depending on the nature of a particular communication and also that a specific communication may not demand that we ask all these questions. The chapters that follow will treat some of these questions in depth and pose further questions.

Why do I want to communicate?

Who am I?

Who is my audience?

    What are the physical, psychological, emotional, spiritual, racial, political, sexual, and other characteristics of the audience I am trying to reach?

    What do they want to hear?

    How well will they respond to the genre I have chosen?

    Where do they live?

    Will the medium I have chosen reach them?

    Who will, and who does, the medium I have chosen reach?

    Is there a more appropriate, or a more effective, or a less expensive medium I can use to reach my intended audience?

What am I communicating?

What is my premise?

What does God want me to communicate?

What are my resources?

What needs to be communicated to my audience?

Will my communication result in action?

Did my communication succeed?

2. Why Do I Want to Communicate?

To communicate effectively, you must know why you want to do it: whether it is a commitment to present the Gospel, a desire to serve the Church, a desire to help others—or a desire to become a celebrity evangelist presiding over a satellite television empire.

Knowing why helps to clarify and empower your presentation. Furthermore, the specific motivation for each communication helps to determine its power and impact.

Have you been called by God to do this? Or has the competition of the electronic church pressured you into using the telecommunications media? Or is it that you feel the media, in particular television, will help to solve some problems of your congregation?

However you ask the question, answer it honestly, so that what you are doing is powered by a sincere knowledge of why you are doing it. Billy Graham, Johnny Carson, and Franco Zefferelli each do what they do for different reasons; however, each knows why he wants to do it, and their work reflects that integrity whether they are motivated by God or by self-interest. Stephen Minot, author of *Three Genres*, has noted:

Contemporary criticism is not generally concerned with why the writer wrote the way he did, and this is one area in which writer and critic must peacefully part company. It is wise for a writer to examine his own motives honestly. . . .

Every writer has his own personal drives, and one can see what variety there is from reading *Writers at Work* (edited by Malcolm Cowley) which contains some of the best interviews conducted by the staff of the *Paris Review*.[1]

For years, I have asked students who participate in my workshops why they want to communicate and videotaped their answers. Later in the course, after each has developed a program for television, we review the initial videotapes.

Many students have no idea why they want to communicate; often, what they produce seems aimless. Many students want to communicate their existence, their feelings, their desires, their loneliness; usually, their work is self-centered, in the manner of home movies, community-access television, or vanity video. Some students want to help others; their presentations are powerful, although sometimes too didactic. Those students who are motivated by God's call often develop the most powerful presentation, once they ask the right questions and learn the language and grammar of television.

Of course, many factors affect the power and impact of a specific communication and also the degree to which a particular motive empowers it. If the communicator is starving, his or her communication of that fact *may be* quite powerful, self-centered though it is in a technical sense.

As the heroic Christians martyrs have demonstrated through nineteen hundred years of Church history, God's call imparts tremendous power. For the past twenty centuries, millions of people have come into his kingdom because of the power of messages motivated by his call.

As the Author of creation, God has given human beings the ability to communicate, so that we can glorify Him. Motivated by God's Word and his great commission, uneducated and previously mediocre communicators have done powerful work. They were able to do so because God's Word is powerful *and* they were in relationship with him.[2] As the Reverend John Stott has said,

For not only has God spoken; not only does God continue to speak through what he has spoken; but when God speaks he acts. His

Word does more than explain his action; it is active itself. God accomplishes his purpose by his word; it "prospers" in whatever he sends it forth to do (Isa. 55:11).[3]

To be motivated by God's call is to be motivated by the Spirit of God—the Spirit of truth, the Spirit of life, the Spirit of justice. When called by God, one speaks with the authority of the Author and Judge of creation, who authenticates what one has to say; the Word of God penetrates the veil of time to reveal the power of eternity. Those who are motivated by God manifest the inevitability, integrity, unity, and durability of God's word.[4]

The very attributes of God's Word empower the communication of one who has been called by God. Love has empowered Mother Teresa to go into the leprous ghettos of Calcutta to communicate the Gospel of Jesus. Faith has empowered Pat Robertson, Mother Angelica, and other television evangelists to lease satellite time to proclaim the Good News. Hope empowers thousands of missionaries from every denomination as they look forward to the redemption of peoples and cultures and of life itself.

Throughout history, Christians like Rembrandt, Bach, and Milton have created great art as a result of, and anchored in, their faith. Michael Aeschliman, writing in *The University Bookman*, takes us on a journey through history as he describes the satiric writing of Malcolm Muggeridge:

Muggeridge's work presents us with a coherent attempt to articulate and defend the Judeo-Christian view of man and satirically to anatomize the cruelties, follies, and idiocies of the modern and contemporary world in light of that view. The vehicle for this satire is some of the most brilliant English prose of our age, a prose that enacts the "grave levity" characteristic of much of the visionary Christian writing and utterance, from the parables of Jesus, through Augustine's mordant wit, Thomas More's gallows humor, down through the centuries, through the Metaphysical conceit, to Chesterton's paradoxes.[5]

Called by God one is communicating the greatest story of

all time, the story of time itself, God's story. His story is not only informative and didactic, it is also the very essence of drama. Drama means to do, to act, and God himself has acted in the creation and redemption of life. God acted in eternity in creation, and in time by being born one of us to die and be resurrected for us. Life is his drama, the drama of the ultimate act by the ultimate Actor. It is a drama that has yet to end, although he has told us the end of his story. This dramatic power can motivate the communicator who is called by God. As George Gerbner pointed out in an article on television and religion,

Storytelling is the great process that makes us recognizably human. A story is the attempt to make the invisible visible—it has to do with relationships, with intellections. We have to have some device to make them visible, dramatic, revealing and embodied in human beings whose characteristics we know and whose actions we understand. We live our lives in terms of the stories we tell.[6]

In the case of the Gospel, God made himself visible in Jesus the Christ. According to Gerbner, that story unites the three basic genres of storytelling: the story about how things work, the story about what things are, and the story of value and action.

The very act of communication requires that one transcend oneself. The opportunity to communicate the very nature of transcendence made immanent, the very nature of reality, is the most powerful motivation.

It is important to remember that to be "called" means something quite a bit different from choosing. One is called to communicate the gospel only when there is primary allegiance to a higher good—God and his plan of redemption for humanity.

This love drives us to proclaim salvation from eternal death even when all the forces of selfishness and temptation are demanding that we be silent or compromise the Good News. This love burns so brightly in our breast that we risk ridicule and persecution to rescue others from the deadly rebellion of this corrupt and fallen world. Without this love one is apt to put off or soft-pedal preaching the Gospel to such a degree that it is of no value in saving lives (although in its compromised form it may serve the purpose of saving face and keeping friends).

And there are other things that will deaden this motivation to preach the Gospel prompted by God's call: Eschatological fatigue is the low-level depression that may follow some time after the initial quickening of the Spirit when one hears God's call for the first time. When one first hears God's call to communicate, one goes forth fearlessly to proclaim the Gospel, announcing and awaiting the imminent return of Jesus the Christ. When the Parousia, the Second Coming, does not occur as soon as expected, one can become discouraged and discount the power of the message—even though it is God in his mercy who postpones the day of reckoning.

Narcissism is the self-love that is sometimes a result of realizing that one is personally called by God. James and John, the sons of Zebedee, fell into this trap of self-aggrandizement, and Jesus put the loving, personal, joyous call that each of them had heard into the perspective of the King of Kings:

If one of you want to be great, he must be the servant of the rest; and if one of you wants to be first, he must be the slave of all. For even the Son of Man did not come to be served; he came to serve and to give his life to redeem many people (Mark 10:43–45, GNB).

Hardening of the heart frequently occurs when one presents the Gospel with great enthusiasm only to be rebuffed and rejected by one's audience, who may be a loved one or a relative. As Jesus notes, "A prophet is not without honor save in his own country, and in his own house" (Matt. 13:57, KJV). This hardening of the heart manifests itself in a lack of zeal and a dangerously lukewarm commitment to God's Word. In going forth to proclaim the Gospel, it is helpful to keep in mind Jesus' prophetic words: "The world will make you suffer. But be brave! I have defeated the world" (John 16:23, GNB).

Of course, the power generated by God's call to communicate is negated by disobedience, whether or not it is willful. Sometimes we simply procrastinate; we put off doing what we have been called to do. A former secretary of mine (a very nice person) would do everything around the office but her job, which was to type and mail letters. Watching her one day, I realized that I was often guilty of the same kind of disobedience: God had given me the job of distributing his message of forgiveness of indebtedness, and for the most part, I did everything but what he had asked me to do. He says that he will feed us, clothe us, and care for us, and our job is to get out the mail—the message of salvation contained in his Gospel.

The power behind the communication of someone called by God is greatly diminished by a lack of faith; it is impossible to give freely of one's time, money, and person when one does not trust God to provide. The motivating power of God's call is also diminished by the tendency to delegate the responsibility to proclaim God's message to someone else, in particular to the clergy. Even though some Christians have been given the gift of evangelism, we are all called to communicate the Gospel.

Many people are motivated by their faith in false gods. George Lucas, who brought the world the successful Star Wars and Indiana Jones movies, is quite clear about his mission to proclaim the occult, transcendental religion of the Force.[7] A casual glance at any of the mass media will reveal that many prominent communicators are promoting a host of pantheistic deities that lead away from eternal life to eternal death.

Another powerful motivation is ideology, as distinguished from religious faith. Throughout history men and women have given their lives in defense of their beliefs. Abolitionists in prison have written and spoken out against slavery. Exiles from their homelands have waxed eloquent about the injustice that drove them out. Often their eloquence has changed the minds of their compatriots and brought a government to its knees.

When Aleksandr Solzhenitsyn was asked, "What is the secret of your art?" he replied, "The secret is that when you have been pitched headfirst into hell you just write about it." In this same article on Solzhenitsyn Norman Stone went on to say,

Solzhenitsyn's descriptions of prison life—*The First Circle, Cancer Ward,* and the three volumes of *The Gulag Archipelago*—are this century's finest exposition of the hideous consequences of totalitarianism, written without obfuscation or self-pity, and often distinguished by their capacity, after all, to see some light at the end of the tunnel. From his arrest in 1945 until his release in 1953 because he appeared to be terminally ill, Solzhenitsyn did go through various circles of hell, and his efforts to make sure that a Stalin never again happened to Russia finally caused him to be expelled in 1974.[8]

Another contemporary example of someone motivated by ideology (or the opposition to ideology) is Haing S. Ngor, who plays the main character in *The Killing Fields*, a recent feature film about Pol Pot's genocidal revolution in Cambodia. When asked why he decided to act in the film, Dr. Ngor recalled:

When Pat Golden [the casting director] ask me how much money I want, I said I don't care about salary. She say $800 a week. I say I don't care. I want to be this doctor. I want to show the world how the communists really were. If any country get into a war, people killed by gun. In Cambodia, we are killed by rice; we are killed by starvation. If I die from now on, O.K. The film will go on 100 years.[9]

With regard to powerful ideological communication, it is important to keep in mind Paul's words to the Colossians: "See to it that no one takes you captive through hollow and deceptive philosophy, which depends on human tradition and the basic principles of this world rather than on Christ" (Col. 2:8).

Related to the power of ideology and ideas to motivate and empower is the desire to help others by providing information, teaching, serving, or otherwise responding to needs. Countless communications have been prompted by this desire. This book, in fact, is motivated in part by the desire to help you communicate more effectively. The feeling that one can help another has driven many film and television producers, writers, and teachers. Many dedicated individuals who were motivated to help others have forsaken fame and fortune.

The desire to entertain is another powerful motivation. It takes on added power from entertainment's own intrinsic power to attract and captivate an audience. To entertain his listeners Mozart composed beautiful music. The dynamic power of storytelling to prove a premise increases the power of a communication and its impact on the audience. Umberto Eco notes that when he wrote *The Name of the Rose,*

I wanted the reader to enjoy himself, at least as much as I was enjoying myself. This is a very important point, which seems to conflict with the more thoughtful ideas we believe we have about the novel. There is no question that if a novel is amusing, it wins the approval of a public.[10]

Fame and fortune are self-centered motivations and are related to other self-centered motivations: hunger, thirst, the desire to overcome loneliness, the desire to be loved, lust, vanity, envy, and so on. These motivations are not necessarily negative just because they are self-centered. As noted in Chapter 1, hunger is a necessary desire, but gluttony is a self-destructive exaggeration of that natural desire.

These self-centered desires may be powerful motivations to communicate *and* the work that results may have a powerful impact on the audience when the communicator knows his or her craft and has addressed all the pertinent ascertainment questions. However, equally well-crafted works that are driven by motivations that are not self-centered are always more powerful and have more impact on the audience, because they are powered by God or address the audience's needs rather than the communicator's needs.

There nonetheless can be great, but not eternal, self-centered communications; this happens when the needs of the communicator happen to coincide with the needs of the audience. Francois Truffaut's films (*Bed and Board, The 400 Blows,* and many others) are a case in point, and Truffaut has set forth his vision of autobiographical films motivated by the desire to communicate the self:

The film of tomorrow appears to me as even more personal than an individual and autobiographical novel, like a confession, or a diary. The young filmmakers will express themselves in the first person and will relate what has happened to them . . . it will be enjoyable because it will be true and new. . . . The film of tomorrow will be an act of love.[11]

Unlike Truffaut's films, most self-centered, autobiographical communications are tedious insights into the not-so-revealing, selfish life of a vain egotist.

It is wise to remember in this regard that each of us is a paradox. Created in the image of God, we have the capacity for seeking and expressing what is good, worthy, and true. However, as sinners, we also tend to embrace what is false, evil, and ugly. We are therefore often attracted by the base, yet we still long for the sublime.

The desire for fame is a potent motivating force. People will go to great lengths for fame, the opportunity to present themselves to the world with such force and power that they become immortalized by, through, or in, their work. As Auntie Mame said in the play of the same name, "I've been immortalized on celluloid." Throughout history, there have been people who starved themselves, others who denied themselves, many who gave up their values, some who sold their souls, and a few who killed, all for fame. Of course, there have been those who perfected their craft and honestly attained greatness in their quest for fame, but many others were merely flashes in the pan, short-lived, soon forgotten. Andy Warhol once said that the new technologies would usher in an age when every person in the world would be famous for at least fifteen minutes. The question for Andy is, Who would, or could, care?

Unless it is a secondary motivation or is modified by another motivation, such as the desire to help, entertain, or uplift others, the quest for fame is nothing more than an extreme case of vanity, simple exhibitionism. At three, our son would try everything possible to attract his parents' attention, exclaiming frequently, "Look at me!" This egotism is cute in a three-year-old, but it is tiresome when exhibited by an endless number of talking heads on a public-access cable television channel, and it is distressing when it motivates vacuous preaching programs and talk shows whose primary purpose is to elevate an individual to stardom. If religious programmers do not have a clear idea of why or what they want to say, their presence on television or cable can appear to be "here I am" exhibitionism.

Television programs, movies, and even radio programs demand a strong central figure, a "star," to sustain and hold an audience. Very few programs have been able to survive without a star to whom the audience can relate. Furthermore, as in the days of Samuel, people still want a strong leader. Therefore, it is easy for a strong, attractive personality to assert him- or herself as the "star" of a Christian communications ministry, whether that ministry communicates through television, movies, radio, print, music, or person-to-person.

The question is not whether there should be a strong central character in a television program, but whether that person is motivated by a desire to serve self, others, an ideal, or God. Humility and a commitment to serve our Lord and others will help us avoid producing communications that serve only vanity.

As Christians, we should avoid even the appearance of vanity video or vanity radio; the taint of vanity detracts from our witness to Jesus, our Lord and Savior. It is easy to fall into the trap of wanting the world to know what a great job we are doing, especially when we feel we have given up much to dedicate ourselves to proclaiming his gospel. It is also easy to fall into the trap of using Jesus to promote ourselves, as Marjoe Gortner so clearly demonstrated in *Marjoe*, an Academy-Award-winning film about his life in which he confessed to being a fraud and using evangelical Christianity to promote himself.

Sometimes there is wisdom in establishing a presence on broadcast or cable television with a simple talk show in expectation of a time when the resources will be available to do real mission or ministry and to ensure that another point of view is heard by viewers. Trinity Parish, the oldest Episcopal church in New York City, produced one of the first programs on Manhattan Cable so that the parish could establish a presence. Ten years later the cable system time that Trinity had secured was very valuable, and the parish was able to produce high-quality programs that truly ministered to the community.

Even during its years of simple productions, Trinity's programs were used by God to communicate the Good News. One Sunday morning, an assistant New York district attorney said that he had been on the verge of committing suicide during an alcoholic stupor when he saw "Trinity Church Service" on the public-access channel. The sermon touched him. He accepted Christ and became a communicant of Trinity Parish, with a new lease on life. The least-watched cable channel with the worst programming became a clear medium for delivery the Gospel.

The desire to make money is a strong motivation and may be the primary motivation for most mass communication in the United States. Anyone who wants to use the electronic media should understand how important the economic aspects of, and motivations for, telecommunications are in this country.

Since the middle of the 1970s, the marketplace approach has been the controlling philosophy at the Federal Communications Commission. Prior to this move toward allowing market forces to govern electronic media, the FCC operated under the diversity of speech, public interest philosophy originally set forth in the 1934 Communications Act. Les Brown, the editor-in-chief of *Channels*, has stated clearly the philosophy of the 1934 Act and the FCC prior to the 1970s:

The public does have rights, because the airwaves over which radio and television stations broadcast belong to everyone. It is the same air as the air we breathe, and no one with a [television or radio broadcast] license may claim it as his or her property. Broadcasters are given the privilege of using these airwaves with a limited number of frequencies, as public trustees. It immediately becomes the responsibility under the law to use the airwaves in ways that serve "the public interest, convenience and necessity" [according to the 1934 Communications Act]. The Federal Communications Commission was created to manage traffic on the electromagnetic spectrum, to award licenses to the most qualified applicants, and to see that the public interest is served.[12]

The 1934 Communications Act was enacted because there is a limited amount of broadcast space on the electromagnetic spectrum. There were more people who wanted to communicate over radio (and later television) than there was room on the broadcast frequencies. In some areas, reception of a clear signal was impossible because of all the people who were broadcasting. To sort out this confusion and overcome the squawk of frequency interference, Congress decided to license broadcasters to particular frequencies. However, Congress was confronted by the problem of the First Amendment guarantee of free speech to all Americans, since only a few people or corporations would receive licenses. To preserve the right of all Americans to express their point of view over the airwaves, Congress made the boradcaster a public trustee over the scarce spectrum space. Congress required the broadcaster to operate with the public interest in mind, and the Federal Communications Commission was set up to attempt to assure diversity of speech through such devices as the fairness doctrine, equal time, balanced programming, noncommercial programming, and community ascertainment.

A 1963 House of Representatives report on the FCC succinctly set forth the legal philosophy underlying the 1934 Communications Act:

Under our system, the interests of the public are dominant. The commercial needs of licensed broadcasters and advertisers must be integrated into those of the public. Hence, individual citizens and the communities they compose owe a duty to themselves and their peers to take an active part in the scope and quality of the television service which . . . has vast impact on their lives and on the lives of their children. . . . They are the owners of the channels of television—indeed of all broadcasting.[13]

However, broadcasters had found, even before the Act, that broadcasting was particularly well suited to commercial speech that sold a product. Motivated by the desire to make money, broadcasters discovered the power of radio, and later television, for advertising. They found that they could structure a program to emotively capture and hold an audience's attention; an advertiser could buy time in or near the program to present a commercial and sell a product.

The program has become the setting for the commercial. Like a flashing sign, the program attracts the audience's attention to the item for sale in the commercial. The program has to not only attract an audience but also enhance the message of the commercial, if the broadcaster wants to sell commercial time to an advertiser at the best price.

If a commercial is attempting to sell toothpaste by claiming that the toothpaste will give the consumer more girlfriends or boyfriends, the advertiser does not want time near a program that discounts the benefit of friends of the opposite sex. On the contrary, the advertiser wants the commercial to run with a program that makes the viewer want more girlfriends or boyfriends so that the viewer will run out to buy more toothpaste. An educational public affairs program on tooth decay, no matter how well produced, will rarely attract the number of viewers necessary to satisfy the broadcaster, who charges the advertiser by how many eyeballs or ears were tuned into the program in question. Motivated by money, the broadcaster wants programs that earn more advertising dollars.

The 1934 Communications Act treats radio and television as tools of communication that will portray reality truthfully by carrying a wide variety of speech. Broadcasters treat these same media as a means for earning money, so their programs must be structured to present a particular view of reality that enhances the sale of goods and services. The Act portrayed the telecommunications media as a forum for diverse speech; broadcasters see it as an agora, a marketplace for commercial speech.

The problem, of course, arises from this colliding of many freedoms in broadcasting: the freedom of speech of all Americans (not just the broadcasters); freedom of the press; freedom of religion; and freedom of the marketplace (though this last is not specifically named in the Bill of Rights). Broadcasters argue that regulations limit their freedom of speech, but the public interest standard rests on the paradox that the rights of the few broadcasters must be abridged to protect the free speech of the many in the listening and viewing public.[14]

Emphasizing programming that serves the needs of the community, the FCC, under the 1934 Communications Act, identified the following program types, in order of importance, as necessary for the broadcaster to carry to serve the public interest:

1. opportunity for local self-expression
2. development and use of local talent
3. programs for children
4. religious programs
5. educational programs
6. public affairs programs
7. editorialization by licensees
8. political broadcasts
9. agricultural broadcasts
10. news programs
11. weather and market reports
12. sports programs
13. service to minority groups
14. entertainment programming

All of these program types, except news, sports, and entertainment, are unprofitable. Due to the powerful pressure of broadcasters, both Congress and the FCC have deregulated radio and are debating whether to deregulate television. Deregulation involves giving broadcasters ownership of the airwaves and removing all requirements to broadcast in the public interest. Deregulation denies everyone freedom to speak unless allowed by the broadcaster. Deregulation would mean that commercial speech would dominate all other speech on radio and television, with greater emphasis on programming that promotes such commercial speech, including sex and violence, since both are very effective in capturing an audience for an advertiser.

For someone who wants to communicate noncommercial speech, being forced to buy time can prove distorting—of both the program itself and the motivation behind it. For instance, if a Christian who is motivated to present the Gospel over radio or television can only do so by buying time *and* to buy time must raise money from the program audience, he or she may begin to structure the presentation of the Gospel so that the audience will give to the program. Unfortunately, eventually such a person may find him- or herself speaking primarily to those who give rather than the audience originally targeted, people who are not converted and are not yet prepared to give.

Right now, thanks to the goodwill of WGST, the local CBS radio affiliate in Atlanta, Georgia, and to the lingering effect of regulation, I host a weekly public affairs program entitled "Religionwise: A Weekly Look at the News Through the Eyes of Religion." Since WGST doesn't charge me for time and I do not have to raise money over the air, I can aim the program at the unconverted, and I can address some prophetic aspects of the Gospel that would not promote audience giving.

On the other hand, I am forced by the public affairs format to emphasize some aspects of the Gospel over others, even though I try to present the full Gospel. In effect, both forms of programming, paid and free, are necessary to present the whole Gospel, demonstrating the wisdom of the diversity of speech approach to regulation of the electronic media.

Broadcasters often compare themselves to newspaper owners, arguing that regulations limit their freedom as members
of the press, but in fact, they are comparing apples and or-
anges. There is no natural or artificial limit on the number of
newspapers there are, and for a relatively small cost anyone
can print, mimeograph, or copy their views and distribute
them. However, the number of people who can use the telecommunications media is limited by the scarcity of electronic
spectrum space, clearly evidenced by the prohibitively high
cost of buying or building a radio or television station. As Joel
Chaseman, president of Post Newsweek Stations, has said:

The let-the-marketplace-decide approach is wrong in principle. It is
clearly not in the public interest for spectrum to be assigned among
potential uses or users on the basis of the highest bid, without regard
for the nature or importance of the use itself. . . .

A new indoor record for the height of bureaucratic arrogance was
achieved recently by a government official who proposed that the
marketplace should determine all difficult questions involved in direct
broadcast from satellite to home—ownership, use, technical standards, compatibility with existing hardware, occupation of scarce
spectrum and even international issues. . . .

What marketplace is this? It costs approximately $350,000,000 from
the design of satellite through the launch of space vehicle to daily
operation, not to mention the purchase or lease by each household or
business of an earth station costing several hundred dollars plus an
additional monthly charge. A very special marketplace indeed, com-
petitive only to those who can afford a billion-dollar entry fee. . . .

Deregulation can not become a synonym for abdication, especially
when the public interest clearly calls for service which is free to all.[15]

Ownership in the communications industry is quite concentrated; therefore, deregulation is not promoting a free market
but strengthening monopolies. With gate keeping concentrated
in so few hands, there is no guarantee that there will be the
free exchange of thoughts and ideas so necessary to sustain a
democracy.

As counsel for the Democratic National Committee, Charles

Ferris, who started the move toward deregulation when he was chairman of the FCC, brought charges before the FCC complaining that Republicans were monopolizing television by buying more time than Democrats could afford. Ferris requested free time on the three networks to counter the Republican spots. He found out the hard way that the marketplace process he had promoted only worked to the advantage of those who have the economic power to control the channels of communication. The diversity of speech principle, by contrast, protects the freedom of speech of all. While in power, Ferris extolled the virtues of the marketplace; when forced out of power, he cried out for freedom of speech for all points of view.[16]

Motivated by the desire to make more money and freed to a large degree from the public interest standard, networks are producing more programs containing sex and violence and featuring themes that were taboo until quite recently, such as incest, homosexuality, and child abuse. When fishing for an audience to sell to an advertiser, broadcasters have found that sex and violence are cheap lures that catch a reasonably large audience without much effort. As John Carman noted in the *Atlanta Journal*,

The formula is obvious. Sell the show on the basis of sin and skin, appeal to viewers' sexual fantasies, tease them with peekaboo shots of their favorite actresses and actors, and then bring down the curtain with the obligatory triumph of conventional morality.[17]

On the other hand, programs featuring a Christian point of view have been relegated for economic reasons to the Sunday morning ghetto (early Sunday morning when few are watching) or the cable ghetto (the channels few people watch), since broadcasters no longer feel any responsibility to feature a diversity of speech in the public interest even when broadcast time is paid for.

To put our country's communications policy into perspective, it should be noted that different motivations drive the systems in other countries. In France, the government is the gatekeeper: therefore, the party in power controls the electronic media, and the primary motivation for communication is political. In the Netherlands, access to the media is allotted to different groups depending on what percentage of the population they represent, so evangelical Christians have a great deal of time on the state television station. In England, the BBC system is paid for by a tax on television sets; therefore, the programming is aimed at satisfying (to a great degree) the wants of the public who pay for the programs as opposed to the wants of advertisers. In the United States, advertisers pay for programs and, in turn, add the cost of that programming into the price of their products; this is, in reality, a hidden tax paid by the consumer.

Because of government funding cuts, public broadcasting in the United States (on television, the Public Broadcasting Service, PBS, and on radio, National Public Radio, NPR) has been forced to rely on corporate underwriting for programming, thereby being caught in the commercial catch-22 to some degree, although "on-air" fund-raising has brought public broadcasting some degree of autonomy.

Having said all this, it should be understood that the desire to make money is not bad or wrong unless it becomes greed that overruns decency and integrity and suppresses other forms of communication. When greed calls for programs that pander to life-diminishing themes and motifs such as prostitution, pornography, sexism, and racism, then it is clear that the motivation is rotten even though it may still empower the communication, impacting the audience by appealing to the worst in them.

Given this examination of some of the motivations for communication, you should be able to ascertain your own motivation. You should be aware of the potential power of your work as well as the pitfalls for those who succumb to a motivation that may be invoked by the chosen medium, especially when that motivation conflicts with God's call. Ask yourself honestly,

Dennis Renault, Sacramento Bee

McClatchy News Service

"THESE LADIES WILL SHOW YOU HOW TO MAKE A GOOD
LIVING WITHOUT GOVERNMENT SUPPORT."

Why do I want to communicate? and evaluate your answer in the context of the other ascertainment questions.

If you are really driven by the desire to make money or the desire for recognition, then do not claim that your motivation is God's call. You can't fool all of the people all of the time and you can't fool God at all. Some double-mindedness undermines the power and authenticity of your work.

You may ascertain your motivation and find that it is not intense enough to power your communication. Your desire to make money, or become famous, or proclaim your ideals may not be strong enough to suffer through the process of using a particular medium, such as film, writing, or television, and/or your motivation may not authenticate and drive your communication.

In Somerset Maugham's famous novel *Of Human Bondage*, the hero, Philip Carey, confronts his desire to be an artist and finds that he is not motivated enough to continue to suffer for his art, even though he has devoted a great deal of time and hard work to his study in Paris. Philip is honest enough with himself to admit that he does not have the talent or the motivation to forge ahead. Monsieur Foinet, the most respected and feared art teacher in Paris, confides to Philip:

"But if you were to ask my advice, I should say: take your courage in both hands and try your luck at something else. It sounds very hard, but let me tell you this: I would give all I have in the world if someone had given me that advice when I was your age and I had taken it."

Philip looked at him with surprise. The master forced his lips into a smile, but his eyes remained grave and sad.

"It is cruel to discover one's mediocrity only when it is too late. It does not improve the temper."[18]

Philip's insight into his talent and his motivation foreshadows our next chapter, where we will look in depth at how to discern our motivational talents. As we shall see, each of us has a motivational talent, which, when discerned, will help us to communicate effectively. Philip's story illustrates that it is not only the type of motivation but also its intensity that empowers us. With drive, Philip might have been able to excel as an artist.

Having dealt with many students who professed a desire to become television producers, directors, writers, or stars, I understand that many have neither a clear idea why they want to communicate nor the drive to see a production through to fruition. Instead, many of them have a vague idea that television is glamorous, and that vague notion is not a powerful enough motivation to see them through.

Vincent Canby notes that Truffaut worked zealously all the time, day and night; he was driven to commit his autobiographical visions to film.[19] In spite of the self-centered nature of his vision, the intensity of his motivation empowered and authenticated his films. The Atlanta Journal and Constitution reported a University of Chicago study as follows: "A study of 120 of the nation's top artists, athletes and scholars has concluded that drive and determination, not great natural talent, led to their extraordinary success."[20]

Therefore, when we ask ourselves, "Why do I want to communicate?" we should also ask the question that logically follows from our answer to that ascertainment question, "How much (or, how badly) do I want to communicate?"—that is, "How strong is my desire to communicate this?" Knowing what your motivation is in a particular instance and how intense it is helps you to determine whether or not that particular communication fits your motivational talent. What motivates a particular communication should follow from those gifts, talents, and desires that God has given you as a unique person. Therefore, next let's look at our motivational talents.

3. Who Am I?

This above all: to thine own self be true, and it must follow, as the
night the day, thou canst not then be false to any man.
SHAKESPEARE, HAMLET

Who are you? What is God's plan for your life? Our oldest
son, when four years old, wanted to be the government (the
president) and a baseball player. Most of the students in my
communication workshops, no matter what their age, come
into the workshop wanting to be the star, the director, or the
producer of their own television program. Philip Carey in *Of
Human Bondage* wants to be an Anglican priest in his youth;
then he decides to become an artist, then an accountant; finally, he finds out that he is called to be a doctor. The question
arises, Does it matter what profession Philip chooses? or what
my son becomes (aside from his father's pride)? or what roles
students take in the workshops?

With regard to Philip, the answer is a resounding "Yes, it
matters!" Maugham has so drawn Philip's character that he
has no alternative other than to eventually become a doctor.
In drama, novels, and other story-telling genres, the dynamics
inherent in a character's structure determine the character's
development and actions as he or she reacts to the other characters within the context of the premise. If an author has done
his or her job of getting to know a character by determining
every aspect of the character's physiology (sex, age, posture,
appearance, disabilities, and heredity), sociology (class, occupation, education, race, and home life), psychology (tempera-
ment, attitude, complexes, motivations, and abilities), and
spirituality, then that character will develop in the story as the
author intended because the character's makeup is such that

he or she cannot do otherwise. If any other alternative is available to the character, then the author has not done the job, and the structure of the character has to be rethought. As Henrik Ibsen describes it,

When I am writing I must be alone; if I have eight characters of drama to do with I have society enough; they keep me busy; I must learn to know them. And this process of making their acquaintance is slow and painful. I make as a rule, three casts of my dramas, which differ considerably from each other. I mean in characteristics, not in the course of the treatment. When I first settle down to work out my material, I feel as if I have to get to know my characters on a railway journey; the first acquaintance is struck up, and we have chatted about this and that. When I write it down again, I already see everything much more clearly, and I know the people as if I had stayed with them for a month at a watering place. I have grasped the leading points of their characters and their little peculiarities.[1]

Philip has to become a doctor; Maugham has constructed Philip so that he will become a doctor. However, what about my eldest son? or the student in the workshops?

Unlike a character in a story, my son—or a student—can persist in pursuing a job or role that is not suited for him. According to some studies, three or four out of five people are in the wrong jobs.[2] However, just because we persist in the wrong job does not mean that we are not designed to excel in a job that suits our motivational talents and gifts. We are.

According to many career counselors, every individual has a unique combination of characteristics that give him or her the ability to excel in a particular career.[3] Of course, different people perform what we might call the same job differently. In fact, saying that a person creates a job is probably more accurate than saying that a person adapts to a job.

As Christians, we realize that these findings by scientists and career counselors are nothing more than an affirmation that God has designed each of us for a particular purpose. God created and is interested in the real world; he came as a carpenter, and he chose some of us to be rulers, some to be bankers, some to be craftsmen, some to be scientists, but each of us to be what he created us to be. He tells us, "I create the blacksmith, who builds the fire and forges weapons. I also create the soldier, who uses the weapons to kill" (Isa. 54:16, GNB). He gives each of us those talents and desires needed to excel in a particular role. He also gives us the free will to choose to flourish by fulfilling his plan for our lives or to choose to be frustrated by rebelling against him and ourselves.

Even before the Fall, work was a part of God's plan for human life: "Then the Lord God placed the man in the Garden of Eden to cultivate it and guard it" (Gen. 2:15, GNB). After the Fall, work became difficult and exhausting. However, in spite of our Fall, God wants to bless us and make us prosper and wants us to rejoice in all that we do because he created us for his pleasure. He rejoices over us, and he loves us. This is great news: God wants us to be joyous and enjoy our work; however, to do so, we must submit to his glorious plan for our lives, give thanks to be content in all circumstances.

In the Church, we sometimes assume that God's plan for us is limited to prayer, praise, worship, social action, evangelism, Bible reading, and the other aspects of spirituality we discern in the New Testament. Living a holy life is a worthy goal (even if it is only fully attainable in heaven); however, since work is part of God's plan for our lives, our sanctification takes place in our living out his plan, not in our escaping the secular work world to adopt a religious role for which he has not created us or called us.

God may call us to be apostles or clergy, but too many Christians upon conversion drop out of the secular world to pursue so-called Christian careers. The institutional churches have recently come to realize that they are partially responsible for this rush to change from a secular to a sacred career by encouraging a low view of the laity and an exalted view of the clergy. (The opposite perspective is also wrong.) Churches must learn to recognize, bless, and ordain nonclerical jobs, as Jesus did. As Martin Luther said, "Be the monk never so holy, his work is no more holy than the farmer in the field, or the housewife at home.''

Another influence causing this leap into the cloth or into so-called Christian professions is the prevailing, but unbiblical, view that wealth and profits are bad, when, in fact, God protects property (''Thou shall not steal''), wants us to prosper, and praises those who make a profit. It is not money that is bad, but the love of it.

As noted in Chapter 1, several speakers at the 1984 Continental Congress on the Christian World View spoke about the powerful influence *Chariots of Fire* had on their lives. One speaker in particular said that he had been an opera singer but left it when he had a conversion experience to pursue Christian ministry. When he heard Eric Liddell say that he knew that his running gave God pleasure, this evangelist realized that his voice was a gift from God that he had not used for many years, so he joined a national opera company *and* continued his ministry.

Several times each year, I come across a successful communicator who has come to know Jesus as Lord and Savior and wants to know how to get into ''Christian'' communications. Many of these influential individuals leave prominent positions at network television stations, advertising agencies, or major newspapers, where they can have an impact on the mass media, to enter the Christian communications industry, where they are either never heard from again or heard only within the Christian communications enclave.

When we come to know him, God frees us from bondage to sin, not so that we can escape from the world, but so that we can witness to him in word and deed in the marketplace where he called us (unless he indicates otherwise). God calls us to ''occupy till I come'' (Luke 19:13) by working in and taking charge of the mass media and all areas of life. His plan is for us to be co-workers with him in redeeming the world by doing what he has designed us to do best in his Name.

Every individual has a specific contribution to make. Every

job that each person performs within our society is important to it, whether that person is a doctor, a corporate executive, a shoemaker, a homemaker, or a janitor—and even though, in our fallenness, we tend to glamorize some jobs, belittle others, and discount the remainder. We should respect every job, even though some jobs demand, deserve, or receive more compensation and/or authority than others. In the biblical model of the world, there is a very definite hierarchy, but that chain of authority is qualitatively different from any social hierarchy because each person is dedicated to loving, respecting, and serving God and each other.

This brings us back to the question, What is God's plan for your life? In other words, What has God designed you to do? and How do you find out what God has designed you to do?

Since each of us has many talents and motivations that come together to determine who we are and in what job we will flourish, we can be defined by that point at which our motivations, talents, physiology, sociology, psychology, and spirituality meet, almost like a character in God's story. Just as Philip Carey's future occupation was clear from his character structure as revealed in the beginning of *Of Human Bondage*, God's plan for us is revealed in those talents and motivations we exhibit throughout our personal history. Even our weaknesses are instruments of God's grace. By discerning and analyzing our characteristics as they reveal themselves in our own history, we can discover what job or role God has designed for us.

At seventeen, Joseph, although he was the youngest brother, clearly exhibited those talents and motivations that would make him the leader of his family, his people, and the Egyptians. He was respectful of authority, responsible, obedient, intelligent, wise, and a man of vision; furthermore, Joseph was motivated by a dream of leadership.

As a youth confronted by a messenger of God, Gideon exhibited the fearlessness, cunning, and drive to save Israel. Later in his life these same characteristics would propel him to become a mighty warrior judge of his people.

Daniel, as a youth, exhibited those characteristics that were to make him a leader and a prophet:

Then the king ordered Ashpenaz, chief of his court officials, to bring in some of the Israelites from the royal family and the nobility— young men without any physical defect, handsome, showing aptitude for every kind of learning, well informed, quick to understand, and qualified to serve in the king's palace. . . .

But Daniel resolved not to defile himself with the royal food and wine, and he asked the chief official for permission not to defile himself this way. . . .

To these four young men God gave knowledge and understanding of all kinds of literature and learning. And Daniel could understand visions and dreams of all kinds. (Dan. 1:3–4, 8, and 17)

From Noah through Abraham, David, and Solomon to John the Baptist, Peter, and Paul, those characteristic talents and motivations that determine each one's role in history can be discerned at the very beginning of their lives, including the weaknesses that must remind us to attribute victories to God rather than to a human being. God has his plan for each of us; all we need to do is to discern it.

There are as many ways to discern God's plan for our life as there are career counselors. Most systems boil down to designating several distinct periods in your life, recalling four or five of your achievements during each period, and then analyzing what motivations and talents went into those achievements. From this analysis, your motivational talents (those talents you are motivated to use), thrust, characteristics, and pattern may be discerned and matched to jobs for which that combination of motivations and talents is a prerequisite.

Research indicates that companies structured according to people's motivational talents are much more productive and successful than companies that hire and organize people on the basis of a job description. The classic example is hiring a secretary because she can type a hundred words a minute without a mistake only to find that she doesn't fit the position because she is motivated to lead and organize the office, not type. If her history had been reviewed with an eye toward discovering her motivational talents, it would have been clear that she was a leader throughout her childhood and was best suited to be an office administrator.

Of course, this is a simplistic example. All of us have many talents, many motivations, and many gifts. Someone, for instance, might be motivated to race cars, read books, compile statistics, and design houses; however, that person may be talented at learning languages, playing chess, and persuading audiences of logical imperatives; furthermore, this same person may have gifts for helping and teaching. It is clear that our hypothetical person should not run off and race cars without considering the total picture defined by his or her motivational talents and gifts. Furthermore, as noted in the last chapter, motivation is often more important than talent, although both should be considered in choosing a profession.

If you want to communicate effectively it is very important that you know what your motivations, talents, and personal characteristics are as they relate to communications. Communication impacts all aspects of life, and there are many different methods of doing it effectively; each requires different motivations and talents. As a medium, television involves a constellation of talents, from financial through electronic to a highly developed sense of time, space, and rhythm to the ability to project an image through time and space to a faceless audience.

To know which method and which medium of communication you should utilize, you should know what your motivational design is. Not knowing your motivational design, you can find yourself frustrated, communicating ineffectively through a medium that is alien to you, in a style that works for others but not for you.

Pick out a few of the better preachers in your community and analyze their preaching. You will no doubt find that some of them are good storytellers, some are good exegetes, some are good teachers, and some are powerful prophets. For you to choose to be a story-telling preacher when neither the method, story telling, nor the medium, preaching, is appropriate to your motivational talents would be extremely frustrating.

In my workshops, students work through a few exercises in which each of them tries a hand at being the star or director, in accordance with their fantasies. They quickly discover whether or not they have the aptitude for their chosen role and whether or not they really like being in that role. More often than not, many find that they really do not want to be the star or the director but do enjoy doing something else, whether it is lighting, set design, engineering, or another important television task. In fact, they find that they excel at those jobs for which they have the right motivational abilities.

This is not a career counseling book, but we need to be aware of our motivational talents if we want to communicate effectively. Not only does the specific motivation for a particular communication, as discussed in the last chapter, flow from "who you are" but the intensity of the motivation for a specific communication is determined to a large degree by your God-given motivational thrust. Therefore, this chapter will acquaint you with a process by which you may discover your motivational talents through practical exercises demonstrating the methods used by several career counselors.[4] There is a specific exercise for determining your role in television production that also applies to film and may be adapted to radio production.

View the system given here as an illustrative guide (which is not definitive) to help you communicate more effectively. Since many of the communicators with whom I have worked like exercises, I include these exercises to help you understand the process. If you are seriously interested in discovering your motivational talents (which you should be), you should consult a career counselor or at least a good book on the subject.[5]

Motivational Talents/Pattern Exercises

Step 1—Past Achievements

This is the first step in discerning your inherent, God-given motivational talents and the picture they form, which determines his plan for your life.

Divide your life into three periods, such as ages 1 to 18, 18 to 25, and 25 to the present. Review each period in your mind, and pick out three or four achievements from each period of which you are the most proud.

Head each of three pieces of paper "My Achievements, Age ___:" and use each form to write down your achievements for each one of the three periods of your life, numbering them 1–4.

Do not get bogged down in detail. Pick things you did that gave you a feeling of accomplishment, not achievements you think someone else would choose.

They key word is *joy*. What did you enjoy doing, felt you did well, and are happy to recall? These achievements may be things that no one else knows about, or no one else would admire. Richard Bolles has this advice:

Keep your eye constantly on that "divine radar": enjoyable. It's by no means always a guide to what you should be doing, but it sure is more reliable than any other key that people have come up with. Sift later. For now, put down anything that helped you enjoy a particular moment or period of your life.[6]

Please note that you are participating in this exerise *for yourself*. It is not a test. It is only a guide. There are no right answers. Enjoy yourself, and let the characteristic patterns of your motivational talents emerge.

Some examples:

"Crocheting potholders and exchanging stories with my grandmother at age nine."

"Writing with an ink pen before anyone else in my class, although no one knew it."

"Diplomatically, bringing my father and mother back together after they had an argument, when I was four or five years old."

"Putting on plays for my brother and sisters."

"Cornering the market in raccoon coats at my college, just before they became a fad."

"Discovering how to enjoy and relate to my children after years of being preoccupied with business."

Step 2—Rank Past Achievements

Look over your list of achievements and choose the five you feel are the most important to you.
Rank these five in order of importance, and write them down numbered in that order.

Step 3—Dissect Achievements

Analyze each of your five most important achievements in terms of the classic questions: who, what, where, when, why, and how.
List the following questions on a sheet of paper for each of the five achievements, leaving space for your answers.

Brief summary of achievement:

When I was involved:

Where I was involved:

How I was involved:

Why I was involved:

What I actually did:

How I did it:

Who else was involved:

How I related to them:

Why I related to them in the manner I did:

What made this achievement important to me:

Step 4—Present Likes and Dislikes

To help discern the pattern of your motivational talents it is important to take into consideration where you are now. Look at your present job, or jobs, and analyze what you like, what you dislike, and why. Head a piece of paper "Present Job," and list the following questions as before:

Brief statement of job:

How I got the job:

Why I took the job:

What I do:

What I like doing:

Why I like doing what I like doing:

What I dislike doing:

Why I dislike doing what I dislike doing:

Step 5—My Vision

List and analyze your vision of what you would like to achieve, if you could, before you die, heading your sheet of paper "Future Achievement" and using a separate sheet for each future achievement:

Brief statement of vision:

What I hope to accomplish:

Why I hope to accomplish it:

What I will do:

How I will do it:

Who will be involved:

Step 6—Discerning Your Motivational Talents

As I have noted, a person can have many motivations (to be a great pianist, for example), many of which may not correspond to that person's talents (no manual dexterity).

Motivational talents are those natural, God-given abilities that you are motivated to use and develop. For example, if our above-mentioned hypothetical person did have manual dexterity, tonal memory, pitch discrimination, rhythmic ability, timbre discrimination, and a love of music, then that person would become a great pianist, if he or she allowed motivational talents to control career choice.

Of course, a person may have talents he or she is not motivated to use, or those talents may be subservient to another talent, or set of talents, because of an overriding motivation. Our hypothetical person may not become a great pianist because he or she hates to perform in public or may be motivated to go into audio engineering because of an overriding interest in the practical solutions to improving the audio portion of television transmission. Therefore, instead of concentrating on motivations and then on talents as many career counselors do, the following exercises will focus on those talents you are motivated to use.

The first step in discerning your motivational talents is to compare what you have discovered about yourself in steps 1–5 with the following lists. These lists are organized according to categories that will help you discern your unique motivational pattern. These lists are not complete and inclusive, but partial and suggestive. (Many career counselors would arrange these lists differently. For more complete inventories of motivational talents or abilities, see the books mentioned in note 5.)

From these lists, pick out the five talents you are motivated to use, and prove that that is the case by analyzing the evidence as revealed in steps 1–5.

Next, rank your motivational talents so that you can discern your basic motivational direction.

Then, in the following steps, discern your motivated faculty, object, relations, and situation.

Finally, bring all this information together to discern your motivational pattern.

Motivational Talents Lists

Your basic motivational talents and the picture they form are common to all your achievements, uniting and empowering everything that you do well and enjoy doing. Compare your achievements, your likes and dislikes, and your vision as set forth in steps 1–5 with the following lists of motivational talents, and pick out five talents you have been motivated to use, like to use, and look forward to using.

Administrative Motivations

Execute	the motivated ability to get things done by following a project or task through to completion.
Expedite	the motivated ability to facilitate and accelerate the process or progress of a project or task.
Govern	the motivated ability to exercise authority in controlling the activities and personnel of an organization so as to keep a straight course and smooth operation for the good of the whole as well as of the individuals who make up the whole.
Manage	the motivated ability to carry on business or affairs.
Navigate	the motivated ability to chart and direct a course through the unknown waters of the future.
Organize	the motivated ability to arrange interdependent parts into a whole.

Oversee	the motivated ability to inspect, superintend, and supervise.
Plan	the motivated ability to develop a method, program, schedule, or scheme of action, procedure, or arrangement.
Prioritize	the motivated ability to rank and prescribe the order in which assignments are to be attended to.

Athletic motivations

Athletic motivations are self-defining; therefore, the following list leaves out definitions. Add to this list any other abilities that belong here and that apply to you.

Catch
Climb
Dive
Fight
Hit
Jump
Ride
Run
Skate
Ski
Swim
Throw
Walk

Cognitive Motivations

Analyze	the motivated ability to study a problem, situation, or the like in detail, in order to determine the solution or outcome.
Appraise	the motivated ability to evaluate or judge quality.

Experiment	the motivated ability to test, to discover some unknown principle or effect, or to demonstrate some known truth, principle, or effect.
Foresee	the motivated ability to anticipate and apprehend events so that prudent action may be taken.
Intuit	the motivated ability to instinctively obtain knowledge.
Investigate	the motivated ability to research by patient inquiry, observation, and examination of the facts.
Learn	the motivated ability to acquire knowledge or skill by study, instruction, or investigation.
Memorize	the motivated ability to retain what has been learned or experienced.
Perceive	the motivated ability to be acutely aware and discerning.
Reason	the motivated ability to think things out systematically and logically.
Synthesize	the motivated ability to combine separate elements into a whole.

Communicative motivations

Argue	the motivated ability to confront and debate others.
Discuss	the motivated ability to dialogue with, interview, and listen to others.
Critique	the motivated ability to correct and perfect communications.
Entertain	the motivated ability to amuse and involve others in flights of fancy through story telling, drama, performing, telling jokes, music, and so forth.

Express	the motivated ability to express feelings, desires, needs, thoughts, ideas, or memories.
Perform	the motivated ability to act, speak, and perform in front of others.
Persuade	the motivated ability to influence and convince others.
Praise	the motivated ability to encourage and commend others.
Preach	the motivated ability to proclaim the gospel of Jesus Christ, or a religious belief system.
Promote	the motivated ability to advertise and enhance the reputation of someone or something.
Prophesy	the motivated ability to confront others with a critical message.
Sell	the motivated ability to communicate about some thing or idea in such a manner that the audience purchases it.
Teach	the motivated ability to lecture, inform, and instruct others by demonstrating, explaining, summarizing, discussing, and/or defining.
Translate	the motivated ability to interpret something to others.

Creative motivations

Build	the motivated ability to create and fashion permanent structures, organizations, and things.
Compose	the motivated ability to conceive and create works of art, music, and literature.

Design | the motivated ability to imagine, visualize, and create visual displays.

Innovate | the motivated ability to introduce something new and make changes in anything established.

Invent | the motivated ability to create physical, chemical, mechanical, and other innovations.

Produce | the motivated ability to create, multiply, and manufacture animals, plants, and things, including gadgets, movies, and so forth.

Solve | the motivated ability to creatively solve problems and improve things.

Leadership motivations

Command | the motivated ability to take charge of people and things.

Decide | the motivated ability to make decisions, to guide and lead others.

Direct | the motivated ability to orchestrate and conduct the activities of others and things.

Encourage | the motivated ability to empower and motivate others to achieve something.

Guide | the motivated ability to show the way to those following.

Influence | the motivated ability because of character and status to exert authority over the minds and actions of others.

Initiate | the motivated ability to start an activity or action.

Prevail	the motivated ability to lead a crusade to defeat adversary ideologies, people, and things.
Recruit	the motivated ability to enlist resources and other people in a common task.

Physical/Manual motivations

Acquire	the motivated ability to accumulate property and things.
Construct	the motivated ability to put together, make, or build something.
Develop	the motivated ability to promote the growth of something.
Exploit	the motivated ability to make use of all aspects of something for profit.
Handle	the motivated ability to hold, move, balance, and manage something using the hands.
Improve	the motivated ability to make something better.
Maintain	the motivated ability to keep something in good condition.
Manipulate	the motivated ability to treat or operate something with the hands.
Mold/Adapt	the motivated ability to shape something with the hands.
Possess	the motivated ability to keep and control things.
Repair	the motivated ability to restore something to good condition after it is broken or has decayed.

Playful motivations

Amuse	the motivated ability to divert, occupy pleasurably, or entertain.

Challenge	the motivated ability to invite someone to engage in a contest.
Compete	the motivated ability to contend in rivalry, as for a prize.
Contest	the motivated ability to struggle for victory.
Enjoy	the motivated ability to take satisfaction in experiencing.
Frolic	the motivated ability to make merry or to play.
Gamble	the motivated ability to play a game for money or another stake.
Master	the motivated ability to become adept at or to subdue something.
Outwit	the motivated ability to surpass in ingenuity or cunning.
Recreate	the motivated ability to change occupation or indulge in diversions for the sake of relaxation and refreshment.
Strategize	the motivated ability to use artifice, science and, intrigue to win a game.
Toy	the motivated ability to trifle, play, or dally with something.

Service motivations

Coach	the motivated ability to assist, instruct, tutor, or prepare someone for a task, game, or examination.
Conciliate	the motivated ability to resolve disputes by causing the parties to agree and become friends by gaining their goodwill, drawing them together, and winning them over to a compatible point of view.

Counsel	the motivated ability to exercise prudence in advising someone based on mutual deliberation.
Facilitate	the motivated ability to make something easy or less difficult for someone.
Feed	the motivated ability to provide food or something else essential for the growth, sustenance, or maintenance of someone or something.
Heal	the motivated ability to help cure or restore someone to health.
Help	the motivated ability to assist, wait on, lend aid to, improve, protect, rescue, relieve, or aid someone.
Mediate	the motivated ability to act as an intermediate between two or more parties.
Nurse	the motivated ability to take care of someone or something.
Nurture	the motivated ability to bring up or train.
Teach	the motivated ability to impart knowledge to someone. (Note that teach is also a communicative motivation.)
Tend	the motivated ability to watch over and take care of someone or something.

Spiritual motivations

Adorn	the motivated ability to add to the beauty, splendor, or attractiveness of something.
Believe	the motivated ability to have faith or religious convictions.
Bless	the motivated ability to praise, glorify, consecrate, or hallow.

Commune	the motivated ability to confer together and have fellowship with God as well as other people.
Dream	the motivated ability to have vision or to perceive the reality of the supernatural.
Explore	the motivated ability to seek for or after a discovery so that the unknown may be made known.
Love	the motivated ability to strongly care for and give selflessly to another.
Meditate	the motivated ability to contemplate and reflect on something.
Obey	the motivated ability to respond in love by executing the commands of someone.
Overcome	the motivated ability to conquer or to succeed.
Perfect	the motivated ability to strive for maturity or to help improve and complete.
Persevere	the motivated ability to persist in any enterprise undertaken in spite of opposition.
Preach	the motivated ability to proclaim the gospel of Jesus Christ, or a religious belief system. (Note that preach is also a communicative motivation.)
Prophesy	the motivated ability to confront others with a critical message. (Note that prophesy is also a communicative motivation.)
Rebuke	the motivated ability to reject and renounce evil.
Rejoice	the motivated ability to feel and give great joy and delight.

Rescue	the motivated ability to redeem or deliver from bondage.
Restore	the motivated ability to heal and make relationships whole.

Symbolic motivations

Account	the motivated ability to value, estimate, or balance a collection of items.
Budget	the motivated ability to estimate income and expenses.
Calculate	the motivated ability to compute.
Equate	the motivated ability to express as equal, reduce to a common standard, or derive an equation that expresses the process of equating by means of symbols.
Estimate	the motivated ability to approximate.
Formulate	the motivated ability to express in a systematized symbolic statement.
Graph	the motivated ability to symbolize using a chart, plot, or tracing.
Measure	the motivated ability to ascertain the dimensions, quantity, or limits of a thing.
Solve	the motivated ability to creatively solve problems and improve things. (Note that solve is also a creative motivation.)
Tabulate	the motivated ability to reduce to a table of figures.

Once you have identified the five motivational talents that most likely apply to you, on a separate sheet of paper for each, write down the name of the motivational talent and the list category it belongs in. Then review steps 1–5, and show that each of these motivational talents are present in your achievements, likes, and vision.

Step 7—Discerning Your Motivational Direction

Your basic motivational direction is the internal guidance system, made up of a unique combination of motivational talents, that drives you in a specific direction. It is the backbone of your God-given structure. Your basic motivational direction is determined by your primary motivational talent and the order of importance of your four other major motivational talents.

To discern your basic motivational direction, simply list your five discerned motivational talents in order of importance by referring to the frequency of occurrence and importance of each in steps 1–5.

Step 8—Discerning Other Motivated Characteristics

You have other God-given motivated characteristics that fill out your structure. From each of the following lists, pick out that particular motivated characteristic that applies to you and then compare it with what you learned in steps 1–5, to demonstrate that that characteristic is your primary motivated characteristic in that category.

Motivated Faculty

Your motivated faculty is that physical or mental power or function, such as touch, that you have been most motivated to use, that you like using and look forward to using, and that is your best-developed faculty.

Allure	the physical power to attract people.
Balance	the power to be poised and to balance things.
Charisma	the quality of extraordinary spiritual power, usually manifest in the ability to elicit popular support.
Coordination	the physical power to function harmoniously and effectively.

Dexterity	the faculty of being able to use your hands with quickness, skill, and ease.
Emotion	the power to feel empathy, sympathy, love, and so forth.
Energy	the inherent power to perform a great deal of work or do many things without becoming tired.
Hearing	the faculty of perceiving, discriminating, and remembering sounds, tones, pitch, timbre.
Intellect	the faculty of using your mind to know, reason, judge, and comprehend.
Memory	the power to remember and recall.
Perception	the faculty of being aware and intuitive.
Rhythm	the faculty of being able to perceive, remember, or emulate cadence, motion, beats, accents, or time.
Sight	the faculty of seeing, perceiving, discerning, visualizing, and remembering images, designs, colors, proportions, objects, and all the real world.
Smell	the power to detect and perceive odors and aromas.
Strength	the faculty of power, endurance, force, and toughness.
Taste	the power to perceive, recognize, and remember the flavor of something.
Touch	the faculty of perceiving by contact.

Motivated Object

Your motivated object is that object which you have been most motivated to use, like using, and look forward to using. This list is not inclusive. Add any objects that apply to you.

Animals
Art
Books
Budgets
Building Materials
Cameras
Electronics
Fabrics
Hardware/Tools
Ideas
Images
Land
Mechanical Equipment
Money
Musical Instruments
Numbers
Organizations
Paints
Plants
Projects
Symbols
Systems
Wood
Words

Motivated Relations

Your motivated relations are those relations with another person, or other people, in which you have been most motivated to be involved, like being involved, and look forward to being involved.

Coach

Healer/Doctor

Helper

Individualist

Leader

Manager/Governor

Mediator

Nurse

Partner/Friend

Server

Team Member

Motivated Situation

Your motivated situation is where you have been most motivated to achieve, like to achieve, and look forward to achieving.

Alone

At ease

Free

In a classroom/lecture/crowd

In competition

Isolated

In a structured environment

Solving problems

Under stress

From each of these four lists, pick out one motivated characteristic that most likely applies to you. Just as you did in the case of the motivational talents, on a separate sheet of paper for each motivated characteristic, write down the name of the characteristic and the list category to which it belongs. Then review steps 1–5 and show that each of these motivated characteristics you picked out are present in your achivements, likes, and vision.

Step 9—Discerning Your Motivational Picture

Your motivational picture is a portrait of who you are produced by bringing together all the information that you have found out about yourself in steps 1–8, where you discerned your motivational talents, direction, and characteristics. Your motivational picture defines who God created you to be and his plan for your life.

To discern your motivational picture, simply review steps 1–8 and fill in a Motivational Picture form like the one shown here.

MOTIVATIONAL PICTURE

Motivational Direction
(primary motivational talent)
_____

Secondary Motivational Talents
_____
_____
_____
_____

Motivated Faculty   Motivated Object
_____   _____

Motivated Relations   Motivated Situation
_____   _____

You may have noticed that you can add to this form other motivated characteristics that you have found in yourself from steps 1–5, or that you can find by increasing the details that you record in steps 1–5 or in similar exercises you can develop.

For instance, you can add your motivated geographic location or your motivated working environment. The more detail you develop, the clearer you will be about God's will for your life.

Keep in mind that these exercises are illustrative, not definitive. To accurately discover your motivational talents, consult a career counselor or an authoritative book on the subject.

Remember, whatever your unique motivational picture turns out to be, it is necessary for you to work at fulfilling God's plan for your life.

Knowing your motivational picture will enable you to communicate more effectively by helping you to determine what you want to say, why you want to say it, to whom, and through what genre and medium: Your motivational direction and motivational talents will tell you what matters most to you and why you want to communicate. Your motivated characteristics and talents will indicate to whom and in what circumstances you are most comfortable and effective. Once you are aware of the nature of the available media, your motivational picture will guide you into using the appropriate medium for your gifts and talents.

Of course, God and unusual circumstances can make you an effective communicator on subjects and in media that cannot be predicted by your motivational pattern. God frequently uses our weaknesses to accomplish his purpose: Moses with his speech problems is a good case in point. However, in most instances, by being sensitive to your motivational picture, you will communicate much more effectively than you would if you ignored it.

For example, an acquaintance of mine is an excellent lecturer/teacher of memory techniques. Reviewing his personal history, it is clear that he has been driven by the desire to memorize (his motivational thrust is to memorize); his secondary motivational talents are to promote, solve problems, teach, memorize (his motivational thrust is to memorize); his secondary motivational talents are to promote, solve problems, teach, and overcome, in that order; his motivated faculty is charisma; his motivated object is images; his motivated relationship is leadership; and his motivated circumstance is in a lecture hall in front of an audience. He knows what he wants to communicate, memory techniques; why he wants to do it, to help others; who his audience is, a live audience whom he can lead; and his appropriate medium, lecturing. He is effective because he is true to his motivational pattern.

In the fall of 1984, the Continental Basketball Association (CBA), the minor league of professional basketball, held an amateur contest to find the official CBA television "color" commentator. About three hundred lawyers, accountants, doctors, salesmen, and even an FBI agent showed up to try out for CBA sportscaster. Having to keep up with a four-minute segment of fast action on a television monitor, one Connecticut man blurted out in frustration, "The players are running around everywhere." A New York equipment operator sat through the four-minute segment in embarrassed silence. Hal Lancaster, reporting on this modern-day "Ted Mack's Amateur Hour" in the *Wall Street Journal*, captured the following comments:

"It's a lot tougher than you think," says Rick Hansen, a computer researcher for International Business Machines Corp. . . . "It looks so easy sitting at home." Adds Robb Larson, the CBA's vice president of entertainment services: "One guy said it was worse than his first date."[7]

Most of the contestants did not take into consideration their motivational talents before they tried out for sportscaster.

As you learn more about the various media, you will be able to discern how you can communicate most effectively through each one. The following exercise illustrates through talent questions the different major roles involved in producing a made-for-television movie. These roles are similar to those involved in feature film production (except for a few changes that will be clear after you study Chapter 7, "What Medium Should I Use?" With further changes, this exercise can be used to discern the talents necessary in radio production. Ask these questions of yourself with reference to your motivational pattern to see where you would fit in a television production.

Television Talent Exercise

For each television role or job, there follows a series of questions that briefly sketch the major motivational talent required for that role. These questions are also useful for recruiting people to produce a television program or a film.

Executive Producer

Can you raise money and secure resources and talent?
Are you good at getting?
Can you wheel and deal?

Producer

Can you get a group of creative individuals to work together and finish a project?

Line Producer

Can you take orders and execute them?
Can you keep track of resources?
Are you careful with your bank balance?

Director

Can you bring the best out of people?

Author

Can you articulate your ideas dramatically?

Scriptwriter

Can you develop ideas into a story?
Can you write dialogue?

Production Manager

Can you keep people working on time?
Can you organize people?

Director of Photography

Can you visualize stories?
Do you recognize authenticity?

Cameraperson

Can you frame a picture?
Can you focus a camera?
Can you compose a picture?

Audio Engineer

Do you like music?
Do you dislike a bad recording?

Soundperson

Do you like sounds?
Can you detect differences in the quality of recordings?

Art Direction

Can you capture a period? a look? a moment in time?

Video Engineer

Can you make sure that the video equipment is doing what it is supposed to be doing?
Can you think and act fast?

Technical Director

Are you good at running a model railroad?

Location Manager

Do you know your way around?
Do you have a good sense of direction?
Can you get the cooperation of people affected by the production?

Prop Manager

Do you enjoy rummaging through thrift shops?
Are you good at treasure hunting?
Can you find just the right thing?

Grip

Do you like to help?
Are you strong?

Gaffer

Are you good with electrical wiring?
Can you fix an electrical appliance?

Secretary/Continuity

Can you keep track of details?
Do you follow through?

Editor

Can you make sense out of chaos and throw away surplus material?

Makeup

Can you see the best in people?
Can you see the character in people?
Can you paint?

Wardrobe

Do you like designing clothes?
Can you capture a look?

Special Effects

Did you have a chemistry set as a child?
Can you make the impossible possible?

Sound Effects

Can you mimic sounds?
Are you aware of noises?

Lighting Director/Engineer

Do you see things in dark (black) and light?

It should be noted that each one of these television production roles is important in producing a made-for-television movie. Without a continuity person, for example, scenes shot on different days will not match, and the movie will fall apart. Every production person is important and worthy of respect.

Having discerned your motivational talents and related them to television production roles, you can do the same with any other medium by simply analyzing the talents required by each role involved in that medium and comparing them with your motivational picture. Furthermore, since every career, job, or activity requires communication, you can analyze the communication talents required in that career, job, or activity and compare those required talents with your motivational picture, keeping in mind that almost any career, job, or activity can be modified to some degree to fit your motivational talents.

One kind of God-given talents we have not considered in

depth is the spiritual gifts that God gives us when we become a member of his Body. These gifts are set forth in 1 Corinthians 12, Romans 12, and Ephesians 4. They are an integral part of "who I am" if the "I" is a Christian. Many of these God-given spiritual gifts relate directly to communications, and you should take the time to review them as set forth in these chapters of the Bible.

Using the same method that you used to discern your motivational talents, you can discern your spiritual gifts by focusing in on those achievements that relate to your Christian walk. Also, the Reverend Robert Noble has produced an excellent exercise for discerning your spiritual gifts. Write to him for a copy.[8]

It has been said that only a fool would distrust his Creator. God has created each of us, giving each of us a unique combination of motivations and talents to that we can glorify him and enjoy his creation. He calls us into his Body so that we can occupy every area of life for him. We should not only praise him with our lips, but also by loving ourselves—who he has created us to be. As Paul says, "Each one should test his own actions. Then he can take pride in himself, without comparing himself to somebody else" (Gal. 6:4).

However, knowing "who I am" and acting accordingly is only part of the process. To communicate effectively we must ask, answer, and apply each of the ascertainment questions. Furthermore, each of us must persevere in being that person God has called us to be in spite of the opposition that is inherent in our fallen world. Trust God and follow him.

> For you created my inmost being;
> you knit me together in my mother's womb.
> I praise you because I am fearfully
> and wonderfully made;
> your works are wonderful,
> I know that full well.
> My frame was not hidden from you
> when I was made in the secret place.

When I was woven together
in the depths of the earth,
your eyes saw my unformed body.
All the days ordained for me
were written in your book
before one of them came to be.

(Psalm 139:13–16)

4. Who Is My Audience?

If you want to send a message, call Western Union.

SAMUEL GOLDWYN

Samuel Goldwyn knew his audience, the majority of the American public who went to the movies for the first sixty years of the twentieth century to be entertained, not instructed. As a founder of Metro-Goldwyn-Mayer he captured that public's attention, sold them tickets, and drew them into movie theaters all over the country by telling stories through film, not sending messages. Goldwyn's Western Union statement sums up many of our ascertainment questions and points out that the medium, the message, and the audience are interrelated—so much so, in fact, that if you vary one, you need to vary the other two.

Frequently, as Goldwyn's comment suggests, communicators use the wrong medium to deliver the right message in the wrong format to an unknown audience. Films and television programs do send messages to their audience, but not in the same way that other media send them, and the messages they send reflect the nature of film and television, through which they are sent, to a greater degree than messages sent by other media. Turn on public-access cable television in any city where it exists, and you will see a number of would-be communicators trying and failing to deliver esoteric messages to nonexistent audiences.

Many Christian communicators are part of this group. Commenting on the 1984 Annenberg-Gallup study "Religion and Television," George Gallup, Jr. notes:

The potential impact of religious TV on our lives is enormous.

But it is a potential that is only partly being realized. Only a relatively small proportion of Americans watch religious television, according to the Gallup and Annenberg surveys. More than half of nonviewers claim to have heard or read little or nothing about religious television. . . .

So it is clear that if religious TV programs are to have a major impact on the religious life of the nation as a whole, programs will have to be created that will appeal to the broad spectrum of churches in the United States and to persons who are only mildly interested in religion. This will mean greater efforts to develop movies and plays with a religious message—perhaps the most effective way of reaching people.[1]

The Annenberg-Gallup study finds that most Americans *do not* watch religious television and that those who do, watch on Sunday mornings. The Annenberg report estimates that 13.3 million people, or only 6.2 percent of the total 214 million potential viewers, watch religious television; the Gallup poll estimates that there are 68 million religious television viewers per month, or 32 percent of the potential viewers. (Note that the difference between the two estimates might be explained by the method of polling: the Annenberg figures reflect a moment in time, and the Gallup figures reflect a period of time, one month.)[2] The study shows that most Christian television programs are not reaching the majority of the American people. Some Christian commentators do not know how to design programs the majority will want to watch; others are not interested in reaching the majority.

Sometimes, in the interest of reaching a mass audience, a religious communicator will purchase prime broadcast television time on a major station to air a religious program. All too often, the religious program is not targeted to reach the station's regular prime-time viewers but Christians who are already converted and support the premise of the program. This kind of program often turns off regular viewers, who might have been reached by its message if the communicator had taken them into consideration in designing the program.

A typical program is this genre grabs the regular viewer's

attention with a powerful, emotional portrayal of the plight of some group, such as teenagers. After this poignant tease, a well-known celebrity will come on the screen and present the problem. At this point, the program could hold many of the regular prime-time viewers if the subject matter of the program was explored in depth and the religious conclusion proved logically, step by step, with attention to who the audience is. Instead, often the star or celebrity jumps quickly to the conclusion and asks for money for the ministry that is presenting the program, thus alienating all but a few loyal fans of that ministry and a few others who are susceptible to the particular message in question. The program is "preaching to the choir," those who are already well versed on the topic being presented and do not want to be bothered with a logical proof of what they already know and believe. Of course, this type of preaching to the choir is effective if the organization's goal is fundraising or informing their natural constituency.

The Annenberg-Gallup study shows that there are basically two different television mainstreams, one religious and one nonreligious, each with their own worldview. The small religious audience tends to watch all the religious television programs offered as well as the same nonreligious programs that the nonreligious audience watches. Even though the values of these two groups differ, both like to watch the same popular nonreligious television programs; the difference is that the religious mainstream adds to that diet religious programs. The producers of the kind of religious program we have been discussing have chosen by their approach, consciously or unconsciously, to reach out to the smaller religious audience of which they are a part and to ignore the vast majority of nonreligious viewers.

If these producers claim they are reaching the nonreligious mainstream, when their program has a miniscule audience, they are fooling themselves, or engaging in "make-believe mission"—especially when their claim is made to entice their supporters into sending money. It is never appropriate to exploit God's name. It is only when it is clear to the audience that the program is a telethon whose basic purpose is to raise money for a legitimate nonprofit organization—and when the program is reaching the intended audience—that the religious producer may be using the medium effectively.

Religious viewers should be aware that when they see a religious program on prime-time television it does not necessarily mean that the program is reaching a mass audience with the Gospel. It simply means that someone has purchased prime network broadcast time.

By contrast, religious communicators who have taken the time and effort to understand the nonreligious television viewer have been able to capture large audiences with high-quality programming. "The Lion, the Witch and the Wardrobe" won an Emmy Award and had 37 million viewers; "Peter and Paul" captured a third of the viewing audience; and 36 million people saw "Jesus of Nazareth." Many feature films with strong Christian themes (intentional or otherwise) have been among the top five or ten most popular films for the year that they were released: for example, *Chariots of Fire* and *Tender Mercies*, which received Academy Awards, and *Places in the Heart*. Local religious telecommunicators who have tried to reach a mass audience have also been successful, one such is Jerry Rose, president of WCFC in Chicago, whose program "Bible Baffle" won a local Emmy Award.

The Christian Broadcasting Network (CBN) has been particularly careful to research the nonreligious audience for reactions to a program, or product, that they want to broadcast or market. For example, Dave Clark, vice president of marketing of CBN, said that CBN wanted to find a way to get non–Bible readers to read the Bible. Through extensive research, CBN found that non–Bible readers considered the Bible hard to understand, mainly because it was in a strange format. Researching their targeted audience, CBN discovered the most popular format, the translation/paraphrase, and even the best cover design to reach the non–Bible reader. For the first five months on the market their Bible, *The Book*, sold more than all other versions of the Bible combined and led sales of all books at several major national nonreligious bookstore chains. By listening to their targeted audience and undertaking an effective national advertising campaign, CBN made *The Book* a bestseller.

Tom Dunkerton, vice president of a large, successful advertising agency, emphasizes that listening to your targeted audience is the key to successful commercial communication. George Gallup, Jr., has been a great help to Christian communicators in this regard by defining and clarifying who our audience is.

During the twentieth century, there has been a small, but vocal, solipsistic movement in some circles of literature, art, music, film, video, and other media, characterized by a conscious disdain for the audience. This movement to create a vacuum, disregarding the "other," or audience, has produced, like every movement, some significant and some popular works, but not by design. Whatever this movement has been called by its various practitioners, it does not represent either a prudent or a biblical approach to communication.

Thomas Hardy wisely points out that a genius communicates what an audience is waiting to hear but has not yet articulated, whereas a prophet communicates what people do not yet realize that they need to hear. Both, however, want to reach their intended audience. Wisdom and God's call demand that we seek to know our audience. Jesus spoke with the authority of knowing who he was and who his audience was. We should strive to do the same.

In Chapter 1, I mentioned the Chinese community television group in New York City who obtained prime cable television time by showing that they would bring a large new paying audience to the cable system. However, being able to deliver a large audience to a radio, television, or cable channel is not always enough to obtain time for a pet program idea.

One group of clergy, representing several major denominations, approached a local radio station for program time and offered to deliver a large listening audience to the station—an audience in excess of the station's average audience for the time period they sought. The station turned them down, pointing out that it was not just the size of the new audience that mattered, but also its demographic and psychographic characteristics. The station doubted that the new audience would buy the products being advertised on the station, or be compatible with the station's targeted audience.

The station management said that they carefully programmed their broadcast day to build and hold an audience: that is, the station aired programs that would capture a targeted audience and then feed that audience into the next program. Also, all of their programs had a distinct rhythm that appealed to their audience, and the clergy program did not share that rhythm. (If you listen to several radio stations, you will note that each has its own distinct sound and rhythm.) The clergy gave up.

A more successful approach might have been made if the clergy had researched the station and its audience and designed their program idea to reach that audience. Another possibility would have been for them to research their constituency to determine how many would tune in to a program compatible to the station's format and how many would continue to listen to the station after the religious program ended. The clergy failed to find out who their audience was, who their own constituency was, who the station management was (and what their broadcast policy was), and who the station's targeted audience was.

"Soaring TV Costs Lead Firms to Seek Better Viewer Data,"[3] read a 1984 headline in the *Wall Street Journal*. The article noted that television was becoming so expensive that companies were anxious to target their television advertising money as carefully as possible by knowing everything they could about the viewing public. These major advertisers wanted to reach and capture not just the biggest audience for the least money ("cost per thousand," or CPM) but also the right audience with the right message. Since it is the program that delivers the audience to the advertiser, these advertisers wanted the programs that ran with their commercials structured to attract their targeted audience.

These advertisers wanted to know exactly who watches the programs and their commercials, who flips channels or leaves the room during their commercials, who buys their products after watching their commercials on a particular program, who is affected by high-impact shows and who by low-impact shows, who is affected by program content and how they are affected, and who is affected by a commercial before or after a sex scene or a scene of violence. They wanted enough research to know their audience.

Once commercial communicators think they know who their audience is, they will do what is necessary to reach it. As reported in *Broadcasting*,

CBS officials said last week they had abandoned a system used in the evaluation of TV movie ideas because the details got out, making it possible for creative types to beat the system, so to speak, by concoting story concepts to meet its specifications.

The system is called TAPE, for television audience program evaluation, and is a service of the British firm TAPE Consultancy Ltd. . . .

[T]he system necessarily assigns comparative values to various program elements, including program type, plot and race or ethnic origin of the principle characters.

Thus . . . the weight given a movie proposal may be "reduced if any of the central characters are other than white Americans.". . . . A white, Anglo-Saxon male is said to be the character with probably the best chance of appealing to the largest number of viewers, and his chances improve—as do any main character's—if he is a little guy fighting the establishment. Chances are lowest for a protagonist who is "someone with a superior intellect who can outwit somebody without even soiling his hands." In general, blue-collar is good; serious music composer is not.

Program types thought to be the most appealing include war movies set in World War II, and thriller action adventure films, such as one dealing, for example, with "a plain girl who has plastic surgery and then sets out to kill all the men who rebuffed her." Placed at the bottom of the list in program appeal are such formats as musicals, science fiction movies and films centering on classical composers or others in arts.[4]

This evaluation plan was drawn up just prior to the shift in public taste away from blue collar to elegance in "Dynasty," "Dallas," and similar programs, away from World War II movies to science fiction movies such as *Star Wars*, and even away from mass murderers to historic composers such as Mozart in the movie *Amadeus*. Moreover, "The Cosby Show" soon became an overnight success, thereby disproving the notion that "a white Anglo-Saxon male" star was the key to a large audience.

Sometimes the interior voice of the communicator is much more accurate in predicting the mood of the mass audience than the best research available. A case in point is George Lucas, whose *Star Wars* was turned down by every major movie studio and every television network, only to become one of the biggest money-making movies of all time when released to the general public. On the other hand, it is wise to remember that even though the polls failed to predict Truman's upset presidential victory over Dewey, most polls since 1948 have been right on target in predicting the preferences of the people.

The common wisdom among commercial communicators is that audiences are attracted by sex and violence. In the never-ending quest for larger and larger audiences, commercial communicators are searching for new controversial social themes— new taboos that will attract viewers, who in turn become more jaded with each titillating new program. The 1984 television season featured programs on prison rape (NBC, CBS), child abuse (ABC, NBC), wife abuse (ABC), white slavery (NBC), call girls (ABC, NBC), lesbian parenthood (NBC), prostitute motherhood (NBC, ABC), and child pornography (CBS). The television critic Arthur Unger has written a not-so-humorous, but profound, fictional press release mocking television's search for the last taboo:

It is estimated that more than 20 million American males throughout the country have spent all or part of their adolescent years on farms.

Recent scientific research reveals that more than 50 percent of farm boys queried admitted that they had at one time or another engaged in some form of illicit sexual activity with one or more animals.

Thus, bestiality is a fact of life which touches one in every 22 Americans, a prevalent social problem which affects over 10 million Americans.

"Something About Daisy" (Sunday, 8–11 P.M.) tackles commercial television's last taboo. It is handled with care and restraint. Great attention has been paid to casting, and the star of recent Borden commercials was recruited to play the lead.

There will be an opening warning which will state: "The following program deals with bestiality and its painful consequences. It focuses on awareness, communication and treatment for affected men and animals. The family is encouraged to view it together. However, due to sensitive subject matter, parental discretion is advised."

There will be a closing notice which will state: "Procedures for prosecution, correction, treatment and criminal justice vary from state to state. This story dramatizes a therapeutic approach to the problem."

At the conclusion of the broadcast, hotlines will be manned in all 50 states by psychologists and veterinarians in order to help those viewers involved in one end or another of the bestiality problem to adjust to their background, become useful citizens and well-adjusted beasts.[5]

Mr. Unger was making the point that television's search for the last taboo was absurd and ultimately self-defeating, but don't be surprised if you see a news release like his announcing a forthcoming program. He thought that bestiality and necrophilia were the last remaining taboos for television to explore to hook an audience. However, at the time he was writing, the movie *Splash*, which focused on the sexual relationship of a young man with a mermaid (i.e., bestiality), was being released at the movie theaters. In *Splash* the key question, asked by reporters and the young hero's brother, is simply what was it like to make love to a fish. Moviemakers titillated their audience with the possibility of bestiality, as they had done before with necrophilia in horror films.

In spite of the lure of increased sex and violence, *Broadcasting* reported in December of 1984 that networks were attracting fewer viewers and that the total Homes Using Television (HUTs) had resumed a downward trend. Because of declining viewership, television networks are seeking more audience data so that they can fashion separate promos for different audiences and "counterpromote" the competition by luring audiences away from the other networks' programs. These same networks are also trying the "hot sell," using heavy repetition to get audiences to tune in and trying tricks such as turning up and fine tuning the audio on commercials.[6]

There is no doubt that technical effects hook audiences and that sex and violence are cheap lures; however, Hollywood and the networks have overused and misused all three, often substituting them for plot and character development. Story telling is the key to successful film and television, but in measuring those elements of a story that appeal to an audience, producers often lose sight of the forest, the story, because of the trees, the elements that make up a story. In fact, noting that the recent wave of blockbusters, including *E.T.*, *Ghostbusters*, and the *Star Wars* trilogy, did not employ sex as a hook, Julie Salamon reports in the *Wall Street Journal*:

It has been 12 years since Bernardo Bertolucci's "Last Tango in Paris" broke the sex barrier for mainstream movies, freeing the men who direct and distribute movies in Hollywood to unleash their own fantasies on the big screen. But most of them miss the point of "Last Tango's" artfully erotic play on sexual and romantic fantasy.[7]

Whatever we may think of *Last Tango*, when a Christian

communicator sells a program concept to a television network, or film studio, his or her audience in terms of that sale is the television (or film) executives, who have their own demographics and psychographics, such as the sexual fantasy syndrome noted by Ms. Salamon. A study by Robert Lichter and Stanley Rothman, under the auspices of Columbia University, found that the executies who run the mass media (television, radio, and newspapers) "were out of step with the public."[8] Unlike the general public, which considers itself very religious (80 percent believe in the deity of Christ), only 8 percent of the "media elite" attend religious services. Ninety-five percent of the public objects to adultery, but 50 percent of the "media elite" sees nothing wrong with it.

For the last few years, the American people have been taking more interest in religion and have been making a much deeper religious commitment.[9] Americans also have been flocking to movies that have great stories and religious, perhaps even Christian, dimensions and little or no sex and violence, such as *Chariots of Fire, Tender Mercies, E.T.,* and *Gandhi.*[10] And in the theater, every year the Royal Shakespeare Company (RSC) comes to the United States and is enthusiastically greeted by sellout crowds who commend the good taste of the RSC and complain about the tawdry nature of American theater.[11]

The demographic, or spirographics (spiritual profile of a target group), gap between the "media elite" and the general public is reflected in the following insight into the history of Michael Landon's television program "Highway to Heaven":

NBC executives laughed at Michael Landon's proposal for a new series called "Highway to Heaven." They knew that a "squeaky clean" show with a do-gooder angel as the main character would be laughed out of American homes. In derision, they labeled the show "Jesus of Malibu."

Landon's pilot for "Highway to Heaven" earned the highest test rating of any NBC show since "Little House on the Prairie," also a Landon show. NBC executives were shocked. They didn't think it would make it—a clean, decent, moralistic show with positive role models for kids and adults.[12]

The success of "Highway to Heaven" and "Little House on the Prairie" demonstrate that the public wants good, uplifting programs. It is an unfortunate fact that when good programming is not available, the television public, including Christians, will watch programs filled with gratuitous sex and violence. Christians, and anyone else who wants good programming should express what they want by not watching pornographic and violent programs. Advertisers are convinced that Christians do not care what programs they watch because they did not follow the Reverend Donald Wildmon's first call to boycott programming with excess sex and violence (although Christians may now be responding to these boycotts).[13] Christians and others who oppose violence and pornography should make their views known by refusing to watch it.

Ninety-seven percent of the households in the United States have television. One third of the television households do two thirds of the daily television viewing, which averages seven hours per day per household. This one third constitutes the habitual watchers of television, for whom being at home means sitting in front of the set. Another third watches occasionally but is not hooked on television. The last third is very selective and watches very little television.

The networks usually concentrate their programming efforts on the third of the public who watch habitually—because they're there, and because the networks have found that it is not cost-effective to try to woo the other two thirds, who seem fickle. Despite recent indications that they are putting more effort into capturing the forgotten two thirds, the networks have largely forsaken the majority of the American people and have settled for the least common denominator. These same television practitioners call their audience "the public," even though most of the public may not be watching.[14] It would be interesting for Christian communicators to demonstrate that the forgotten two thirds can be attracted to television by quality programming like "Highway to Heaven."

Audience research goes by many different names: demographics, physical and social statistics; psychographics,* psychological perceptions, preferences, and statistics; and spirographics, spiritual characteristics and statistics. Whatever name is used, audience research is an attempt to discover as much information as possible in order to make accurate predictions of how the audience will react in the future and to design communications with those factors in mind.

The originator of the method called psychographics, for example, discovered that people tend to form a personal, anthropomorphic mental image of a company. His research showed that when a random sample of individuals was asked about a particular company, such as Kentucky Fried Chicken or Bell Telephone (before the breakup), almost all of them saw the company in the same anthropomorphic terms, as the same distinct person, such as the Colonel for Kentucky Fried Chicken or a friendly elderly female operator for Ma Bell.

The researcher who made this discovery found that he could increase the sales of a company by changing the image people had of it. For example, if the viewing public saw one of their local television stations as a radical Ralph Nader, but preferred a kindly Walter Cronkite father-figure and, for that reason, watched the competing station, this researcher would have the station change those specific factors that produced the unpopular image. When the right image was evoked in people's minds, they could change their viewing habits and tune in to the client station. In time, the audience preference would probably change, but any change can be identified and reflected in advertising and programming decisions that affect the image of the station.

Even a cursory study of television network news shows will

---

* The term psychographics referring to a psychological profile of a target group was coined by David Clark, V.P. of CBN.

demonstrate that they each present a definite personality to the public. After a careful study of the evening news, Walter Karp found that NBC represented "old-fashioned, midwestern Republicanism: upright, decent, cautious" and was the most popular network news shows in the Midwest; ABC projected a very low-key, somewhat right-wing interventionist foreign policy image and appealed to the Western states; and CBS represented the liberal, democratic point of view and found its greatest support in the East.[15]

The networks have spent millions of dollars trying to understand their targeted audience. However, you can find out a great deal about your own targeted audience for very little money. First, define who you want to reach by asking the right ascertainment questions; then find out as much as you can about your targeted audience through existing surveys, your own research, and/or objective, common sense discernment.

The following exercise will help you define who you want to reach. The ascertainment questions in this exercise expand upon the questions posed under Call and Impact in Chapter 1. After this exercise, we will look at sources for information about your targeted audience, how to conduct your own simple survey and objective discernment of your audience.

Defining My Audience Exercise

This exercise is simply your way of targeting your audience. As with all our exercises, you should adapt it to your own needs by revising, adding, or subtracting questions.

Demographic Questions

Demographic questions, as defined herein, relate to the physical and social characteristics of the audience you want to reach.

	Yes	No
Do I want to reach		

the general public? ____ ____
a specific group of people? ____ ____

If you want to reach the general public, then your audience is fairly well defined by the research available in almanacs, through major polling organizations, and through news services.

If you want to reach a specific audience, then:
Do I want to reach
men? ____ ____
women? ____ ____
both? ____ ____

For example, is your audience the Daughters of the King, an Episcopal women's group, the Brotherhood of Saint Andrew, an Episcopal men's group, or the Community of the Cross of Nails, which contains both men and women?

Do I want to reach a specific ethnic or racial group? ____ ____
If so, what group? _____

Ebony, the Goethe Institute, and the Japan-America Society all want to reach specific racial or ethnic groups. Their communications are shaped by their targeted audience.
Do I want to reach
married couples? ____ ____
parents? ____ ____
single people? ____ ____

Marriage Encounter aims at reaching couples; computer dating services aim at single people; and diaper services aim at parents.

Do I want to reach a specific age group? ____ ____
If so, what age group? _____

Most television advertisers want to reach people eighteen to thirty-five, because that age group spends the most money.

Do I want to reach people in a specific
occupation, such as lawyers, military personnel, or students?   ___ ___
If so, what occupation?   _____

The Fellowship of Companies for Christ, the Christian Legal Society,
the American Legion, the AFL-CIO, and Campus Crusade for Christ
all have targeted audiences according to occupation.

Do I want to reach a specific income
group?   ___ ___
If so, what income group?   _____

Rolls-Royce and Ford commercials, for example, aim at different
audiences.

Do I want to reach a specific recreational
or athletic group, such as skiers or
runners?   ___ ___
If so, what group?   _____

Ski clubs and riding clubs target their audiences, who may, in fact,
belong to both groups.

Does my audience live
on a specific block?   ___ ___
in a specific city?   ___ ___
in a specific state?   ___ ___
in a specific region?   ___ ___
in a specific country?   ___ ___
on a specific continent?   ___ ___
in a specific hemisphere?   ___ ___
If so, where?   _____

Where your target audience lives affects both your communication
and the medium you choose to deliver your communication. Language, dialect, idiom, and usage vary from region to region. The size
of the area where your audience lives will determine to a degree what
medium is the most cost-effective for reaching your audience.

Is my audience
scattered over a large area?   ___   ___
clustered in groups?   ___   ___
spread evenly over an area?   ___   ___
If so, where?   _____

The distribution of your audience will help determine the best medium for you to use. If your audience is thinly spread over a large area, then low- powered FM radio or broadcast television might not reach them, but satellite teleconferencing, telephone teleconferencing, newsletter, or mail might be appropriate, depending on your answers to the other ascertainment questions.

Does my audience have any unique physical characteristics, such as poor eyesight,
diabetes, or above average height?   ___   ___
If so, what are they: _____

Weight Watchers, Retarded Citizens, and the Special Olympics reach out to individuals with distinctive physical characteristics.

How large is my audience?   _____

The size of your audience will affect how you communicate and what medium you use. If you are communicating to only a few people, you may be advised to use the telephone, the mail, or direct presentation. If your audience is extremely large, you may have to choose between television and radio.

Can my audience be moved?   ___   ___
If so, where?   _____

If your audience can be brought to a central location, you might be able to communicate with and to them in a lecture, in seminars, or one-on-one.

When is my audience available?   _____
What time of day?   _____
What day or days of the week?   _____
What time of year?   _____

When your audience is available will affect your communication and your choice of medium. Television is much less expensive late at night and early in the morning, and so are phone calls. Your audience will respond differently at different times and in different seasons.

Psychographic Questions

Psychographic questions, as defined here, relate to the psychological perceptions, preferences, and characteristics of the audience you want to reach.

	Yes	No
Do I want to reach uniquely gifted individuals?	—	—
If so, what is their distinguishing gift?	_____	

Mensa, which is made up of individuals with a genius-or-above IQ, and Toastmasters International, which is made up of gifted public speakers, are two of many organizations that seek to communicate to a select group of uniquely gifted individuals.

Do I want to reach a specific political or ideological group?	____	____
If so, what group?	_____	

The Young Conservatives reaches out to a different audience than the Students for Democratic Action or Mothers Against Drunk Driving.

Do I want to reach a particular social preference group?	____	____
If so, what group?	_____	

The Social Register and Mother Jones are addressed to audiences with different social preferences.

Do I want to reach a group with a particular artistic preference?	____	____
If so, what group?	_____	

Your presentation and your medium will vary depending on whether you want to reach music lovers, art afficionados, or bibliophiles.

Do I want to reach an audience who pre-
fers a particular genre or format, such as
stories, poetry, or reports?   ___   ___
If so, what group?   _____

If you are aiming at people who prefer science fiction novels and
films, your communication will reflect that audience's preferences.

Do I want to reach an audience who pre-
fers a particular medium?   ___   ___
If so, what medium?   _____

Advertisers often aim at a group distinguished by its medium preference, such as high-brow magazine or radio lovers.

Do I want to reach a group with specific
psychological needs?   ___   ___
If so, what needs define my audience?   _____

Self-improvement, "how-to," and "health" books aim at audiences
who need success, accomplishment, or security.

Spirographic Questions

Spirographic questions, as defined here, relate to the spiritual perceptions, preferences, and characteristics of the audience you want to reach.

                                                 Yes   No
Do I want to reach a specific religious
group?   ___   ___
If so, what group?   _____

Christianity Today is aiming at a different audience than the *Christian
Science Sentinel*. You may want to target a specific religious audience
for evangelism.

Do I want to reach a group with specific
spiritual needs?   ___   ___
If so, what group?   _____

If you are trying to reach a group with specific spiritual needs, such as alcoholics, divorced persons, or those seeking spiritual renewal, then your communication will reflect the nature of your target audience.

My Portrait of my Audience

After you answer all the demographic, psychographic, and spirographic ascertainment questions, draw a portrait of your audience by listing in order of priority the *five* most important *characteristics* you want your audience to have. This portrait of your audience will assist you in framing your communication and in choosing the appropriate medium.

Once you have targeted your audience according to characteristics you have defined, you need to get to know who they are, what their perceptions, preferences, and unique characteristics are, especially their wants and needs, so that your communication will have maximum impact. Also, you will want to find out what your audience thinks about the subject matter of your communication. Thorough research will help you to avoid alienating your audience (assuming that alienating your audience is not your purpose) and will give you clues on how to make what you present appealing to your audience.

For instance, if you want to reach motorcycle riders to sell them insurance and your research shows that 90 percent of them disdain security but love to impress members of the opposite sex, then you might structure your communication to emphasize that macho motorcycle riders can really impress their broads by having insurance made out to their girl friend and then ride recklessly. Or if you are trying to reach these rebels for Christ, you may want to emphasize that, as the song says, Jesus hung out with the hard-line gang, and it takes more courage to walk with Jesus than to reject him. Of course, if your research tells you that motorcycle riders are not reckless, but instead are reserved, you will want to modify your communication accordingly.

The following ascertainment questions will help you to find

out what you need to know about your targeted audience. Add to and subtract from this list to fit your communication.

Sample Audience Ascertainment Questions

These audience ascertainment questions suggest the type of information that you will want to discover about your audience so that your communication will have maximum impact.

Subject Matter Questions

Your subject matter is the theme, central idea, and focal point of your communication. If, for example, the Church is your subject matter, then when asking these questions, replace "the subject matter" with "the church."

How does my audience perceive the subject matter of my communication?

What image does my subject matter conjure up in the mind of a typical member of my audience?

What does my audience think are the positive attributes of may subject matter?

What does my audience think are its negative attributes?

Under what circumstances is my audience positive about my subject matter?

Under what circumstances is my audience negative about it?

What factors, genre, format, characteristics, people, or things give my audience a positive feeling about my subject matter?

What factors, genre, format, characteristics, people, or things give my audience a negative feeling about it?

What related subject matters do they prefer?

Why do they prefer them?

What related subject matters do they like less than my chosen subject matter?

Why do they like them less?

Needs Questions

These questions are adapted from the needs outlined in Chapter 1.

Does my audience need:

	Yes	No
food?	——	——
clothing?	——	——
shelter?	——	——
security?	——	——
protection?	——	——
love?	——	——
community?	——	——
respect?	——	——
recognition?	——	——
success?	——	——
accomplishment?	——	——
to know Jesus?	——	——

What else does my audience need?

What does my audience need to hear, see, or have communicated?

Wants Questions

What does my audience *want* to hear, see, or have communicated?

What are my audience's dreams and desires?

What are my audience's goals?

Demographic, Psychographic, and Spirographic Questions

Review the Defining My Audience Exercise and answer any questions that you did not use in targeting your audience by revising the questions to reflect the point of view of your audience rather than your own point of view.

For instance, you may have targeted skiers as your audience. You should find out if that target audience is made up of men only, men and women, or women only, where they live, what their religious preference is, what their profession is, and so forth.

To find out the pertinent demographic, psychographic, and spirographic information, you will want to ask your targeted audience all of the relevant questions suggested in the Defining My Audience Exercise from your audience's point of view. Therefore, instead of asking yourself Do I want to reach a specific occupation group? you would ask What is your occupation? and, instead of Do I want to reach a specific political group? you would ask, What is your political preference? giving your targeted audience several options, including "none."

Once you have found out everything you should know about your audience, your communication should reflect that information; but under no circumstances does that mean that you should compromise the Gospel message. At the Areopagus, Paul structured his presentation of the Gospel message so that his audience could understand it, but he did not compromise that message. To put our communicates in a context that our audience can understand is wisdom, but to compromise the Gospel is foolishness.

Even if you don't have the money necessary to commission a research organization to find out everything you need to know about your audience, you can find out a great deal about your audience by reviewing existing data. In fact, you can often draw a very objective portrait of your audience by comparing data from several different research organizations. Even the best ones approach the subject matter of their research from a particular point of view. The Annenberg-Gallup study of religious television details information obtained by two different research organizations; by comparing the information obtained by each, an accurate picture of religious television emerges.

The following sources will help you to begin your search for the information you need. This list is not exhaustive. Once you start looking, if you haven't done so before, you will find many sources of information and research readily available for very little cost.

Sources of Information on My Targeted Audience

* The Yellow Pages of your local telephone book will not only help you find the right organizations to contact for information about your targeted audience, but you will also discover, if you haven't already, that the information there can help you to know your targeted audience.

  Reference books, such as almanacs, dictionaries, encyclopedias, histories, handbooks, resource guides, and compilations or listings, can provide you with a wide variety of information on your targeted audience.

* Newspapers, newsmagazines, journals, and trade publications, like *Broadcasting*, for instance, may provide you with almost all the information you need regarding the radio and television industries and their respective audiences. Most of the pertinent television and radio research of A. C. Neilsen, Arbitron, and the other television and radio researchers is published in *Broadcasting*. Whatever you discover in other sources, keeping up with the news is an invaluable help in knowing your targeted audience, because they are as much a product of history and current events as you are.

* Polling, research, and census institutions and organizations may be able to provide the information you need from existing studies, making it unnecessary for you to commission research on your target audience. Inquire of several

organizations; for instance, the Gallup Organization undertakes a yearly study of the state of religion in America, which will provide you with excellent information. The United States Bureau of the Census is another excellent source.

• Universities, schools, and colleges are not only great places to find existing information and research, but they are also primary sources for original research undertaken by the faculty and/or students on their own or due to your timely suggestion. For instance, Dr. Robert J. Schihl, at CBN University, has done an excellent study of the contemporary television audience entitled, "Man/Woman of Today: Survey of Potential Religious Audience" (CBN University, 1984).

• Libraries are great places to find out almost anything. A few enjoyable hours spent researching your subject matter and your targeted audience may give you most of the audience information you need and/or point you in the right direction for obtaining it elsewhere.

Let's assume that you want to reach teenagers. Contacting the Gallup Poll in Princeton, New Jersey, you find that teenagers watch a tremendous amount of television and do very little reading.[16] Contacting the Annenberg School of Communications, you find that there is an existing study on adolescent television program preferences that shows that young adolescents prefer comedy programs but, as they grow older, begin to switch to drama, police, and variety programs.[17] Therefore, to reach young teenagers, you might want to produce a television comedy. If you want to reach older teenagers, you might decide to produce a television police drama. Most of the information you need on your targeted audience is readily available.

It is possible that you will review all the existing sources of data and not find the information you want, or it may be that you need more specific information on your targeted audience. In either case, you may decide to conduct your own survey.

Without going back to school to take a course in statistics, probability, or survey techniques, you can obtain credible, objective, reliable information about your targeted audience by performing your own survey, as long as you plan it carefully in advance, keeping in mind that your questions must be as neutral as possible so that they do not affect your research results. Tom Dunkerton of Compton Advertising has found that a survey of sixty people is just as good as a survey of several hundred people; the key is to listen to their answers very carefully. The following procedures will help you perform your own survey.

Procedures for Conducting your Survey

Define the purpose of your survey.

With reference to the five characteristics you are using to define your audience, state exactly what information about your audience you want from your survey.

Determine the medium you will use to conduct your survey.

Will you conduct your survey by:

	Yes	No
telephone?	——	——
mailed questionnaire?	——	——
personal interview?	——	——
other?	——	——

Determine who will conduct your survey.

Often, short of hiring a polling organization, it is advisable to have a friend or an objective person conduct your survey. Better still, have two or more people conduct it.

Determine whom you will poll.

It is important that you are as careful as possible in determining your sample of individuals who share the characteristics of your targeted audience, and that you weight that sample statistically to conform to the real world.

For instance, if your targeted audience is the churchgoers who live in your city, obtain the mailing lists of some of the major churches in your city, and choose your sample from those lists. Or it your targeted audience is skiers in the United States, obtain the mailing lists of several ski magazines, and select at random individuals from those lists to poll.

Carefully prepare your questions.

Write and revise your questions until they say what you want to say and are as neutral and objective as possible. Your questions can easily destroy your survey by influencing the answers you obtain. Be careful, because you want the correct information, not information that supports your personal misconceptions and keeps you in the dark about who your audience really is.

Determine how you will tabulate and interpret the results of your survey.

Review the results, weight the results, and review the results again so that you are very clear about what the survey is telling you about your targeted audience.

Having researched the existing information available on your targeted audience and conducted your own survey, you will still have to rely on your own objective perception of who your audience is and what effect your communication will have on them. Research can only take us so far, since people are continually changing and your communication will help to change them.

Television networks have often produced expensive programs based on extensive, accurate research, only to find that they flop after a few weeks on the air. On the other hand, independent producers have come up with tremendous popular successes by flying by the seat of their pants into a gale force wind of opposing research. For instance, for years sports movies were considered the kiss of death at the box office; then along came *Rocky*, which grossed millions of dollars.

This is not to say that the key to success is launching programs that fly in the face of opposing audience research. Rather, research must be analyzed in light of your own discernment of your targeted audience, so you have to be objective about your prejudices and preferences.

Actually, if we were to review the television network or motion picture company failures, we would probably find that it was not the audience research per se that failed but the personnel who formulated the survey and interpreted the results. For instance, looking back at the TAPE system on which CBS relied, it appears from the success of subsequent programs like "Highway to Heaven" and "The Cosby Show," which did not conform to the TAPE findings, that the prejudices of the British firm affected the audience research. Since we can make research say what we want it to say by allowing it to reflect our prejudices, we must be careful not to do so.

Putting ourselves in the place of our audience can be an excellent device for understanding our audience, if we can maintain objectivity. Although not everyone can be their own critic and some communicators find it very difficult to be objective, some of the greatest work has resulted from someone imagining his or her audience and placing himself or herself in that role. Umberto Eco, the author of the best-selling book *The Name of the Rose* tells in a postscript to his book how he created his own reader rather than write for the already well-informed devotee of mystery, or detective, novels.

To put yourself in the place of your audience, monitor your radio, television, film, and book habits, especially those media through which you want to communicate. For example, if you want to communicate through television, then monitor what types of program you watch (such as news, entertainment, or game shows), what particular programs you watch, what your reaction is to them, why you watch the programs you watch, when you watch, how the commercials affect you, how the program format affects you, how the technical effects affect you, and how much television you watch. Make yourself the survey audience; formulate the appropriate questions and answer them as objectively as possible. Common sense and objectivity will go a long way in telling you what you need to know about your target audience.

Whether or not you have the ability to be or to imagine your own audience, solid audience information will help you to convince the gatekeeper of the medium you choose that he or she should give you access to that medium, whether the gatekeeper is the program manager of your local radio station or a television executive. Those gatekeepers hold prejudices and misconceptions just as you and I do, and if you can show them, in love, that there is an audience for your communication that complements their audience, they will be more open to giving you access.

For example, financial backers of expensive presentations are willing to be shown facts that indicate that what you plan to do will make money. Suppose you want financial backing for a play; you will strengthen your case if you show that almost as many Americans attend live theater as movies. In fact, in 1984, 115 million Americans went to see plays, whereas 134 million went to movies, 100 million went to museums, 60 million went to the opera, 58 million went to dance performances, and 58 million went to classical music concerts, according to a Louis Harris and Associates survey commissioned by Philip Morris. If you were producing in 1985, this data would help you.

Knowing who our audience is will improve our communications as long as we remember to obey the Author of communication.

Get wisdom, get understanding; do not forget my words or swerve from them.

(Prov. 4:5)

5. What Am I Communicating?

If a man will begin with certainties, he shall end in doubts; but if he will be content to begin with doubts, he shall end in certainties.

FRANCIS BACON

How often have you said your piece, stated your argument, given detailed instructions, or tried to communicate an intensely felt emotion, only to find that your audience has not understood? All of us who have communicated to an audience have experienced that sinking moment when we find out that our audience has not understood our most basic point. What we communicate is frequently not what we want to communicate.

Performing a scene in an acting class is an excellent way to discover problems. If you have never done so, try performing an emotional scene in front of a group of strangers. Our clothes, our posture, our grooming, our state of mind, our self-control, our objectivity, and our environment interact. Knowing our lines, knowing what we want to get across, is only the first step. For an actor the other steps involve getting in touch with one's feelings, being relaxed, putting on makeup, getting into costume, going on stage, pacing the delivery, reading the audience, and physically expressing the appropriate feelings within the context of the play. For other communicators, the other steps involve applying the answers to the pertinent ascertainment questions and constructing a communication that is logical with reference to the medium one has chosen.

In my workshops, each student videotapes a scene to demonstrate how the medium affects communication. When they review those scenes, they see that many evidence what is called a lateral reversal effect, something the student producer didn't expect and that created distortion. Lateral reversal effects are perceptual tricks played by our eyes and minds that, for example, cause subjects to look heavier on screen right, diagonals to suggest up or down depending on the direction of their slope, and pictures to look static composed one way and dynamic the other way. Such effects can change the meaning of a scene by affecting the audience's perception.

With regard to diagonals and slope, the following illustration is instructive:

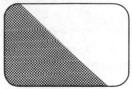 

Both these lines are the same in every respect except the direction of their slope. Our left-to-right perceptual orientation causes us to perceive the one on the left as having a downward slope and the one on the right an upward slope. In fact, neither line goes up nor down. Every environment is made up of lines. Videotaping an environment without regard for the lateral reversal effects that could be lurking therein can cause interesting perceptual consequences that will alter the meaning to some degree.

When Richard Burton performed in his first movie scene with Elizabeth Taylor (in *Cleopatra*) he thought that she couldn't act because she was so low-key. However, when the film rushes came back from the laboratory that night, he noted that her acting was very powerful, whereas his appeared exaggerated and unnatural. Watching the rushes, he realized that he was accustomed to acting on a stage, where he had to project his emotions to the back of the theater; film magnified everything he did. Underplaying the part, as Elizabeth was doing, was what was necessary to achieve a natural yet powerful effect on screen.

Translating a communication from one medium to another can drastically alter the message. In her review of the BBC television program "The Jewel in the Crown," adapted from the novel by Paul Scott, Martha Bayles notes:

The trouble is, the obsessive reconstruction of events which occurs in Mr. Scott's fiction is hard to bring off in the relatively literal medium of film. When we see something happen on film, we assume it really happened that way. Granted, this is a pretty obtuse reaction, but film makers usually have to respect it. There is no real cinematic equivalent to the novelist's device of having characters ruminate in different voices about an event they can neither fathom nor forget.[1]

Not only does the medium affect our message, but our delivery can make a difference in the way the audience perceives it. Even a slight mispronounciation can make the difference between life and death, as in the Old Testament Book of Judges where the revengeful Gileadites slaughtered the fugitive Ephraimites because they could not pronounce the password, *shibboleth*.

In line with the axiom that actions speak louder than words, some popular advice books emphasize that our manners affect how our communications are perceived. Manners and sign language, such as hand signals, vary around the world, and the misuse of a sign or signal or a breach of local etiquette can drastically affect a cross-cultural communication.

Several years ago our company, Good News Communications, was producing a film on location in Brazil for an international missionary organization. On location, we hired two local Brazilians to work as grip and gaffer. Our Brazilian crew did not speak any English, and we did not speak Portuguese. While filming, we communicated by the same hand signals we use in the United States. When we drove the Brazilians back to the television studio where they worked, we were informed that they had a grievance against us. We were shocked and embarrassed when we discovered that the American signal for "OK" meant something quite different in Brazil. The Brazilians thought throughout the filming that we had been making nasty signs at them. We explained, apologized, and made amends to our Brazilian crew—and learned an uncomfortable lesson about the consequences of poor communication.

Other recent advice books have stressed that we should *Dress for Success.*[2] Clothes communicate. Mahatma Gandhi chose to wear nothing more than a loincloth, to proclaim to the world that he was one with the poorest of the poor in India. In many countries, people perceive clothing as invested with supernatural power and react to certain kinds of clothing as good or bad omens.

Noting that the visual media, such as television, focuses on the surface of people, Prof. John Phelan argues, "It may be that Fidel Castro's battle fatigues, Colonel Quaddafi's operatic uniforms, and Ronald Reagan's rancher outfits say more to the world and of the wearers themselves than any speeches they may make."[3]

Because every communication excludes what it does not include, omissions create powerful secondary messages in the mind of the audience. In an Annenberg School of Communication study, "Television and Viewer Attitudes About Work,"[4] it was found that the environment portrayed on television blacks and other minorities were generally excluded from professions with high prestige. These omissions had a profound effect on specific demographic groups; some groups were demoralized by the exclusion, and others affirmed.

In a similar study, a little black girl was recorded as saying that she wants to be a doctor so that she can travel a lot, have a big house, a pool, a plane, and a yacht. Her perception of the medical profession had been totally distorted by its portrayal on television. Instead of being attracted to medicine as an opportunity to heal, serve, and help, she was drawn to medicine as a way to acquire things.

Prompted by the growing body of research showing the adverse effect of television on children, ABC hired the co-directors of the Yale University Family Research and Consultation Center, Drs. Jerome and Dorothy Singer, to design a course that would teach children that violence on television should not be imitated and that they should not make gener-alizations about minority groups based on television models. (ABC initially offered this course, which consisted of video-tapes, lesson plans, and workbooks, to schools for $1,197. As someone has noted, it's not often you can make money trying to solve a problem you created.)[5]

To capture an audience, the networks have learned that it is important for programs to present an attractive image. Even though that image is frequently not real, certain demographic groups within the viewing audience believe that what they are seeing *is* real. This can create envy in the hearts of some groups, who believe they are being excluded from the good life everyone else enjoys. When our television programs are exported overseas, a similar problem is created.

This process of different demographic, psychographic, and spirographic groups being affected differently by the same television program is called "mainstreaming." Mainstreaming reflects the ways in which different psychographic groups react to sex and violence on television. For example, sex and violence is used primarily as secondary material within a television (or film) communication to attract an audience, punctuate events, and/or move the story along. Alfred Hitchcock advised film-makers to begin every movie with a bang (a gunshot, battle, or explosive scene) to get the audien's attention. The viewers of such violence are mainstreamed in three different ways: most viewers are not affected at all; some viewers become anxious and paranoid about the real world; and a few viewers are attracted by the violence, sometimes to the degree that they emulate it in the real world.

It is this third, small group of viewers that we read about in the news, who burn their spouse in bed, shoot someone, or rape a child after seeing the same act portrayed on film. These viewers are often referred to as addictive personalities. They are easily and powerfully influenced by those acts, such as sex or violence, or those things, such as alcohol or drugs, to which they are psychologically susceptible.

However, most viewers pay no attention to sex and violence on television. Recent research has confirmed Marshall Mc-Luhan's prediction that "the media explosion" would cause most people to experience a "perceptual numbing," "a stubborn insensitivity to all but the most extreme experiences in life."[6] Dr. Robert Coles, a child psychiatrist at Harvard University, has found that children are particularly susceptible to perceptual numbing, and those children who watch a great deal of television turn off their minds to what they are watching.[7]

The middle group consists of those viewers who identify with the victims of violent acts. These viewers experience increased fear, anxiety, and anger from watching violent acts on television or in films.[8]

Since a camera excludes everything beyond its field of view, television journalism is technically biased in its reporting. During my junior year at Dartmouth College, there was a small student takeover of the administration building to protest the war in Vietnam. In the middle of the night, a friend woke me to say that the National Guard was evacuating the administration building. The landscape was empty except for a few observers like myself, a handful of National Guardsmen, the thirty students who had occupied the building, and the television news crews. However, the next day on television the operation looked like a major military maneuver. Frightened alumni and parents from all over the country started to call the college. The television news team made such tight shots of the scene in the midst of the small crowd that the event looked larger and more important than it actually was. I realized then the meaning of the axiom that a protest really occurs only if the television cameras are there.

Time is another factor that causes information to be omitted from television news. Not only does the program time limit the amount and depth of information that can be presented, but the short lead time on late-breaking news stories causes serious omissions.

Several years ago, just after I finished studying law at New

York University, a friend who was a network news researcher called me to find out who was legally at fault for abandoned buildings in New York City: the landlords, the tenants, or the city government. I told her that urban law was a complex field and she should take a few days to research the subject. She said that she had to prepare an editorial by that evening, which meant she had about two hours to do the research. She did not have enough time to research the subject thoroughly, or to treat it accurately in the evening editorial. The editorial appeared, placing the landlords at fault, a politically safe assumption since the tenants were the networks' major audience and the city had the political power. The limitations imposed by the clock forced a television editorial seen by millions of people to take sides without considering the legal and economic problems that conspired to precipitate the abandoning of buildings.

Beside inherent technical limitations that can distort communications, television, movies, and radio are more prone than other media to willful distortion of reality because such distortion is so easy to do and because the distorted product appears so truthful. Editing, close-ups, shadow shots, reverse shots, and other conscious camera techniques can distort the meaning of a scene. Notwithstanding the bungled "Watergate tapes," changing the meaning of a video, film, or audio recording is simple and practially unnoticeable. Every film, video, and audio editor has condensed a real event on tape (or film) so that it fits into the allocated program time, and even the participants in the event don't notice the editing. As Reuven Frank, former president of NBC News, warns: "I can't imagine the general viewer getting so sophisticated with techniques that they could discount them."[9]

It is interesting to note that surveys consistently show that people regard television as the most believable news medium. Since 1961, the Roper Organization has found that people would be most inclined to believe television news if they received conflicting reports of the same news story from television, radio, newspapers, and magazines. Also, people rank television above churches, police, newspapers, schools, and local government when asked which organization is doing the best job.[10] People believe that if they see it on television it must be true.

Jerry Mander approaches what is real on television from a humorous perspective:

There is a widespread belief that some things on television are "real" and some things are not real. We believe the news is real. Fictional programs are not real. . . . Talk shows are real, although it is true they happen only for television, and sometimes happen some days before we see them. . . .

Are historical programs real? Well, no, not exactly. . . .

Our society assumes that human beings can make the distinctions between what is real and what is not real, even when the real and not real are served up in the same way, intercut with one another, sent to us from many different places and times and arriving one behind the other in our houses, shooting out of a box in our living rooms straight into our heads. . . .

As I write these lines, my son, Kai, is seven years old. He still asks me if the Bionic Man . . . is real or not. . . . I told him that the Bionic Man is not real. . . .

"Isn't that a person on the screen?" he asks.

"Well, yes. . . . "

"Are quiz shows real?"

"Yes."

"Are they happening now?"

"No."

"When did they happen?"

"I don't know, maybe a week ago."

"Do they really win those prizes?"

"Yes, I think so." . . .

There have been . . . reports showing adults are having only a slightly less hard time separating what is television from what is life.[11]

He goes on to say that television is the only window on the world for most people, so they think that what they see on television is what is going on in the world.

Not ony does the medium you choose affect your communication, but the genre or format also affects it. If you choose the story as your genre, your communication will be perceived by your audience in a different manner than if you choose the documentary format. A documentary may be perceived as reality, even though you have edited it to reflect a particular point of view; a story may be perceived as fiction, yet be closer to the truth and/or cause a more pronounced emotional change in the audience.

The importance of learning how to communicate what we want to communicate is so great that thousands of courses have sprung up, on and off campus, to help individuals develop their skills so they can improve their careers, their family relationships and their lives. One business communications trainer asks:

Every time you speak you are shaping the future of your company and even your own career—

How do you shape up?

• Do you come across as crisp, thoughtful, well-organized and appealing . . . or do you have that sinking feeling that you are putting everyone to sleep?

• Are you the same person in front of an audience as you are with friends and associates . . . or do you suffer a drastic personality change?

• Can you give a speech reading every word on a page—while appearing to your audience to be talking from notes? . . . or is it painfully obvious that you are reading?[12]

Most of these courses deal with external aspects of your communication, each of which has to be perfected for you to be effective. However, the key to communicating exactly what you want to communicate is properly constructing the engine that drives the communication itself.

The engine of your communication is your premise, which you must prove in a logical, impressive way, given your genre and choice of medium, so that your audience will be affected in exactly the way you want. In most cases, an impressive proof of your premise will require lots of interesting illustrations (verbal or pictorial) and plenty of technical, dramatic, or literary effects.

Here is a brief outline of the most important steps in preparing your communication. Each genre and medium will require it to be modified by adding or subtracting steps or substeps. However, these basic steps should prove valuable in planning any presentation.

15 Basic Steps to Communicating Effectively

1. Make a brief note of what you want to say, your idea, conviction or key thought, in light of who you are, why you want to communicate, and your well thought out research and ascertainment. This idea, thought, or statement must be something that you believe and want to communicate.

2. Ask and answer the appropriate ascertainment questions to target your audience, determine your genre and medium, and plan the execution of your communication.

3. Rephrase your idea or key thought into an active premise you can prove, taking into consideration your answers to all the pertinent ascertainment questions.

4. Identify the elements needed to prove your premise, most of which are inherent within it. In drama, these elements are your characters, conflict, climax, and resolution.

5. Structure these elements, taking into consideration your audience, genre, and medium and your answers to the ascertainment questions that are appropriate for your communication.

6. Outline the proof of your premise.

7. Illustrate your proof with stories and images appropriate for your genre, medium, and audience.

8. Top and tail your proof with an introduction and a conclusion that reflect your genre, medium, and audience.

9. Write out, plan, or script your communication, punctuating it with effects, technical, dramatic, or literary, to capture and retain audience interest.

10. Prepare, storyboard, and/or rehearse your communication.

11. Produce, storyboard, and/or rehearse your communication.

12. Edit, review, and revise your communication

13. Deliver, distribute, broadcast, publish, or present your communication.

14. Survey your audience to find out how effective your communication was and how it can be improved.

15. Review and revise your communication to improve it, if possible.

These steps and the processes therein are for your significant communications, those you design to convince, motivate, convert, entertain, and instruct. Simpler ones, such as requests, conversations, and exchanges of information, occur informally and do not require the planning envisioned here. However, you may find that some of your simple communications would have been more effective if they had been planned better.

If you review some of your more successful informal communications, you may find that you have unconsciously (or consciously) incorporated many of the processes listed in this outline, perhaps after several attempts at the same communication. Most of our casual communications have, for example, motivating premises that give them power and direction, such as "Eating food makes me happy by sustaining my body" or "This information improves my performance." These unstated premises drive us to communicate our desire for food, shelter, knowledge, and whatever else is important to us at a particular point in time. Here we will focus on significant rather than casual communications, but the same principles apply to both.

The Premise

The key element is your premise. It is the motivating power that drives your communication. Your premise is an active, dynamic statement of the argument that you will prove. It is the essence of your work. Within your premise are the key elements of your presentation. Simply stated, your premise is a sentence—with an active verb, a subject, and an object—that summarizes your point.

Lajos Egri discusses the role of a premise and those elements that emerge from it in the context of a dramatic play:

A play can be judged before it reaches actual production. First, the premise must be discernible from the beginning. We have a right to know in what direction the author is leading us. The characters, growing out of the premise, necessarily identify themselves with the aim of the play. They will prove the premise through conflict. The play must start with conflict, which rises steadily until it reaches the climax. The characters must be so well drawn that, whether or not the author has declared their individual backgrounds, we can make out accurate case histories for each of them.[13]

There are any number of ways to arrive at your premise. You may have an idea, or a conviction, that you will convert into premise. You may be intrigued by an obligatory scene, event, or situation and want to develop it into a premise. To convert your scene, or idea, into a premise, look for the drama, the meaning, the conflict, and the purpose inherent in it; then state that purpose, meaning, and conflict in a simple, active sentence.

Suppose your idea is to communicate that God is love. Ask yourself what your purpose is in communicating that idea.

Your answer may be that it is to show your audience that God loves them, us, humanity, and/or the world. Be as specific as possible; refine your purpose in light of the answers you have found to your ascertainment questions in combination with the question, How does God love them, you, or us? Your answer may be that he loves us by comforting us in sorrow, by delivering us from fear, by forgiving us our transgressions, or by rescuing us from drug addiction, depending upon your answers to your ascertainment questions.

For our example, let's say your purpose is to demonstrate the forgiveness inherent in God's love. In light of your answers to the ascertainment questions, state your premise in a simple but specific sentence such as "God's love forgives the transgressor."

What does that mean? What is the conflict inherent in that statement? Forgiveness must mean that a wrong was committed that has alienated the wrongdoer, perhaps because of his or her feeling of guilt, or knowledge that a just judgment awaits. God's love conflicts with and triumphs over that alienation by forgiving the individual from judgment and healing him or her of guilt.

Your premise gives you the direction, the basic elements, and the conclusion of your presentation. In our example, the direction and the conclusion are inherent in the active verb *forgives*. Since you are going to demonstrate how God's love forgives the wrongdoer, you will conclude at that point where the forgiveness is a reality for the transgressor. The initiating force in your communication is God, and the object is the forgiven transgressor. The conflict is the negation of the verb/object combination, which, in terms of your premise, is the transgressor's alienation that resists forgiveness. By resisting the direction and conclusion of your premise, the conflict forces your proof and propels your communication along.

Let's assume that you decide, because of the audience and medium you have chosen, to demonstrate your premise through a story. You could choose to make the wrongdoer a young woman who decides to run away from home to live the good life. After several adventures, she ends up destitute. She feels guilty for running away. You might decide, because of your audience, to represent the subject of your premise as the father who manifests God's love. His love for his daughter causes him to go search for her. She sees him, but avoids him because of her guilt and fear of judgment. In the process of avoiding him, she is thrown in jail. The father finds his daughter, spends all he has to pay her fine, and takes her home. When the father finds the daughter and forgives her and she accepts his love and forgiveness, your premise is proved, and the story is resolved, although you may want to top and tail your story to highlight the message of your premise.

You may want to prove your premise in another genre. You may decide to do it in a sermon filled with illustrations, or you may write a theological text to prove your premise, carefully analyzing, step-by-step, how God forgives transgressors. Whatever method you choose, by rephrasing your idea into a premise you have given yourself a clear direction to follow. Any idea, scene, thought, or conviction may be converted into a premise that will drive your communication to a powerful conclusion.

In every story, the premise can be found by analyzing the story. In the Star Wars trilogy, the evil Empire is taking over the universe. A young man who is full of goodness, perseverance, and integrity is forced to fight the Empire. He wins. "Good triumphs over evil" is clearly the premise. Every film or television program with that clear-cut premise "Good triumps over evil" tells a different story by proving that premise in a different way. However, it is the process of proving the premise that satisfies the expectations of the audience.

Every one of Jesus' parables has a premise. As an exercise, you may want to try to discover the premises in some of Jesus' parables. Every one of Shakespeare's plays, every good story, and even every commercial has a clear-cut premise. Try to find and state the premise in the next movie or television commercial you see.

Many well-produced films, television programs, or other

media communications fail, not because of the quality of the production, but because of an unclear premise, a double premise, or some other defect in the premise. The movie *2010* was beautifully produced, but failed because three fourths of the way through the premise changed, and the second premise was never proved through the medium of the story to the audience's satisfaction. The first part of *2010* told the story of how "Cooperation triumphs over adversity"; then, after proving that premise, a second premise, "Supernatural being(s) bring peace," was introduced that took the movie in another direction.

As Lajos Egri notes, without a clear-cut premise, no idea, thought, or conviction is strong enough to carry you through to a logical conclusion.[14]

A badly worded, or false, premise will force you to fill space with pointless and irrelevant material.

A communication with more than one premise is confusing, because it is trying to go in more than one direction at once.

An anthology, variety, or series of separate and distinct pieces will have separate premises for each, but none should have more than one premise.

A premise that says too much is ambiguous and therefore says nothing.

A premise that does not take a position is ambivalent and says nothing.

Don't write what you don't believe.

In most communications, you should not mention your premise directly; however, your audience should know what it is, and, whatever it is, you must prove it. (Commercials and advertisements are exceptions.)

In story-telling genres, if there is no clear-cut premise your characters will not live, because without a clearly defined premise, it is impossible to know your characters.

No one premise expresses the totality of universal truth.

Every premise is limiting. For example, poverty does not always lead to crime, but if you have chosen the premise that poverty leads to crime, it does in your case, and you must prove it.

The elements of a premise are a subject, an active, transitive verb, and an object. The verb must be active and present tense, not future or past tense, to give direction to your communication. If the verb is past tense, the goal has already been achieved, and there is nothing to prove. If the verb is future tense, your premise is purely speculative.

Furthermore, the verb must be transitive to motivate your communication. An intransitive verb states a fact and portrays a static picture, giving you no basis for proving your premise and reaching a conclusion. To say "Jesus is love" is a static portrait of a fact; however, to say "Jesus loves you" sets up a dynamic situation; starting with Jesus, there has to be a demonstration of his love for whoever "you" is, and the questions how? why? where? when? what? become relevant and necessary to answer. Here is a list of some sample premises:

Hope triumphs over despair.
Greed consumes itself.
Great love conquers death.
Ruthless ambition destroys itself.
Jealousy destroys love.
Love conquers jealousy.
Poverty encourages faith.
Faith conquers fear.
Honesty defeats duplicity.
Pride leads to a fall.
Good triumphs over evil.

In every premise, it is conflict that provides the forward drive. To prove your premise you must disprove the negation of your premise, and this process propels your communication. If there is no negation and no conflict possible in your premise, your communication will be stillborn—it will have no direction and no goal.

To illustrate this, try asking two friends to stand five feet apart, facing each other, and tell each other in as many ways as they can "I love you" for no less than two minutes. After a very short time, this dialogue without conflict will become very boring. However, if you ask one to convice the other of his or her love, and you ask the other to resist, the dialogue will be very entertaining, and one or the other will have to relent, thereby establishing the premise for that brief scene as either "love triumphs over rejection" or "resistance destroys love."

Some Christian radio and television interview programs are boring to all but a few loyal supporters because the host avoids conflict, loses sight of the value of loving conflict. In these boring programs, the host and the guest spend all their time affirming each other, so that the program remains static and uninteresting. If the host will define what he or she wants to discover in the interview, the premise, in such a way as to probe who the guest is and why the guest is there by asking the tough questions that elicit what the audience needs and wants to know, there will be a real dialogue. The interview will be interesting because there is conflict built in, even if only on the level of a premise like "Curiosity discovers important information."

This conflict does not have to be mean, petty, or angry, as so much conflict is on nonreligious television. The conflict can and will be loving if the tough questions, which prove the host's premise, are asked in love. A thoughtful host can ask tough questions in a loving way to reveal the interesting story every guest has to tell. The conflict in the interview is merely the vehicle by which the guest proves his or her story to the host and the audience. Without a clear-cut premise, there will be no such conflict, and neither the host nor the audience will have any idea what the host is trying to communicate.

In a drama, the subject of the premise is the protagonist, who initiates the action of the verb and carries that action through to the conclusion; he or she takes the lead in the movement of the story, creates the conflict, and makes the story move forward. The protagonist knows what he or she wants and is determined to get it. The protagonist can be the hero, the villain, or any other character in the story. The protagonist may not be the central character, but without the protagonist the story founders.

The antagonist is the conflicting force inherent in the premise who opposes the protagonist. The antagonist can be the hero, the villain, or any other character in the story, except the same person as the protagonist. The antagonist has to be as strong as the protagonist so that the conflict between the two will carry the story forward to its natural conclusion. If the antagonist gives up at any time, the story will die. There must be a unity of opposites between the protagonist and the antagonist.

All these elements are embodied in your premise and are important to understand and define clearly if your audience is to know exactly what you are trying to say. If you have decided to communicate dramatically through a story, then you must define your characters carefully and get to know them inside out. If you are using an interview, then you must know who your guest and the topic you will be discussing. If you are preaching a sermon, you must be clear about all the elements you will use to prove your premise.

Once you have determined who you are, why you are communicating, and what the idea, scene, or conviction is that you want to present, every other element, including your premise, should be structured in light of all your answers to the ascertainment questions that apply to your communication. Use the information you have discovered by answering the questions to shape your presentation. If your audience likes to ski, frame the elements of your story or your proof in terms of skiing. If your audience is preoccupied with the human condition, design your premise and your proof with that in mind. Designing your premise and its proof in light of the answers to the pertinent ascertainment questions does not mean that you need to dilute the gospel; rather, it simply means that you need to consider the most effective way to communicate the Gospel to the audience you are trying to reach.

A few years ago Pat Robertson of the Christian Broadcasting Network told a meeting of Christian communicators that he had researched the audience who watched his program the "700 Club."[15] He found that they were primarily women his age who were attracted to him as a personality. He realized that as he grew older his audience would grow older and sparser as some died off. His commitment to preach the Gospel was clear; however, the question was how he could redesign the program to broaden his audience without losing the audience he already had. The answer was to add a co-host who would appeal to another demographic group and to re-format the program in other ways to appeal to a broader audience. These changes did not compromise the Gospel; instead, they improved his effectiveness in proclaiming the Gospel.

Recently, I lectured at a church school on the nature of television and the Christian response. When I walked into the lecture hall, I found myself facing a much younger crowd than I had imagined. Immediately, I had to reshape my talk to communicate to these students, or they would not have understood what I had to say. Structuring my talk for that audience did not change the thrust of my lecture; however, it did improve its effectiveness.

As you construct your communication, use your imagination and allow yourself to be emotional. Powerful emotions and images will give life to any presentation whose premise is well defined and proved. Whether you are using radio, film, or a newspaper, concrete, emotional images created in words, pictures, and/or sounds will create a powerful impact on your audience. Allow yourself to imagine your audience and their reaction; that will help you to make your communication more interesting.

Effects—technical, literary, and dramatic—help to capture and hold an audience, and every communication should be punctuated by them. Even if it is only a turn of phrase or a change in perspective, effects help you to retain the attention of your audience.

In television and film, both real-time media that reach out to their audience, technical effects are particularly important. The producers of the children's program "Sesame Street" use a "distractor machine" to find any places in a particular program when the attention of a group of test children wanders. If the children's attention wanders, the producers will insert another technical effect to sustain interest.

Watch several minutes of different television programs, and count the technical effects per minute: cuts, camera moves, action, and scene changes. You will find that most programs have ten to fifty technical effects per minute to capture and hold attention, and those with fewer effects will not keep your attention unless the premise, its execution, and the emotive images that constitute the fabric of the program are unusually powerful.

Aside from the effects you use, where appropriate, keep your communication simple. As the acronym KISS notes, Keep It Simple, Stupid. This does not mean that you should force yourself to communicate in a manner that is alien to you. Anything that is unnatural will fail. Be true to yourself—your own voice, your premise, your medium, your audience, and your characters. Where appropriate, be brief. Capture the tone, language, and grammar that will be most effective.

Be truthful in constructing your presentation, true to its demands on you and to your demands on it, taking the time to edit, cut back, and/or elaborate as needed to be perfectly clear and coherent. Articles abound in literary mgazines urging one to be ruthlessly plain and natural; just as many articles appear urging writers to recapture the beauty of the romantic flights of fancy of the great nineteenth-century novelists.[16] There is room for both if they communicate effectively, clearly, and coherently what the author is trying to say. In "Is Fiction the Art of Lying?" Mario Vargas Llosa notes:

In fact, novels do lie—they can't help doing so— but that's only part of the story. The other is that, through lying, they express a curious truth, which can only be expressed in a veiled and concealed fashion, masquerading as what it is not. . . .

Every good novel tells the truth and every bad novel lies. For a novel "to tell the truth" means to make the reader experience an illusion, and "to lie" means to be unable to accomplish that trickery.[17]

For a communication to be true is for it to be true to the rules you have set up as its creator, given that you have very good reasons for setting up those rules.

If at one point in planning your presentation you feel that you want an objective reaction to it, do not succumb to the temptation to have your friends review it. They will be prejudiced and will not give you an objective evaluation. If you do for some reason have to have your friends review your work, ask them to stop when they feel bored; that is the point where you have failed.

If you state your premise clearly, define all the elements contained therein with great precision, and carefully prove your premise, then your premise will powerfully drive your communication no matter what genre and medium you choose. If you follow the fifteen steps, or your own variations, in light of your answers to the ascertainment questions, you will say what you want to say to your audience.

Finally, remember: "Ask the Lord to bless your plans, and you will be successful in carrying them out" (Prov. 16:3, GNB).

6. What About Genre?

The first sign that a baby is going to be human comes when he
begins naming the world, demanding stories that connect its parts.

KATHRYN MORTON

Babies are human because God created us in his image, not
because they demand, or tell, stories. Communication, however, is an important part of the uniqueness of humankind,
and the human drive to communicate through a variety of
forms, formats, and media is remarkable.

Communicating effectively requires learning and applying
basic principles that are the language, grammar, rhetoric, techniques, and rules governing each genre and medium. There
are three levels of principles for each communication:

General principles, those that apply to most communications.
The principles that apply to the specific genre.
The principles that apply to the specific medium.

In Chapter 5, we looked at the general principles. In this
chapter, we consider the key principles that apply to certain
genres. In the chapters that follow, we will consider the key
principles that govern selected media.

The notion of genre is a simple way of talking about the
different kinds, types, or formats of communications. George
Gerbner has reduced human communication to three genres:
stories that tell about how things work, stories that tell about
what things are, and stories of action.[1] Aristotle was probably
aware of three ultimate categories, drama, epic, and lyric,
which have evolved into drama, fiction, and poetry according
to some contemporary literary critics.[2]

Others have proposed different generic classifications, such as comedy, epigram, satire, epic, and tragedy. Northrop Frye, author of *Anatomy of Criticism*, classifies literature into mythic, heroic, high ironic, low ironic, and demonic, a system that promotes a better understanding of the import of a story.[3]

Here, we need a practical classification to help us communicate more effectively; therefore, the most commonly used forms of contemporary communication will constitute our genres: the story, the commentary or sermon, the report, and the instruction. This chapter will look briefly at the key principles that apply to each of these.

We will look briefly also, at a few key principles that govern certain subordinate communication genres: the commercial or promotion, the contest, and the interview. These are classified as subordinate because they are subcategories of one of the other communication genres, their principles differ only slightly from one of the other genres, or they are a combination of two or more genres.

Other genres of communication, such as poetry, music, and conversation, and subgenres, such as science fiction, romance, comedy, and tragedy, will not be treated. If you have chosen to use one of these, you will want to research the principles that apply by consulting some of the many fine books available. Remember Schopenhaver's adage: "Write the way an architect builds; who first drafts his plan and designs every detail."[4]

The Story

A story is a connected narration of real or imagined events. There are many types of story, including science fiction, romance, myth, fairy-tale, tragedy, and adventure. The full range of story telling is limited only by the human imagination, yet there are principles that apply to all stories, and all stories can be classified in categories or subgenres.

Stories have an internal logic driven by a premise acting

through characters and conflict to move the plot from a beginning point of attack through one or more crises to a climax that resolves into a resolution. There are a wide range of variations on this approach, but the key principles apply to almost all of them. News reports are often called stories, and some are; however, the descriptive reporting of events is a separate genre with its own principles that will be considered when we discuss the report. Here are the steps and key principles involved in constructing your story. (For an excellent, step by step analysis of the art of dramatic writing, see Lajos Egri's book by that name (cited n. 13, chap. 5):

Constructing Your Story

1. *Formulate your premise.*

Chapter 5 discussed and demonstrated how to find, formulate, and state your premise. Your premise is the essence of your story.

You can find premises all around you. Look at an interesting situation, and ask what motivates it. The best premises and characters come out of genuine experience.

Look at a strong, even militant, character, and ask why that character is motivated to do what he or she is doing. Look at an idea, and ask what that idea means translated into action. Your premise expresses the motivation, the action, and the reaction, through a subject, an active verb, and an object that drive your story to its conclusion.

2. *Define your environment, subgenre, style, and point of view.*

Your environment must be real, even if it is far, far away in time and space.

Before you start constructing your story, you must define in detail the environment in which it takes place. The environment and the laws that govern it create the illusion of reality in your story. The more you know about when and where your story takes place, the more real your story will be to your audience. The novel *Time and Again* by Jack Finney[5] has an implausible plot where the hero is able to will himself back in history, but it works because Finney has defined the setting of the novel with such meticulous care.

Many movies, especially science fiction, fail because the setting is only partially realized. The Disney movie *The Black Hole* has many scenes where the sets look like sets—unreal, with no sign of having been lived in. *The Return of the Jedi*, on the other hand, has outlandish sets that look real because time was taken to make them so through detailed definition.

You must learn, define, and obey the rules of the subgenre your choose.

Whether you choose to construct your story as a romance, science fiction, comedy, contemporary stream of consciousness, history, or as a detective story, you must obey the rules that the subgenre imposes.

Note that the principles of the genre to which the subgenre belongs apply as well as the principles, or variations on them, that define the subgenre itself.

Select your style to fit your premise, your environment, your characters, and your subgenre.

The style, rhythm, and tone you establish is as important as your plot. A satiric or low ironic style may be appropriate for a detective story but not for a portrayal of Jesus' ministry, unless you are attacking the Gospel, or you have chosen Judas Iscariot's point of view.

Here are some stylistic keys:

In the mythic style, God triumphs, or the hero triumphs due to an act of God.*

In the heroic style, the hero triumphs because he or she is superior.

---

* Note that Northrope Frye (see n. 3) would consider this a genre, but the styles suggested here can be used in the context of any subgenre of the story genre.

In the high ironic style, the hero triumphs because of a quirk
of fate.

In the low ironic style, the hero fails because of a quirk of
fate.

In the demonic style, the hero is hopelessly overwhelmed by
evil.

Here is a brief list of effects within a style and how they can be
created:

To shock, you must make the incredible credible.

To create irony, the audience's assumptions must be contrary
to the outcome.

To create a paradox, logic must be contradicted by fact.

To create satire, the normal must be exaggerated.

To create suspense, withheld information must confront the
desire to know.

Your point of view affects your characters.

The first person point of view involves the audience in the thoughts
of one of the characters. The first person ("I") is not necessarily the
protagonist, or the antagonist. "I" can be any character in the story.

The first person point of view may be pure stream of consciousness,
but the rules of story telling still apply. The first person may be
established in a neutral style, which overcomes the limitations imposed by the "I" speaking in dialect. If you choose a first person point
of view, you must define that person in the same detail as you would
define any other character.

The third person is the most common and flexible point of view.
The third person allows for different perspectives, involving the audience with different characters, or establishing an omniscent perspective.

3. *Define your protagonist*.

Your protagonist is the driven, driving subject inherent in your
premise who forces the conflict that moves your story to its
conclusion. Your protagonist takes the lead in your story, knows

what he or she wants, and will act to get it. Not only does your protagonist want something badly enough to act but will go after it until successful or completely defeated.

Your protagonist must have something very important at stake, must act out of necessity, forced by who he or she is and by circumstances to do what he or she does.

Your protagonist has one highly developed motivation—love, hate, revenge, greed, envy, caring, faith, or hope—that drives him or her to act until successful or defeated.

Even if the motivating characteristic of your protagonist seems passive, it must be active in terms of your premise and the situation. For instance, if your protagonist is motivated to patiently endure, then he or she must be willing to act on that motivation even if it brings martyrdom, as is the case with many Christian martyrs.

Your determined protagonist will not grow as much as the other characters. The other characters will grow a great deal, even from one emotion to its opposite, because of the strength of will of the protagonist.

If your premise is "Love conquers death," for instance, your protagonist must love enough to do everything possible, including die to save the beloved from death. Your protagonist could be a loving father who risks his life to save his son who has fallen through the ice, a loving mother who will give up everything to save her family from destruction, or Jesus, who gave his life so that death would be defeated.

4. Define and orchestrate your characters.

You must know your characters inside out. Get inside your characters, live with them, find out and define what makes each a unique individual.

Well-orchestrated characters are one of the primary reasons for rising conflict in any story. It is the differences that distinguish each of your characters that move your story from start to finish through conflict. You may have two apostles, two tax collectors, or two thieves in your story, but they must be different; they must contrast with each other so that they will move the story along. The contrast between them must be inherent in their characters, that is, the way you defined them.

Orchestration is simply creating well-defined, strong characters who are in conflict and therefore move your story. Through this conflict your characters will grow and your story will develop, proving your premise.

Use the Character Definition Form, or a modification of it, to define each of your characters. Your story is built by your characters, so be as thorough as you can. The difference between a simple and a sophisticated story is primarily the complexity of the characters. Visualize your characters as if they were people you have known all your life.

Character Definition Form

Name of character:_____

Physical Characteristics:

Sex_____

Age_____

Height_____

Weight_____

Hair_____

Eyes_____

Skin_____

Race_____

Ethnic Group_____

Appearance_____

Posture_____

Unusual Characteristics_____

Background:
Class_____
Education_____
Home_____
Occupation_____
Nationality_____
Politics_____
Relationships_____
Marital status_____
Hobbies_____
Parents_____
Relatives_____
Children_____

Psychological characteristics:
Ambition_____
Preferences_____
Motivations_____
Temperament_____
Attitude_____
Fears_____
Wants_____
Likes_____
Relationship patterns_____
Talents_____
Qualities_____
Intelligence_____

Emotional state_____

Religious characteristics:
Beliefs_____
Hopes_____
Faith_____
Worldview_____
Cares_____
Religious background_____
Religious environment_____

5. Define your antagonist in opposition to your protagonist.

Your antagonist opposes your protagonist. He or she wants to prevent your protagonist from acting—from doing what your protagonist is driven to do. The will of your protagonist must clash with the will of your antagonist, and they must be strong and equally driven.

Your antagonist and your protagonist must be locked in opposition. There must be a unity of opposites that can only be broken by the death of the motivating characteristic in one or the other of them. Either one must be completely defeated for your story to reach its natural conclusion. Because of the strength of will of these two characters, the initial conflict between them must lead to a crisis, which must lead to a climax, which must lead to a resolution.

If one or the other of these two characters gives up early, your story will stop. If one or the other is a pushover, if they are unequally matched, then you have no story, because there will be no conflict to drive the plot. Compromise is out of the question unless it is the result of a completely realized conflict that has proved your premise. If one character is determined to win and the other doesn't care, there is no challenge, no battle, and no story. A strong person pitted against a weak one is a farce, unless the weaker has the courage, will, and hidden ability to put up a real fight and perhaps win.

Every character will fight back under the right circumstances. It is up to you to catch your character at that point where he or she will carry the premise through conflict.

Your antagonist is inherent in your premise. Your antagonist is what your subject/protagonist must oppose to fulfill his or her goals. The antagonist reacts against the action of the subject. Depending on the outcome determined by your premise, either the antagonist must change for the protagonist to reach his or her goal or your protagonist must change in the face of the antagonist's opposition.

6. *Define your starting point, a crisis, which must lead your story to a climax, which must result in a conclusion or resolution*.

If you want your story to move and to capture your audience, you must choose the right point of attack—that moment in time and space when your protagonist is at a critical turning point at which action must be taken to achieve his or her goal, thereby initiating the action of the premise. This turning point is a crisis point where a decisive change must occur. Because of your premise, this opening crisis can only lead to the climax inherent in your premise, which must be resolved in such a way that your premise is proved.

No story starts at the beginning: there is always something that occurred before the story began. Genesis starts with God acting to create our universe, but it does not tell us what was going on in eternity before God decided to create. In the beginning of Genesis, God, the protagonist, is at a turning point where he acts to create the heavens and the earth.

Rather than ramble, looking for a place to begin, start your story at the moment when the conflict starts, when the protagonist acts. This moment occurs when circumstances and motivation force it to happen. The protagonist acts out of necessity: something extremely important is at stake, such as love, survival, health, or honor. This point could be where your protagonist has made a decision, has reached a turning point, or where something important is suddenly at stake.

Whatever precipitated this moment has already occurred when your story begins. Your story grows out of whatever happened to cause your protagonist to act, and that action forces the climax, which proves your premise in its resolution.

7. Develop rising conflict.

Your story builds through rising conflict, that is, a series of conflicts, each building in intensity on the previous one until the climax is reached and the premise proved. Each conflict moves your story forward through action and reaction, attack and counterattack, which in turn cause change, growth, and new conflict until you reach the proof of your premise. The first conflict in your story comes from your protagonist consciously trying to achieve the goal you determined by your premise.

Conflict will grow out of your characters who are in opposition. The more evenly matched your characters are, the more real rising conflict will move your story to its resolution.

Conflict exposes your story and your characters.

Through conflict your characters and your story are revealed and exposed. Each dialogue, every interaction between characters, reveals who they are, what their background is, what the environment is, what the plot is, and where the plot is headed.

Conflict causes change and growth.

Every conflict causes change. At no two points in your story are any of the characters, or situation, the same. As a result of conflict, each character will change emotionally, psychologically, and spiritually. Growth occurs continually until the story proves your premise.

In your story, if your premise is "Love conquers hate," the conquered character must grow from hate to love. To do so he or she must go through every step, every change that leads from hate to love: hate—dislike—annoyance—understanding—interest—attraction—caring—love. Each conflict will move this character along the road from hate to love, where his or her growth will be complete.

Avoid static conflict.

Static conflict will bring your story to a halt. No dialogue, effects, descriptions, or rhetoric will move your story if the conflict is static. Conflict is static when

—one or more of your characters can't make a decision. Each has to grow from one emotional, psychological, or spiritual point to another in your story. If they stop at one of the intermediate steps along the way because they can't make a decision, you will have static conflict and your story will stop.

—your story lacks the motivating force of a premise.

—your characters have exactly the same point of view because you have not orchestrated them by defining them carefully as unique individuals.

The exercise suggested in Chapter 5 in which you ask two friends to try to tell each other that they love each other for two minutes is an example of static conflict. Since they are both starting with the same point of view, there is no conflict to generate a story. Here is an example of a character who is indecisive. These characters and this story are going nowhere because Jack is indecisive:

Jane: "Do you want to go out, darling?"
Jack: "Maybe."
Jane: "When will you decide?"
Jack: "Sometime."
Jane: "Do you care?"
Jack: "I don't know."
Jane: "When will you know?"
Jack: "Soon."
Jane: "Will you tell me?"
Jack: "Sure."

Avoid jumping conflict.
Jumping conflict is when

—one, or more, of your characters has skipped one, or more, of the important stages of growth through which he or she must pass to reach the conclusion inherent in your premise.

—you are forcing people in your story to do things that are not within their uniquely defined characters.

—you have not given one or more of your characters a chance to grow steadily and realistically through rising conflict.

—you have not thought through the process of proving your premise.

—you have not defined your premise clearly.

Here is an example of jumping conflicts:

Jane: "Do you want to go out, darling?"
Jack: "Maybe."
Jane: "Well, if you don't know for sure, I'm walking out on our marriage."
Jack: "But I'll make up my mind."
Jane: "It's too late, you inconsiderate slob." (*She leaves, slamming the door.*)

To avoid jumping conflict, determine the stages of growth through which each character will progress from where they are emotionally, psychologically, and spiritually when the audience first meets them and to where they must end up, as dictated by your premise. As your characters grow through conflict, they are allowed to choose only those solutions to each conflict that will help prove the point of your premise. For instance, if your character has to go from rebellion to submission in your story, make sure that you have predetermined each one of the stages that he or she must pass through in the process: rebellion, alienation, loneliness, insecurity, fear, need, longing, desire for help and protection, submission.

Conflict foreshadows itself.

Each minor conflict in your story leads to the next conflict, because none of the intermediate solutions will resolve your story until your premise is proved. Each conflict foreshadows the next conflict because it contains the seeds of the next conflict by the very nature of how you have defined and orchestrated your characters in light of your premise.

Conflict is the product of the tension inherent in your characters. Every conflict contains all the elements of a story in brief.

8. Use dialogue to quote a character's words or thoughts.

You have defined each of your characters; each character defines the dialogue he or she utters. Dialogue that does not flow clearly and validly from the character who uses it is unnatural and defeats your story, unless it is being used as an effect. If dialogue is an effect, it still must be true to the character of its real source.

Dialogue reveals who a character is and hints at who he or she will become. Each character should speak in his or her own language and dialect, but too much dialect will usually sound phony and should be avoided. Informal, natural dialogue is most effetive.

Rising conflict produces healthy dialogue that foreshadows the direction in which the premise is leading.

Dialogue should be concise and succinct. In most cases, surplus words weaken. Sacrifice brilliance for character. Do not preach through dialogue unless that preaching reflects who a character is and occurs naturally in context. Never overemphasize dialogue. Don't be didactic.

9. *Observe, experience, and create the illusion of reality in your story, even if that reality is set in a cosmos far, far away.*

The Commentary or Sermon

A commentary on radio or television, a discourse, a form of documentary, an editorial, a homily, or a sermon is an orderly, logical communication of an opinion. This genre because many communicators have the notion that the only work involved in using it is having a brilliant opinion and then presenting it through their chosen medium.

An undisciplined approach to expressing opinions has caused Webster's to give a negative definition to one of the names by which this genre is called. In *Webster's New Collegiate Dictionary* (2nd ed.), the second definition of *sermon* concludes, "a homily; hence, an annoying harangue." A sermon should be an annoying harange only if that is intended. Otherwise, it should be a powerful, effective discourse. Here are the steps and key principles involved in constructing an orderly and logical commentary, sermon, or discourse:

Constructing Your Commentary or Sermon

1. Formulate your opinion based on the evidence.

If you have an idea, let it point you toward the right evidence. Then put your idea aside.

If you don't have an idea, but a subject, text, or evidence on which to comment, try to restrain yourself from forming an opinion until you have thoroughly studied your subject, text, or evidence.

If you don't have a subject, but must come up with a commentary or sermon (as many of us do week after week), choose your subject by noticing what matters to you:

Events:

Anything outside of you that presses upon you and concerns you, such as a natural catastrophe (food, famine, etc.), a crime, a occurrence in your community, a new film, or a government action.

Needs:

Anything that your audience, the community, the country, or people in general need. Human interest is the key here.

Notes:

Reminders of moments of inspiration. Keep notes and review them when you need a subject.

Once you have your subject, text, or evidence, study it, think about it, and pray about it, asking yourself, in this exact order:

1. *What does it mean?* What did it mean when it happened or was written—not what you want it to mean, but what the evidence, the

subject, or the text really means? To get at what it really means, dig, analyze, and ask What? Why? Where? When? How? Who?

2. *What does it say?* What is the message of the subject, the evidence, or the text for my audience, where they are today? Imagine your audience and relate the evidence, the subject, or the text to them.

3. *What do other commentators or communicators think about the evidence, the subject, or the text?* Do not consult other commentators or communicators until you have answered the first two questions to your satisfaction.

From your answers to these questions, isolate and formulate your opinion. To do this, ask yourself:

What is the main thrust of the evidence, the text, or the subject? Think and pray about this question, and your answers to the previous questions until you have your opinion and long to communicate it.

The worst commentaries, sermons, or discourses are half-baked presentations of one or more opinions based on insufficient evidence, or based on evidence that is strained and forced in an unethical and ultimately unconvincing manner to fit an opinion.

In sermons, a problem often develops when a biblical text has been taken out of context and forced to support a twentieth-century opinion. An extreme example would be using the text "Blessed are the poor" to support poverty, greed, and hard-heartedness. Another example, equally absurd, would be to use the text "Love your enemies" to support lawless anarchy or tyranny. This process, which has been called isogesis, stands in contrast to biblical exegesis, in which the sermon emerges from the text.[6]

2. *Formulate your premise*.

Find the premise in your opinion, and state it so that you can prove it using the evidence, subject, or text upon which your opinion is based.

3. *Research all the evidence that supports your premise*.

To make sure that you have all the pertinent evidence to prove your premise, ask and answer the following questions:

Who?

What?

Where?

When?

Why?

How?

What evidence is missing?

What evidence supports the negative of my premise?

4. *Organize your evidence to support your premise*.

This step creates the structure of your discourse, sermon, homily, or commentary.

Once you have found all the pertinent evidence, arrange it in such a way as to serve your premise. Reject the irrelevant. Subordinate your evidence to your premise in such a way that it will illuminate and prove it.

In choosing a structure, consider all the pertinent ascertainment questions; particularly important is who your audience is and what medium you will use. There are several methods you can use to organize your evidence, but remember that you must be logical no matter what structure you choose:

Intrinsic:

This method lets the evidence impose its own structure and organization.

Don't impose an artificial structure on the evidence, let the evidence, in light of your premise, dictate its own structure. Review all your evidence and meditate on it until an outline emerges that proves your premise. In some cases, your evidence and premise will give you no choice but to structure your communication in a particular way.

Importance:

Outline your evidence under your premise in order of importance. This method resembles news articles or reporting. Give the most important point first and then the remaining evidence, texts, and proof in descending order of importance.

Aristotelian:

Aristotle organized his arguments for maximum impact on his audience by moving from his least important proof to his most important proof. In this way, his arguments gathered power as he progressed, proving his premise.

Causal:

Outline your evidence in terms of cause and effect. This is similar to the method used in proving your premise through a story. Start with an action, event, or fact, which causes a reaction, which leads to another reaction, and so on, building to a climax and a conclusion.

Chronological:

Histories and newsmagazines use this method, in which the evidence is organized and grouped according to the time of occurrence. This structure tends to legitimize the proof being presented, since people witness reality in chronological terms. (You could also organize the evidence in spatial terms—for instance, moving around the scene of a crime.)

Acts 2:

Peter uses a powerful seven-step method of organizing his sermon in Acts 2 that causes his audience to ask, "Brothers, what shall we do?" (Acts 2:38). This seven-step evangelistic sermon structure is used throughout the New Testament. In response to the crowd questioning the outpouring of the Holy Spirit on Pentecost, Peter uses the following seven steps to present the Gospel:

1. *What God said* through his prophets would happen, is happening.
2. *What happened* was that Jesus came and was accredited by God to you by miracles.
3. *What the people did* was put Jesus to death by nailing him to the cross.
4. *What God did* was raise Jesus from the dead.
5. *What I(we) am(are) doing* is witnessing to the fact of the resurrection.
6. *What you can do* is "repent and be baptized, every one of you, in the name of Jesus Christ so that your sins may be forgiven" (Acts 2:38).
7. *What God will do* if you repent is give you the gift of the Holy Spirit.

This seven-step structure starts and ends with God and tells his story, past, present, and future, as it pertains to each individual in the crowd. This structure logically answers the crowd's question and presents the Gospel.

As an interesting exercise, compare contemporary evangelistic presentations of the Gospel with Peter's to see where they differ and how those differences affect their impact.

5. Prepare your sermon or commentary.

Prepare your commentary, sermon, or discourse in detail. Be as complete as possible, but at the same time be concise, specific, and definite. Visualize your audience, and aim your communication at them. Keep the medium you will use in mind, and work to utilize that medium's assets and minimize its limitations.

Prove your premise by disproving the negative of your premise. Weigh the defects in your argument and in your information. Address those defects wisely, emphasizing the strengths of your proof. Use your evidence, as well as appeals to emotional evidence, basic human needs, biblical principles, and recognizable values to build your discourse.

Remember to observe

Economy of language

Clarity of thought

Forthrightness of opinion

6. *Illustrate*.

After you have prepared your communication, use stories, quotations, and anecdotes to make your abstract thoughts concrete. Illustrate your discourse after it is in semifinal form, because you want your communication itself to dictate what illustrations are necessary, not the other way around.

If you are working in an audiovisual medium, use visual and verbal images. If you are preparing a film or television documentary, a great deal of your evidence may be photographs or film or video clips. Since you have used that visual evidence to prepare your presentation, it is already part of it. In most instances, you will still have to illustrate. Do so, with discretion.

Never let your illustrations become overpowering; however, use enough illustrations to capture and hold your audience.

After you have illustrated your communication, determine what rhetorical devices you need, if any. Would a question enliven your presentation? If so, use one, but don't go overboard. Repetition may help, if appropriate. Humor is quite powerful in the right place. Devices and effects create rhythm and hold interest when used judiciously.

7. *Top and tail*.

Now that you have prepared your communication and illustrated it, prepare an introduction and a conclusion.

Your introduction will hook your audience, capture their attention, and get them to tune in to what you are about to say. Alfred Hitchcock would have us start with a bang. He meant that literally, but it can also be taken figuratively: Challenge your audience. Wake them up. Hook them. Use stories, anecdotes, personal material, facts, needs, wants, questions, prayers, humor, or whatever else is appropriate to get their attention.

Your conclusion is not the same as a recapitulation or a summary. If the body of your commentary or discourse communicates logically to the mind, your conclusion goes to the heart. It should elicit the response you intend—the appropriate action, or decision, on the part of your audience. Be emotional. Be worshipful. Open fire on the enemy. Ask your audience to do what you want them to do. If you have structured your sermon or commentary properly, they will.

8. Rehearse, Review, and Revise.

Whether your work is intended to air on television or be presented in an auditorium, practice it in front of critics who are looking for flaws. Be honest. Review it. Revise it.

In most cases, presentations that could be terrific fall apart at this point because the communicator doesn't have, or take, the time to review and revise. If you do so, you will be pleased with the results.

9. Familiarize yourself with every aspect of your communication.

If your discourse is live, or taped live, know it so well that it becomes part of you. Then drop it for a while so that it will be fresh when you present it.

If your communication is an article or a documentary, skip this step.

10. Produce and distribute your commentary.

Put your sermon, commentary, documentary, or discourse into final form. Make last-minute changes. Produce, print, record, film, or write it. Then give, broadcast, present, publish, or distribute it.

The principles of the medium you have chosen apply here; they will be discussed in the following chapters.

11. Pray.

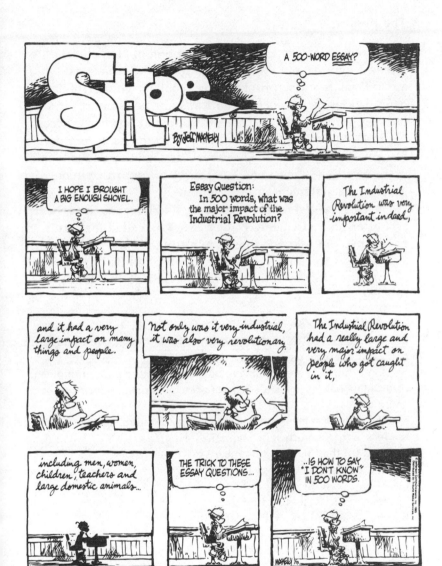

SHOE. *Reprinted by permission: Tribune Media Services, Inc.*

The Report

The report is a statement or description of fact, evidence, or received information. This genre includes proclamations, which are official reports (prophetic or secular), church bulletins, news articles, some documentaries, some newsletters, and the many reports we give to others throughout our lives. According to *Webster's New Collegiate Dictionary* (2nd ed.), to report is "to give account of. . . . ; to repeat, as something heard, said, or received as a message." A report is not an opinion disguised as a statement or description.

The essence of a report is accuracy and integrity. In a speech just after his retirement, Walker Cronkite called for "truth in packaging" for television news reporting. At the Radio-Television News Directors Association Convention in New Orleans six months after he retired, Cronkite said to the newspeople present:

> I don't think we are fulfilling our mission when, in highly competitive local markets, we seek to shock and titillate with crime and other stories of doubtful significance. . . .
> I don't think we are enhancing our respectability with entrapment, confrontational journalism when its principle purpose seems to be to entertain. . . .
> [T]he title of anchorman, or woman, by the employment of news readers without sufficient claim to be journalists . . . [should be changed to] the title of "announcer" or "news reader." . . .
> [T]he burdens of success [are] its dangers of arrogance and complacency. . . . [O]ne proof of that success is a growing public appetite for news on television and radio. . . . [W]e have been responding to that increased appetite with a lot of junk food.[7]

Fifty-four percent of the American public depend on television news for information, as opposed to 25 percent who depend on newspapers, 14 percent on radio, and 2 percent on magazines.[8]

Ben Wattenberg, in his book *The Good News Is the Bad News*

Is Wrong, says that the news media has a bad new bias that is damaging its credibility.[9] Georgia Congressman Newt Gingrich has suggested that if Edison's invention of the light bulb were reported by today's press, the report would lead off, "Candlemaking today received a severe blow, which may lead to wisespread unemployment in the industry."

The rule of thumb for television news used to be, "Avoid unnecessary sensationalism. Remember that the newscaster is coming into the home as a guest."[10] Times have changed, but this rule should still apply—it will, if people demand good reporting. Here are the steps and key principles involved in giving an accurate and effective report or proclamation:

Constructing Your Report

1. If you don't have an assigned subject, choose one based on your audience and God's will.

In many cases, you will have an assigned subject on which to report. It may even be that God will speak to you and tell you what to proclaim. But if you do not have a subject on which to report, find one by

—observing the events around you.

—researching what is going on in your church, community, town, country, and in the world.

—consulting the wire services: Associated Press, United Press International, and Pacifica News Service.

—typing in to a computer information service, like the Source, Compuserve, or Dow Jones, for example.

—consulting television news services, if appropriate.

—read newspapers, magazines, and everything you can get your hands on that is appropriate.

Ask what is important for and to your audience in light of

God's will. Think backward from the point of view of your audience and the Lord.

If your audience is your congregation, they will be interested in births, weddings, the sick, church activities, and other items that are current and that apply to them.

If your audience lives in the farm belt, they will be interested in farm news, weather, equipment, and agricultural events.

If you have a radio or television program and the station has placed you in an early-morning, weekday time spot, you audience will probably be business men and women who want financial news. If you have a midday program, your audience will probably be women who want to know about the home, school, and fashion. If your program comes on late at night, your audience will want news that will affect them tomorrow.

2. *Research the subject of your report.*

Find out everything you can about your subject so that you can be as accurate as possible in your report.

Do your own research, where possible. Don't trust secondary sources, opinions, guesses, and third-party evidence.

Ask the traditional journalistic questions, sometimes known as the six *W*'s: Who? Where? What? When? Why? How?

Find out as much as you can about any people involved. These are the characters in your report. Know them so that you can report accurately. Marguerite Young, in *Conversations With American Writers*, has confessed:

I often have to hold myself back in writing nonfiction, because it is stranger than fiction. You can never assume that you know the logic of a character in nonfiction. You may think so, but there are surprises.[11]

Make lists of

Facts

Evidence

Information

Pluses

Minuses
Interesting factors
the Familiar
the Unfamiliar
Relationships
Similarities
Differences
What's missing

3. Formulate your premise to summarize your subject or report In an active statement.

Dramatic action affects all life. Whatever the subject of your report, it involves, results from, or results in action. Formulate your premise to express the action inherent in your report, and let that premise motivate your reporting.

4. Organize and condense your information or message.

News reports, memorandums, documentaries, proclamations, and other reports are usually organized in one of the following orders:

Importance:

Start with the most important information, and proceed, step-by-step, to the least important information.

Topic:

Structure your report according to the natural topics inherent in your information or message.

Chronology:

Structure the report in the order in which events occurred.

Geography:

Structure the report by a systematic and logical geographic progression. For example, if you are reporting on a new church building, walk your audience through that building.

As you structure your material, condense it, retaining the essential descriptive facts or information necessary to report clearly and concisely on your chosen subject.

If you are reporting through television or radio, your report must be very condensed, because the television or radio audience will only see or hear the news once during a short program and will be unable to absorb a great deal of detail. All-talk radio and all-news cable television allow slightly more detail.

On the other hand, because of the state of education in the United States today, many times you must provide more detail than you woud have to the average audience fifty years ago. For example, it is important to identify the players in reports on government, and recipes, which used to assume that the cook would preheat the oven and grease the pan to bake cookies, now must tell people to do so.[12]

5. Formulate your opening summary statement.

Your opening sentence should be a summary of your report. Make it simple and clear.

6. Compose your report.

Report, don't editorialize.

Describe what you are reporting on clearly, concisely, and vividly. Use the present tense and active verbs, where possible, to give your report life. Use natural, colloquial, everyday language.

Avoid repetition, rhetorical questions, tongue twisters, abstract statements, and words with unclear meanings. These may be great devices for an opinion piece, but they detract from a report.

Make sure that your terminology is correct. Use *alleged murderer* not *murderer* for someone who has not been convicted.

Television is visual; therefore, be visual and use visual evidence and information. Make sure that your pictorial material is applicable and factually accurate. Material can portray an event but do it so as to make the event something that it wasn't.

7. Review and revise.

8. Present your report.

Presenting your report has to do with your medium of choice, but prayer should be part of it—and of every step in constructing your report.

9. Update when necessary.

Always be prepared to update your report as new facts come out. Most reports acts as background for future reports, so keep them on hand, ready to update.

FUNKY WINKERBEAN *by Tom Batiuk.* © *by and permission of News America Syndicate.*

The Instruction

The point of most instruction, or teaching is not just to pass on facts and figures (*P*—physical or factual—experience); but also, to help the audience to develop cognitively (*LM*—logical-mathematical—experience) so that they can use the facts, figures, and experience to live a better life. To lecture, instruct, or teach implies educating, from the Latin *e* (out) and *ducere* (to lead)—to lead the audience out of the darknes of ignorance into the light of knowledge.

Instruction differs from the genres previously discussed because it needs feedback, or action and reaction, to promote cognitive development in an audience. Persuading your audience to do something, reporting on facts, or even getting your audience to remember information is not the same as helping them to grow cognitively through action and reaction.

Since television does not impact *LM* experience, it must be combined with another medium, such as a live instruction, a feedback telephone, or a study guide before it can be used successfully as a medium for instruction.

Here are the steps and key principles involved in constructing an effective instruction:

Constructing Your Instruction

1. *If you don't have an assigned subject, choose one based on your audience and God's will, keeping in mind that you can cover many subtopics, or subjects, in one instruction.*

When you do not have an assigned subject and God has not called you to teach on a specific topic, determine your subject by ascertaining

—who your audience is and what they need to hear;

—what God wants your audience to hear; and

—what your field of expertise is with respect to your teaching talents, your call, and your motivational talents.

The nature of an instruction allows you to cover a wide range of material, information, topics, and evidence. In most cases, the audience of an instruction is interested in learning and will want to understand the subject in depth. Even so, you need to make your instruction as interesting as possible to engage your audience. Remember, "Everything which is written is meant either to please or instruct. The second object is difficult to effect without attending to the first."[13]

Instruction is presented to a variety of audiences in a variety of settings: such as, adult education, technical schools, discipleship training programs, Sunday Schools, and so on. Knowing your audience and your talents is essential to teaching effectively.

2. Research your subject.

You must know your subject before you instruct others. Go to the library; go to your local bookstore; research; dig. Live with your subject until you know it so well you can answer intelligent questions about it from a three-year-old or a thirty-year-old.

3. Formulate your premise.

Your premise will give your instruction a cohesive direction and ensure that it is logical. If you are presenting a series of instructions, formulate a premise for the entire series.

4. Organize your material, and structure your instruction.

Structure your instruction so that the subject, material, and subtopics come across clearly and coherently. In most cases, you will want to organize your instruction topically, that is, according to those topics and categories that logically emerge from your subject matter, given your premise.

Structure your presentation to build interest and intensity, so that your conclusion is driven home to your audience.

Prove the opinions, assumptions, and conclusions you offer in your instruction using facts, values, and authorities that your audience will recognize and respect. Build the credibility of your arguments and propositions. Within your instruction, propose and answer any opposing arguments and deal with other solutions, divergent approaches, contradictions, and false conclusions.

At the same time, keep your instruction simple, clear, and concise. State your opinions in a direct, forthright manner, distinguishing them from facts and from the opinions of others.

Keep your format flexible, capable of modification, expansion, and clarification to meet the needs and reasonable demands of your audience, but don't allow your audience to sidetrack you from the goal of your premise.

5. *Structure inquiry and response into your instruction.*

Since cognitive development requires work, structure questions and interaction into your instruction. However, prepare your presentation so that your audience will receive the essential information and conclusions even if they do not participate, because many will not. More of your audience will participate in a live instruction than in one done through television.

In a live presentation, interaction includes being responsive to your audience. On television, feedback is difficult, but possible with a local instructor with a study guide, through phone-in questions and answers, or by mail.

Feedback by mail has many obvious drawbacks, including the lack of immediacy. The network educational television program "Sunrise Semester" had a disappointing six correspondence students out of the millions of potential television viewers in 1980.

Try not to confuse your audience by playing devil's advocate with facts and proven conclusions. Make sure that they know your point of view, the correct answers and the incorrect answers.

Avoid discussions that are phony and pretentious, but don't hold back real discussions just to keep your instruction on track.

If you are not presenting your instruction yourself, or you are presenting it through a medium that separates you from your audience, prepare your instruction to allow for feedback, and make sure your audience knows what is fact, what is debatable, and what is speculation.

Avoid spreading your instruction too thin by going off on tangents. Set a clear time limit to inquiry and response. Try to prevent the audience from taking over.

Jesus took three years to instruct a small group of disciples. Be prepared to help your audience develop cognitively through two-way communication.

6. Illustrate your instruction.

Most people have a short attention span, and visual and verbal illustrations, stories, humor, and anecdotes will help to hold your audience's attention and enhance the effectiveness of your instruction. Drama, sound effects, visual effects, and rhetorical devices will also help.

Television is a very good tool for illustrating an instruction. If you need to show how something works or what something is, television, film, film strips, slides, and photographs are helpful. For example, if you are teaching a class on how to repair an automobile engine, only a few students at a time can watch an actual maneuver; however, television or film can allow many students to watch a close-up of the operation. Students who can't afford to fly to Israel can learn a great deal about the Holy Land from a videotape, a film, or even a slide show.

Illustrations should augment and enhance an instruction, not replace it. Television is especially seductive in this regard. Try to see television or video as a moving blackboard; even with sound, you need a mechanism for feedback and interaction to involve your audience. Imagine writing $E = MC^2$ on a blackboard and expecting your students to understand the theory of relativity! Students need to be able to wrestle with the concept with someone who understands it so that they can integrate the ramifications of the theory into their cognitive framework.

7. Prepare your instruction.

Prepare your instruction with room to improvise, and be creative in your presentation, if appropriate. Make it logical. Keep your rhetoric simple, direct, and understandable. Be entertaining. Visualize your audience as you prepare, and practice presenting it to them in your mind to keep it lively.

8. Top and tail.

As with a commentary, you need to prepare an introduction thatr will hook your audience and a conclusion that will drive your points home to your audience's memory.

9. Prepare guides and tests.

Prepare teacher's guides, study guides, and examinations that will help your audience to comprehend and assimilate your instruction. Each guide should clarify the key material, facts, conclusions, and other items that you researched and used to structure your instruction. Tests should highlight facts and proven points that your audience needs to remember and help your audience to use what they learned.

10. Review and revise.

Check and double-check until your instruction works. Be as self-critical as you can.

11. Present or produce.

Be flexible and responsive if you are giving a live presentation of your instruction. Whatever medium you are using, produce or present your instruction obeying the principles governing that medium.

12. Seek feedback.

Seek feedback so that you can update and improve your presentation. If possible, survey your audience or study the answered tests and ongoing audience responses. Just as your audience cannot grow cognitively without action and reaction, neither can you as the communicator.

Subordinate Communication Genres

The commercial, the contest, and the interview have a great deal in common with the genres we have considered, especially the basic steps necessary to construct presentations in these genres. Therefore, we will look only briefly at the key principles that apply to each of these.

By calling these subordinate genres, I do not mean they are less important than the other genres discussed, since each of them is a widely used, powerful communications format. They are classified as subordinate because they are subcategories of one of the other communication genres, a combination of two or more, or differ only slightly from one of the others.

The Commercial or Promotion

"I don't mind the commercials. It's just the programs I can't stand," said John Crosby, former television critic for the now-defunct *New York Herald-Tribune*. Advertising, promotions, public service announcements, sales pitches, and fund-raising are an integral part of life. Whether it is a duck enticing its mate in an old Walt Disney nature film, a congregation seeking funds for a new building, or a bureaucrat selling superiors on a new procedure, the commercial or promotion is a necessary and frequently used genre of communication.

THE FIRST COMMERCIAL

"FIRST COMMERCIAL." © *1985 Nurit Karlin. Reprinted from Channels Magazine.*

The point of a commercial or promotion is to persuade the audience to buy the product being sold or the concept being promoted or to commit to do so in the future.

A commercial or promotion can be presented in the form of any of the genres we have considered—testimonial or report, dramatization or story, sales pitch or commentary/argument, or instruction or "how to"—as well as in formats that we will not consider, such as the musical and the comedy. A commercial or promotion can be a hot, hard, direct sell, or a soft, evocative, feel-good, emotive enticement to buy into whatever is being sold. Whatever approach you choose, here are some key principles to keep in mind:

Key Principles for a Commercial or Promotion

1. Know your product, concept, or whatever you are promoting or advertising. If you don't know it to start with, familiarize yourself with it.

2. Target your commercial or promotion at a specific audience. A rifle shot is preferable to buckshot; therefore, know your target audience.

3. Formulate a powerful premise by finding the inherent drama and benefit for the buyer in your offer. By listening to your audience, you will find attractive and interesting features your product has that make people want to buy it. (Tom Dunkerton, at Saatchi & Saatchi Compton, notes that many of the ideas for Proctor & Gamble commercials came from the consumer, who suggested what was interesting about the product during surveys. People buy products that will benefit them; therefore, make your product benefit(s) clear to your audience in the premise.

4. Be so clear about the product or concept you are selling that everyone who sees or hears your commercial will know exactly what you are offering.

5. State the benefits of your product to your audience in a believable manner. You want your audience to believe that your product will benefit them. You can be honest and people will not believe you, so be believable above all.

6. Appeal emotionally to your audience by making your commercial or promotion warm, human, lifelike, tempting, slick, catchy, attractive, or funny.

7. Use the five steps of persuasion:
   Get attention
   Hold interest.
   Present the problem.
   Show that the product solves the problem.
   Conclude with a strong emotional or logical appeal telling your audience to buy—now.

8. Be positive. Most audiences fail to pick up on a negative sales pitch or promotion and tend to hear negative as positive.

9. Don't compare. Comparisons promote and advertise your opposition.

10. The visual take precedence over the verbal. Many researchers have shown that people believe what they see over what they hear.

    The producers of "Sesame Street" showed to several different age groups of children pictures of an ant growing to be as large as an elephant, with a clear voice track saying that it would be impossible for an ant to grow to be as large as an elephant. After the viewing, the majority of the children thought that an ant *could* grow to be as big as an elephant. The negative voice track had no affect on them. They saw it: it happened.

    Make sure that your visuals support your verbal communication.

The Contest

The contest, game, or sporting event is a story whose outcome is unknown and is dependent on two or more individuals who participate in solving the premise through conflict. The contest is a popular genre because the audience can participate by predicting the outcome with as much certainty as the creator or the contestants.

Like a story, a contest has a clear-cut premise, such as "The better player beats the poorer player" or "The stronger contestant defeats the weaker"; something at stake, such as fame or fortune; and a point of attack, which leads through action and reaction to a climax, which leads to a conclusion in which one or more of the participants wins and the other(s) lose. Unlike a story, a contest has characters (the contestants) whose inherent characteristics are only partially known, even though they have been evenly matched to the degree possible.

A contest communicates information, values, goals, and the principles of play to your audience. For instance, I asked my good friend, the game inventor Paul Gruen, to design The Lion and the White Witch game, based on C. S. Lewis's *Chronicles of Narnia*. This game has built in to it biblical principles such as loving your enemy and helping the poor.

Whether you are designing a contest, a game, or a sporting event through which you want to communicate, here are some key principles to keep in mind:

Key Principles for a Contest

1. Know what values, goals, information, and principles you want to communicate.

2. Formulate your premise to define the goal of your contest.

3. Structure the values and principles you want to put across into the rules and events of your contest. For instance, in The Lion and the White Witch we wanted the contestants to learn to help others, so Paul made a rule that if someone was captured no one could move forward until that captured player was freed, either by another player or by possessing the appropriate Lion card.

4. Structure the information you want to communicate into the events, setting, questions, and/or answers in your contest. For instance, Bible trivia games structure information into the board setting and into the questions and answers.

5. Keep the rules simple.

6. Be visual. Use colors, charts, boards, pictures, and other visual material to grab and hold attention.

7. Build in action.

8. Make it fun.

9. Block out the contest, set the format, and prepare for all possible moves or answers.

10. Test your contest out on children. If they like it and want to keep playing, then it works. If not, revise it.

11. For sporting events, prepare background and commentary material to add color to the event.

The Interview

The interview is like a story in that there is a premise, a protagonist, and an antagonist. It is like a commentary in that your opinions direct the interview and are communicated to the audience. It is like a report in that you are trying to find out and report information. It is like an instruction in that there is feedback and response. It is like a contest in that the outcome is usually uncertain.

An interview can be formatted as one-on-one, a panel of several investigators, a symposium of several experts, a group discussion, a debate, audience participation, or a press conference. Whatever format you choose, here are some key principles to keep in mind:

Key Principles for an Interview

1. Formulate your premise, which will determine the direction of your interview. Your premise is your ultimate goal, what you want to find out or prove.

2. Prepare as much as possible, and learn as much as possible about all the parties and issues involved.

3. Ask the tough questions that your audience wants to hear. Ask, "Why?" Be determined to find out as much as possible. You are the protagonist, who initiates the conflict. Go to it, with love.

4. Ask questions that require personal responses, preferably personal stories. As a secondary source, your guest can be replaced by an encyclopedia, but as a primary source, your guest is a direct connection to the proof of your premise. Introduce your audience to your guest and the proof of your premise by seeking personal responses from your guest. For example, ask, "How do you know?" and "What is your experience?" questions that prompt your guest to include him- or herself in the answer.

5. Use visuals and effects as appropriate.

Whatever genre you choose, learn and apply its unique rules and principles so that you can use it to communicate effectively. With work, dedication, and inspiration, you can construct powerful communications.

II. HOW TO COMMUNICATE SUCCESSFULLY THROUGH THE MEDIA

7. What Medium Should I Use?

The medium is the message.

MARSHALL MCLUHAN

Each medium has its advantages and disadvantages. To communicate how something looks, an oft-quoted ancient Chinese proverb tells us that "a picture is worth a thousand words." If, however, we want to communicate the true nature, or ontology, of some person, event, or thing, then a few words, such as "the Word was made flesh and dwelt among us" (John 1:14, KJV), say more than a thousand pictures.

Each medium can be seen primarily as a communications tool capable of accomplishing one or more functions. (Also note that each medium is itself composed of one or more tools: from pencil and paper to compose a note, to the sophisticated cameras, recorders, editing machines, satellites, and other hardware and software necessary to produce and broadcast a television program.) A tool is in itself neither good nor bad; however, every tool can be used for good or evil purposes. A hammer, for instance, can be used to build a school, or to hurt another person.

The value of a tool is determined by how we use it. When we use a tool to perform a function the tool performs well, then the tool is very valuable. But, if we use it to do something it was not designed to do, it is of little or no value to us. An ordinary screwdriver is very useful for driving screws; it is of some value in scraping paint off the side of a house; it is of little value when used to hammer a nail; but it is of no value at all in gripping a nut.

Like other tools, each communication medium has certain functions that it performs well, others it performs to a lesser degree, and many it may not perform at all. For example, a television newscast can give us an immediate visual experience of an event; a newspaper cannot. Moreover, each medium can be used for good or for bad. Adolf Hitler's propaganda provides an excellent example of the malevolent use of various media.

Like some tools, certain media can be harmful when used to perform an inappropriate function, or when just overused. Some media, such as television or film, like some sophisticated chemical, biomedical, and electronic tools, have an environmental impact due to their very nature, an impact that may be harmful under certain circumstances to certain groups.

To determine what medium you should use, you must first ask what functions each medium performs and how well each one performs a particular function. You know that with your limited resources you want to reach a specific audience living in a specific area with a specific communication to achieve a specific effect; therefore, the question you need to ask is, What medium will best accomplish my goals? Its ability to accomplish your goals depends on

the nature of the medium
the nature of the genre you choose
the nature of your audience
where your audience lives
the size of your audience
the cost of the medium in money, time, and energy as measured against both its ability to accomplish your goals and the cost and effectiveness of other media that could accomplish those goals.

This last factor could be phrased as the question, Is there a more effective, less expensive medium I should use to reach my intended audience?

Every medium has a specific audience, or market, that it

reaches under normal circumstances. Comic books, Christian television, and rock music radio reach different audiences, with some overlap. Some media reach markets and demographic groups that are also reached by other media; television, for instance, reaches many groups who can be targeted by other media, such as newsmagazines.

Furthermore, different channels, or modes, of the same medium will reach and impact different audiences. PBS television reaches a different audience than NBC television. Mass mailing a form letter will impact a different audience than a personal letter.

The genre you choose will affect who it is you reach through a particular medium. Television comedy will reach teenagers more effectively than game shows or news programs; however, these same teenagers may be more interested in reading newsmagazines or romance novels than humorous novels. Also, certain media are better suited to communicate certain genres. Poetry works well in print but seldom succeeds on television.

In deciding which medium to use, research what demographic groups the media you are considering reach at the time of your presentation, keeping in mind that the reach of many media changes over time. Also determine through up-to-date research which genre reaches your targeted audience best through which medium. The questions you should ask are Who will the medium and genre I am considering reach? How effectively will my medium and genre reach my targeted audience?

To understand how the nature of each medium affects how well it will accomplish your communication goals, it is instructive to look at how an audience mentally receives and processes something from a particular medium from the point of view of psychological research into cognition (which scholars used to call epistemology). Building on the research of the child psychologist Jean Piaget, Robert Morse has found that television is capable of transmitting concrete physical information to children but not capable of teaching or educating them by promoting cognitive growth.[1] Television educates in the sense of transmitting information but not in the sense of promoting cognitive growth.

Morse shows that television, in fact, inhibits cognitive growth and may cause cognitive impairment. Morse is careful to point out that his study is concerned with the effect of the medium of television, not the content of television programming, the sex and violence that is the subject of so much research. Morse concludes that the very act of watching is harmful to the cognitive development of children and affects adversely their moral, social, emotional, and religious development as a consequence. Furthermore, he concludes that television "debilitates an important cognitive function in adults, the one that permits abstract reasoning—and hence related capacities for moral decision making, learning, religious growth, and psychological individualization."[2] In other words, excessive television watching can be harmful.

Let's take a moment to examine Morse's logic. Initially, he points out what we all know: cognition does not equal thinking; rather, thinking is a part of cognition, and cognition itself is the process of knowing. He likens this process to the building of a house step-by-step from the ground up from a blueprint, or to adding colors to our mental palette, which he notes must be done correctly in the right order or the result will be muddy. The palette corresponds to the stages of cognitive growth, similar to Piaget's designation, only renamed:

Sensation (approximately ages 0–2): the first stage of cognitive growth, the child's sole means of processing reality is his or her senses.

Imagination (approximately ages 2–7): in which the child's cognition is dedicated to the elaboration of the symbolic function, as manifested in the acquisition of language or in symbolic play, and limited by being serial and one-dimensional.

Relation (approximately ages 7–11): in which children acquire the ability of simultaneous perception of two points of view, so that they can master quantities, relations, and classes of objects, although at this stage, there is such a strong correspondence between their thoughts and reality that they assume their thoughts about reality are accurate and distort the facts to fit what they think.

Reflection (approximately ages 12–15): in which abstract thought gains strength, although at the beginning of this stage, there is still incomplete differentiation, as a result of adolescents' inability to conceptualize the thoughts of others, as exemplified by the assumption that other people are as obsessed with their behavior and appearance as adolescents themselves are.

These stages of cognitive development represent a growing differentiation between person and object. Cognition takes place by adaptation to reality; that is, by resolving conflict by integrating new material into the cognitive structures through what is called assimilation and accommodation. Cognition takes place through action and adaptation only when a conflict is caused by the entry of a new element of reality.

Cognitive structure changes through its own functioning— through being active. You have to exercise reasoning, and the environment must provide nourishment for this. The medium of television provides not nourishment and therefore prevents reactive reasoning, thus causing damage to cognitive growth.

Referring to Piaget's research, Morse notes that there are two modes of experience that will result in learning:

P (physical or factual) experience, which impresses itself on us from the outside and causes the appropriation of discrete facts or individual pieces of information and

LM (logical-mathematical) experience, which actually has to do with generating structures that help us to integrate and organize all of our experience, including the individual facts learned through *P* experience.

Cognitive development occurs through maturation and *LM* experience. Cognitive development cannot possibly occur through maturation and P experience. One may have P experience ad infinitum with no resulting cognitive development. The access of LM experience requires concentration and action.

Television presents people with P learning but not LM learning. People expect P experience from television; they expect to be entertained and to be receptive to the information that television presents. Programs are designed to make it impossible to direct the experience, to focus attention, or to concentrate. Programs are designed to grab and hold the audience by making concentration impossible. Morse points out that "Sesame Street" employs a "distractor machine" to ensure that viewers' minds do not wander from the program. The pace is determined by the program, not the viewer. There is no time to stop, review, react, enter into dialogue, or concentrate.

Television precludes one's following thought processes at one's own proper pace, circling around a sequence, moving forward and back to compare this idea with that, to verify and test; it disallows much in the way of essential, internal "talking back."[3]

Morse cites evidence that television watching causes changes in brain hemisphere dominance:

It is established that, no matter what the program is, the human brain wave activity enters a "characteric" pattern . . . once the set goes on, the brain waves slow down until a preponderance of delta and alpha brain waves becomes the habitual pattern. The longer the set is on, the slower the brainwave activity.[4]

An Australian National University psychological research team, headed by Merrelyn and Fred Emery, found:

The evidence shows that human beings "habituate" to repetitive light-stimuli (flickering light, dot patterns, limited eye movement). If habituation occurs then the brain has essentially decided that there is nothing of interest going on—at least nothing that anything can be done about—and virtually quits processing the information that goes in. In particular, the left brain "common internegative area" goes into a kind of holding pattern. "Viewing is at the conscious level of somnambulism."[5]

Increased vocabulary as a result of the *P* experience offered by television does not show advanced cognitive development on the part of children, contrary to what many parents think:

Language is, then, deceptive as an index to thought. Teachers of middle class children are often misled by the verbal facility of these youngsters into believing that they understand more than they do. . . . According to Elkind, attempts to teach children concrete operations have been almost uniformly unsuccessful.[6]

Children who are heavy users of television demonstrate decreases in the capacity for creative imagination, concentration, and delayed gratification. With regard to imagination, they are less able to form "mental pictures," and they engage in less "imaginative play." With regard to concentration, children become "lazy readers" of "nonbooks" with greatly decreased attention spans (you have to exercise concentration, or it atrophies). With regard to delayed gratification, the children have less tolerance for getting into a book (or other activities.)

In effect, the symbolic function, perception, and abstract reasoning are damaged in a manner that resembles dyslexia, and the rapid increase in reading disabilities, or dyslexia, may be, in part, attributed to heavy television viewing. Television inhibits eye movement and, thereby, the acquisition of reading skills. Morse notes that

psychologically, the effect of television's damage to the symbolic function is devastating. Because cognition (and especially the capacity for self-reaction) is, by definition, the means whereby we become conscious, the child so severely afflicted will remain largely unconscious.[7]

Reasoning along these lines, Morse concludes that television causes cognitive impairment that has a deleterious effect on the child's moral, social, emotional, and religious development. With respect to moral development, Morse notes that Kohlberg outlines six stages of moral development: the punishment-and-obedience stage; the instrumental-relativist stage; the interpersonal concordance or "good boy–nice girl" stage; the "law and order" stage; the social-contract, legalistic stage; and the universal-ethical-principle stage.[8] We progress through these stages as we mature, and this progress, or moral development, is dependent upon cognitive development.

With regard to social and emotional development, a child needs dramatic play, which, as we have noted, is inhibited by television. Furthermore, a child must do or act, not just be done to (as is the case with watching television), or there is impairment of social and emotional development. In the area of psychological maturation, the ability to suppress detrimental emotions is impaired.

With regard to religious development, impairment of the symbolic function results in the "clogging of the filters of religious perception," so that the child's doorway to experience of the transcendent is blocked.[9] Furthermore, television watching causes the viewer to see reality as illusory, or nominalistic, whereas Christianity has a real ontology because God created a real world in which real events occur independent of our consciousness and our imagination. Television therefore inhibits a Christian ontology and worldview.

Morse's findings with respect to children are corroborated and summarized in an article by John Rosemond, circulated by the Southern Association of Colleges and Schools:

The next time your child watches television, look at him instead of the screen. Ask yourself, "What is he doing?" Better yet, since the chances are he won't be doing much of anything, ask yourself, "What is he not doing?"
In answer, he is not:
  Scanning.
  Practicing motor skills, gross or fine.
  Practicing eye–hand coordination.
  Using more than two senses.
  Asking questions.
  Exploring.
  Exercising initiative or imagination.
  Being challenged.

Solving problems.

Thinking analytically.

Exercising imagination.

Practicing communication skills.

Being either creative or constructive.

Also, because of television's insidious "flicker" (every four seconds, on the average, the picture changes), television does not promote long-term attention.

Lastly, because the action shifts constantly and capriciously backward, forward and laterally in time . . . , television does not promote logical sequential thinking.

So what? Well, interestingly enough, the deficiencies noted above are characteristic of learning-disabled children, children who don't seem able to "get it all together" when it comes to learning how to read and write.[10]

With respect to adults, Morse notes that television saps cognitive strength, analogous to what happens in nursing homes, where inactivity leads to cognitive impairment. After an hour or two of television watching, people come away cranky, irritable, tired, and ready to explode. Discussing the addictive, hypnotic power of television, we are reminded that in television, images are projected at us in which we ourselves become the vanishing point.[11]

By demonstrating the negative aspects of television, Morse underlines its powerful ability to capture the viewer's attention; convert the viewer from one product or point of view, to another; motivate the viewer to buy a product or to do something; influence the viewer; and to impart to the viewer P information. Part of the problem with television lies in its very effectiveness at performing these functions. The powerful, emotional images propel the P experience into the viewer's mind in real time, with no time for the viewer to reflect, react, or review the P information he or she is receiving. As a result, many viewers can be converted from one product to another (and even from one political candidate to another, as evidenced by the voter swings after the Nixon-Kennedy debates and the

Carter/Reagan debates)* and then motivated to go out and buy that product, which the viewer may not need.[12] Many viewers are influenced to look at the world in the way television does since their information about the world is filtered through the unique nature of the television medium.

Morse's analysis of the cognitive impact of television is important to consider when reviewing the appropriateness of any medium, because within his analysis are the pertinent questions to ask regarding the nature of a medium:

How well does the medium in question communicate P experience to the audience?

How well does the medium in question communicate LM experience to the audience?

How well does the medium in question capture the audience's attention?

How well does the medium in question enhance the audience's concentration?

How well does the medium in question allow internal review, reaction, and reflection on the part of the audience?

How well does the medium in question promote creative imagination on the part of the audience?

How well does the medium in question promote delayed gratification on the part of the audience?

How well does the medium in question promote action on the part of the audience?

How well does the medium in question convert the audience?

How well does the medium in question motivate the audience?

---

*The Roper Organization and other researchers have tabulated the extent of television's impact on voters. After the Carter/Reagan debates, 36 percent of those surveyed who voted for Reagan said that the televised debate was helpful in their deciding who was the best candidate to vote for, according to a report entitled "Evolving Public Attitudes Toward Television and Other Mass Media 1959–1980" (Television Information Office, 745 Fifth Avenue, New York, NY 10022).

How well does the medium in question influence the audience?

Using these questions together with the other pertinent criteria for determining the ability of a specific medium to accomplish your communication goals, you will be able to choose the most effective medium for your purposes. The Medium Determination Chart at the end of this chapter lists advantages and disadvantages of several selected media, taking into consideration the factors and questions we've discussed. You should add other media that might be appropriate for your communication and also add to the list for each medium factors that relate to your targeted audience.

There are many other media, such as signs and billboards, that could be analyzed, but space on the chart doesn't permit. You should analyze all the possible media in terms of your targeted audience and the nature of your message. By asking the right questions, you will discern which medium is best for you, your audience, and your communication.

At the same time as you determine which medium to use, you should determine which genre you will use. Medium and genre are closely related. Quite often you will want to choose your genre first, then your medium.

Once you discern which medium is appropriate, you need to apply both the general principles of effective communication and the unique principles that constitute the "grammar and rhetoric" of the medium you have chosen. Often, inexperienced people will undertake to use a medium such as television without learning its grammar, or they will undertake to employ a particular genre, such as the story, without learning the principles that apply to it. In effect, they try to reinvent the wheel, producing unsightly vehicles for communication in the process.

Even if you hire someone else to produce your communication for you in a particular medium ("hands off" production), your knowledge of the medium will help you choose the right producer; structure your communication properly for that medium, and work with the producer to guarantee the most effective presentation. Many media require a constellation of skilled people to produce effective presentations. These talented individuals must be given the freedom and respect to exercise their talents and be encouraged to work together. If you do choose "hands off" production, try to keep your hands off those areas that are the responsibility of the people you have engaged—the producer, writer, editor, gaffer, actor, director, and others. It is never wise to delegate authority and then undermine it. It is also unprofessional. Each person has a role, let him or her fill it.

Understanding the gatekeepers of the distribution systems for many media is crucial for obtaining access to those media. Make friends with the gatekeepers—the program managers at radio stations, or the program producers at the networks—and they will help you to get on the air. A noncombative attitude is helpful.

Neither the medium nor technology will produce powerful communications. Only creative, dedicated, industrious people do this effectively, using whatever medium is appropriate, or available, to do so. Shakespeare didn't have a word processor. He himself was repsonsible for his great plays and poems. You yourself are the key to effective communication. Yesterday, you used a pencil; today television; tomorrow holograms? Whatever medium you use, use it well.

New technology continues to present us with new opportunities. Many new technologies try to *change* what people do, and fail. On the other hand, new technologies that *help* people to do what they like, or need, to do more easily and conveniently usually succeed. These successful new technologies change *how* people do (e.g., the calculator), *where* people do (e.g., the Sony Walkman), and *when* people do something they like or need to do (e.g., the home videocassette machine, which gives people the freedom to watch what they want when they want). Books work very well, so videotext has not been an attractive replacement, but computer information services are popular because they expand the use of the computer. Qube* failed because people want television to entertain them, not challenge them by asking questions, but people enjoy participating in game shows because they give them a chance to play and win.

Knowing how to use your chosen medium will not guarantee that you will communicate effectively. Many craftspeople know how to use their tools but are unable to create excellence because they do not know the principles of design or because they are not inspired. Effective communication requires not only knowledge of your medium but also inspiration, honest ascertainment, and application of the principles that govern the genre you are using. However, if you are inspired and also have applied the principles outlined in the previous chapters, you are more than two thirds of the way to doing the job.

The four chapters that follow will look at how to use four selected media, each used to illustrate a whole category of media. The basic principles and functions that you need to know in order to use each of these will be examined. For those media that appeal to two senses, the eyes and ears—like film, multimedia, slide shows, and video—the focus will be on television. For those media that appeal just to the ear—such as audiocassettes and the telephone—radio will be the representative medium. Live, in-performance media of communication—such as lectures, preaching, and plays—will be considered in terms of public speaking. Those media that communicate words visually—such as books, newspapers, magazines, and brochures—will be examined under the generic title print, with a focus on one of the more common forms of print used by Christian communicators, the newsletter.

The examination of each medium presents an introduction to the category of media it represents. They will help you

---

*Qube was Warner Amex Cable's two-way interactive cable television channel, which allowed viewers to answer questions and otherwise interact with the channel. Warner Amex dropped Qube for lack of viewer interest.

determine what you need to know to communicate effectively through these media or related ones. Sometimes a few distinguishing characteristics of one or more of the related media are noted; you should extrapolate and consult other sources on how to use a related medium effectively.

Whatever medium you choose, you need to develop "hands on" experience it. After learning about a medium, practical experience (i.e., *LM* experience) is what will help you to really know how to use it.

These chapters are not intended to be exhaustive. Instead, they will cover basic principles and point you in the right direction.

The graphic media—such as signs and photographs—will not be treated; nor will we consider music or multisensory experiences, such as "The Power."

Medium Determination Chart

Visual Media

Medium	Advantages	Disadvantages
Broadcast TV (in general)	Good at communicating *P* experience	Does not communicate *IM* experience
	Great at capturing and holding attention	Inhibits concentration
	Great at converting	Inhibits review, reaction and reflection
	Great at motivating	Inhibits imagination
	Great at influencing	Inhibits delayed gratification
	Great at reaching large mass television audience	Inhibits audience action
	Reaches around the world	Expensive for small audiences
	Cheap for very large audience—low CPM* possible	Requires time to produce
	Very accessible to audience	Difficult access for most communicators
	Powerful communication tool	Can mainstream groups in negative ways
	Immediate	Poor medium for educating and discipling
	Emotive Experiential	Difficult medium for telling what things are in fact
	Visual	
	Great for story telling	
	Great for selling	Inhibits cognitive development
	Good for outreach and mission	

*Cost per thousand viewers

Network TV	Attracts largest audience Most entertaining High quality Advertiser support guarantees production quality Greatest reach	Does not attract some demographic groups, such as most CEOs** Difficult access for communicator Expensive
PBS	Attracts certain demographic groups that may be desirable to communicator Easier local and national access than network TV Large reach (274 stations)	Difficult funding Smaller audiences than network TV Difficult for communicator to deal with myriad of independent stations Some signal quality problems in some markets
Independent stations	Large audience Easier local and national access than network TV for communicator	Uncertain demographics

---

**Chief executive officers

Cable TV	Growing audience	Only a few channels watched
	Easier access than network TV for communicator	Gatekeeper controls programming
	Good signal quality	Laying cable is expensive and subject to theft
	Many channels	
	Targeted audience	Many of the same disadvantages as broadcast TV
	Public-access channels good for narrow casting	Many homes don't have cable
	Two-way communication possible that removes some of the problems associated with broadcast TV	Public-access channels are not watched
	Immediate	
	May be used for art	
	May be used to establish a presence or image	

Satellite TV	Good for teleconferencing	Special equipment needed to receive
	Good for reaching a large audience that is scattered over a large area (direct broadcast satellite and teleconferencing)	Same problems as broadcast TV
		Expensive for communicator to access
		Limited audience
	Two-way communication possible	
	Good for sharing	
	Good for communicating *P* experience to a targeted audience	
	Teleconferencing is inexpensive (CPM) for reach a large spread-out audience	

Video	Inexpensive	Expensive means of reaching a large audience unless they are buying the tapes
	Can be interactive and provide some *LM* experience	
	Can provide review, reaction, and reflection	Incompatible formats
	Can be used for personal, interpersonal and spiritual development	Playback limited to small groups
		Quality requires expense
	Can reach a specific audience scattered over a large area	Quality requires maintenance
		Not immediate
	Can be an art form	
	Can be used to share information	
	Can promote creativity	
	Tape is reusable	
	Instant playback	
	Portable equipment	
	Can involve many people	
	Easy access	
	Can promote change	

Film	Good at communicating *P* experience	Does not usually communicate *LM* experience
	Great at capturing and holding attention	
		Inhibits concentration
	Good at converting	Inhibits review, reaction, and reflection
	Good at motivating	
	Good at influencing	Inhibits imagination
	Reaches around the world	Inhibits delayed gratification
	Large audience possible per viewing	Expensive for small audiences
	Equipment easily available	Inhibits audience action
	Involves many people in production	Expensive to produce and duplicate
	Visual and auditory	No feedback
	Emotive and experiential	Quality requires time, talent, and money
	Great for story telling	Hard to edit or change
	Good for art	Complex distribution

Slide and Multimedia	Can capture attention Can promote creative imagination Can be very emotive and experiential Can enhance concentration Can be viewed by large audience per viewing Easily revised Equipment readily available Can be very powerful Can involve audience action Can communicate *P* experience Can be used as an art form	Can be complex and cumbersome May be difficult to distribute Can be expensive to achieve quality Takes time to achieve quality Does not allow audience to review, react, and reflect Does not promote delayed gratification
Drama and Performance	Can be very experiential and involve audience Can communicate some *LM* experience Can create rapport between audience and actors Can enhance concentration Can be inexpensive Can travel if few sets Can promote creative imagination Good for story telling	Does not communicate *P* experience as well as broadcast TV Does not convert and motivate as well as TV Hard to move a large production with sets Requires time and talent to do well No time for review and reflection

Auditory Media

Radio	Inexpensive	Cannot communicate *P* experience as well as TV
	Can reach large audience around the world immediately	Does not capture attention
	Easy access for audience and communicator	No time for review and reflection
	Large regular audience	Does not convert and motivate as well as TV
	Flexible	Is not as emotive as TV
	Promotes creative imagination	Not visual
	Can communicate *LM* experience	
	Can promote concentration	
	Can influence audience	
	Emotive, but less so than TV	

Audiocassette	Provides *P* and *LM* experience	Does not capture attention—audience must be self-motivated to use
	Enhances creative imagination	
	Easy to distribute to small, scattered audience	Distribution to large audience requires marketing
	Provides for review and reflection	Cannot react with communicator
	Provides some delayed gratification	Not immediate
	Enhances concentration	
	Can involve and influence audience	
	Inexpensive	
Telephone	Great for personal communication with small audience	Expensive for large audience and over time
	Can communicate *LM* experience	Not great for communicating *P* experience
	Can enhance concentration	Not experiential
	Can react with communicator	Normally not emotive
	Can promote creative imagination	Takes time to reach a group
	Can influence, convert, and motivate	
	Immediate and intimate	

Print Media

Books	Great at communicating *LM* experience	Audience must be self-motivated to read
	Enhances concentration	Requires work
	Promotes delayed gratification	Limited audience
	Promotes creative imagination	Does not capture attention
	Provides for review and reflection	Not immediate
	Can provide some feedback	Can be expensive to market to large audience
	Can be a powerful influence	Can be static
	Inexpensive	Not normally experiential
	Simple production	
	Variety of formats	
	Long life	
	Worldwide reach to those who read	
	Distribution can be controlled	
	Good for story telling	
	Good for telling what things are	
	Good for telling how things work	

Newspapers, Magazines, Pamphlets and Handouts	Inexpensive	Limited distribution
	Provides *P* experience and *LM* experience	Does not capture attention as well as TV
	Enhances concentration	Quality requires time and talent
	Review and reflection	Quickly dated
	Enhances imagination	Not very emotive
	Enhances delayed gratification	Few people like to read
	Moderate influence	
	Can reach designated audience cheaply	
	Can reach widely scattered audience	
Letter	Inexpensive	Does not capture attention under normal circumstances
	Simple to produce	
	Provides for cognitive development	Good letters take rare talent
	Personal	Not as influential as TV
	Review and reflection	

Public Speaking Media

Preaching and Lecturing	Powerful, personal	Requires rare talent
	Interactive	Easily boring
	Provides for cognitive development	Does not capture attention as well as TV
	Good for converting and motivating	Limited reach
	Influential	Limited audience
	Immediate	
	Emotive	
	Involves audience	
	Inexpensive for small audiences	

8. What About Television?

Television is the most powerful force in the world today.

PAUL KLEIN

There is no doubt that television is a powerful medium. In 1983, television viewing per household exceeded seven hours per day.[1] People rely on television for news, sports, entertainment, and a window on the world. Television lets people know what to buy, where to go, who to vote for, and how to look at the world beyond their five senses.

Frequent research confirms the powerful impact of television and movies on the behavior of individuals and thereby on the nature of our society. In the early 1960s, Professor Alfred Bandura of Stanford University demonstrated in his pioneering research that preschool children imitate the aggressive behavior they observe on television.[2] Recent research by the Behavioral Sciences Branch of Extramural Research Programs at the National Institute of Mental Health (NIMH) confirms Bandura's findings, showing a "connection between the viewing of televised violence and later aggressive behavior."[3] Edward Donnerstein of the University of Wisconsin and Neil Malamuth of the University of Californa at Los Angeles say that their research into violent films "has shown conclusively that viewing violence—especially sexual assault—has notably spurred male viewers to violent acts toward women."[4] Professor Mary Magee of Hunter College of the City University of New York has found:

Wife and child abuse are highest among men who (a) watch a lot of television and/or (b) watch predominantly action-adventure "television fare."

Anxiety-related crimes, automobile accidents, and illnesses (mental and physical) occur most frequently among people who watch a lot of television.

Anxiety and anger among heavy users of television are measurably higher than anxiety and anger among light users of television.

These heavy-viewing groups are those in which the largest increase in violent crime has occurred over the past few decades.

Literacy is lower among heavy users of television than among light users.

Among the heavy users of television, the feeling is strong that certain material goods are "necessities," whereas light users of television usually consider the same material goods "luxuries."

Among heavy users of television the incidence of alcohol and drug addiction and abuse is significantly higher than such incidence among light users.[5]

Newspapers constantly run stories on the powerful effects of films and television programs. As Charlotte Johnson reported in the *Atlanta Journal*, John W. Hinckley, Jr., said that his shooting of President Reagan was "a love-sick re-enactment of the plot of the movie 'Taxi Driver.' " In that movie, the actor Robert De Niro told Jodi Foster, "If you don't love me, I'm going to kill the President." After *The Deer Hunter* was released, fifteen young people died imitating the Russian roulette scene in that film. She goes on to list further examples:

In the early '70s, a group of Boston youths poured gasoline on a derelict and set him afire—a re-enactment of a scene they'd seen in the movie "Fuzz."

In 1973, here in Atlanta, a young woman was killed by a 17-year-old boy who mimicked the actions of a suspect in the TV movie "The Marcus-Nelson Murders."

In 1978, in California, four teenage girls assaulted a 9-year-old girl in imitation of a scene in a two-hour drama called "Born Innocent." In that drama, female reformatory inmates appeared to assault a teenage girl sexually with a wooden rod. The imitators used an empty beverage bottle.[6]

Television executives often discount the effect of sex and violence. To say that violent programming does not affect the viewer is equivalent to telling a corporate advertiser that television commercials don't affect the viewer. If that were the case, advertisers would not spend millions of dollars to advertise on television. As George Gerbner has noted, "Television is a hidden curriculum for all people financed by hidden taxation without representation . . . you pay when you wash not when you watch."[7]

What is the spiritual and psychological impact of television on the millions of people who do not act on what they see, but have their perspective of reality distorted? By the time a person has reached nineteen years old, he or she has seen twenty thousand murders. What is the long-term impact on our culture of sex and violence in programming? According to Gerbner, "Television is that ritual myth-builder—totally involving, compelling and institutionalizing as the mainstream of the socializing process."[8] If television, with its focus on sex and violence, is building the conceptual framework of our society, our society is in trouble.

There is no doubt that television, film, and the other audiovisual media are powerful, but Paul Klein is wrong: God is the most powerful force in the world today. As his disciples, we should redeem, occupy, and use these media to proclaim the good news; they have been used to proclaim bad news for far too long. As Robert E. A. Lee said in *Media & Values:*

> It takes a very special communicative gift to convey the mystic reality of communion between human beings and their God. But there's a challenge if there ever was one for the producer—to return the missing dimension of religion to movies.[9]

Religious television has a very small audience, and that audience continues to support the sex and violence program fare on nonreligious television. To capture a larger audience, Christian communicators will have to break out of the religious ghetto by producing high-quality film and television programs that will attract a large audience.

It should be noted here that even though the audiences are

small by network standards, religious programs have had a powerful effect on our society. Many people have become Christians because of these programs, and there is growing evidence that society is altering its course from self-destructive to life-affirming partly because of the impact these programs have had on millions of viewers. However, there is much more to be done.

Television technology is continually changing. By the time you read this, much of the equipment being used as I write may be obsolete. However, if you learn the basic principles and techniques of television production you will be able to use whatever equipment comes along.

These techniques and principles will help you to use the other audiovisual media as well; however, you should acquaint yourself with the unique principles and techniques of those other media to use them effectively.

To understand the techniques and principles that apply to television, let's examine the steps involved in producing the most complex form of television, a network television movie. A made-for-television movie requires the most skill, the most equipment, the most money, and the widest range of artistic and technical creativity and decision making. Reviewing the basic steps for producing a television movie will give you an overview of the medium and allow us to at least touch on most of what you need to know.

FUNKY WINKERBEAN by Tom Batiuk. © by and permission of News America Syndicate.[7]

Producing Your Television Program

The following steps will take us through the process of producing a hypothetical network television movie from idea through follow-up. The assumptions made throughout will guide you through the basic principles and techniques of television production.

Reviewing your Choice of Television as your Medium.

To reach your decision to produce a television program, you had to work through the appropriate ascertainment questions, discern your talents, target your audience, formulate your communication, determine your genre, and choose your medium— television. You decided that you are called to communicate the Gospel to a mass audience, and that you have the motivation and talents to do so.

At first, you may have considered doing an interview program, but realized that that genre would limit your audience because television is best suited to communicating stories, commercials, variety, contests, sports, and current news. Lack of audience appeal has caused television executives to relegate most public affairs programs to poorly watched time periods, PBS, or certain cable television channels. Producing your program for a secondary time period, cable, or PBS would limit the size of your targeted audience. (Remember, however, that PBS or cable offer advantages if you are targeting professionals or an audience who could be persuaded to watch a cable channel.)

You may have considered producing a commercial, but you decided that that genre did not give you the broad impact you wanted and, ten, thirty, or sixty seconds was not enough time to logically present what you have to say. Sports, contests, and variety programs did not give you the logical, emotive power you wanted. Although your communication was good news, it did not lend itself to a current events format. Therefore, you decided to use a story genre, a television movie.

"Rights," Financing, and your Access to Network Television

Once you decide to use network television the question arises, How are you going to get your program on the air? This question should be answered before you go to the trouble and expense of producing your program. Your answer may change your mind about producing a network program; it may also affect how you produce your program.

This question also involves rights and financing, two of the basic building materials of television programs. Networks have to fill twenty thousand hours of programming time every year and need new ideas to capture and hold their audience. On the other hand, there is a tight concentration of power in the hands of a few producers, agents, and network executives who have very little contact with religion* and make it very difficult for a producer with no track record to break into the network program schedule.

For forty years, a religious program producer had reasonable, though difficult, access to the networks because they scheduled a certain amount of religious programming as part of their obligation to operate "in the public interest, convenience and necessity" (as required by the 1934 Communications Act). Since the late 1970s, the FCC has been relaxing the public interest obligations of broadcasters. Therefore, to get on the air today you have to sell the networks on your concept, convince them that they should air material with religious content, and/or buy air time. As Benjamin J. Stein pointed out in the *Wall Street Journal*:

Now, television has never been really big on religion, but at least in

---

* Only 7 percent attend church or synagogue, according to a survey by Lichter and Rothman at Columbia University.

the past the Cleavers went to church with Ozzie and Harriet. . . . Those vestiges are gone now, almost completely, and whatever dramatic imperatives put religion into moral decisions in drama from Shakespeare to sitcoms have disappeared. I am still trying to find out how this happened, and how prime-time network television became an island without religion in an ever-more-religious America. It has something to do with the people who make television, something to do with network skittishness, and something to do with politics.[10]

At this point, you may decide to reconsider using network television. You could retarget your audience and use a medium that is easier to access, such as cable television, PBS, independent television, Christian television, or even feature films.

You should not aim for network television unless that is the right medium for you and your communication. However, if your communication demands network television and you have the patience and stamina to do it, you can get your program on the air, with God's help. "Jesus of Nazareth," "Peter and Paul," "Who Will Love My Children," and "The Lion, the Witch, and the Wardrobe" are good examples of programs produced by relatively unknown producers who secured air time on networks.

The key to network television is your story. George Haineman, a former vice president of NBC, stresses that television is "a once-upon-a-time, story-telling medium." A strong story will help you to convince strongly talented people with good track records to be part of your production—as stars, director, or perhaps, co-producer. They will help you to convince foreign, cable, and independent television to prepurchase and an advertiser to sponsor your production, which, in turn, will help you to convince a network to put you on the air.

With a Strong Story

You can go directly to one of the three *networks* and have that network finance and air your production. The network will want to oversee your production at every stage, and will want poeple who are successful at attracting viewers involved. The network will want your program to be compatible with its image and advertising at the time the program airs.

Normally, a network can only be approached through an *agent*, such as International Creative Management or the William Morris Agency. The networks sometimes have been successfully approached directly with a story that is extraordinarily strong. Even an agent will want a strong story, or your story will collect dust on the shelf. You must believe in your story for good reasons that you can demonstrate to the agent in no uncertain terms.

Agents push what's hot because it sells more easily to the networks. If you are unknown, you may have to team up with a known commodity, a producer or director with a track record, to break through the psychological barrier at the agency. On the other hand, agents are on the lookout for new talent and new ideas. The key is a story that is saleable, since agents work for money.

Instead of approaching a network first, you can go to an *advertiser* and have that advertiser sponsor your program by buying the air time and paying for program production. The advertiser will want hot, bankable people involved in your production, and will want your story to enhance their image and/or promote the sale of their product. There are more advertisers to approach than there are networks.

You can go to a *cable* movie channel, such as Home Box Office or Showtime and have them prepay for the right to air your program before or after it airs on the network. You can use that prepayment to finance your production, which, once produced, you can try to sell to a network. Finished productions have the advantage of being known commodities; unfinished program concepts have the advantage of offering hope in a risk-oriented industry.

You can go to *foreign* television or film companies and have them prebuy the right to air your program in their countries. Again, you can use that presale to finance your production, which, once produced, you can try to sell to a network.

You can involve a major, known *producer* in your production, who will put the financing together, co-produce your program with you, and help you to sell it to a network.

You can go to a *stockbroker* or investment banker and have a production underwritten, which, once produced, you can try to sell to a network.

You can go to *friends* or acquaintances for private financing for all or part of your production.

You can go to a *church* or denomination, for underwriting to finance all or a part of your production.

You can go to a body of *believers* for donations to finance your production.

You can use any *combination* of the above non-network sources for part of the production financing, which will help you to sell your program to a network for the remainder of the production costs. This is a common approach that gives you some bargaining power and control.

You can involve any combination of the above non-network sources of financing to such a degree that you can use their money to finance your production and buy the air time from the network.

The story is the key. You can obtain a good story by writing one, hiring someone to write one, or buying the rights to a book, play, life story, or event (from those who were involved). Here we run into another key, "rights."

Rights

Jim Day, one of television's pioneers and a founder of WNET and educational television, boils network television down to rights: the legal right to produce a good story as a television program, of which a known star and/or director and/or producer will want the right to a piece of future profits, which the networks will want the right to air to capture an audience to sell to advertisers, on which advertisers will want the right to advertise to sell their products, which foreign stations, cable systems, movie channels, and independents will want the right to play after it is shown on network television, to which many companies will want the merchandising rights, and which the public will pay for the right to see by buying the advertiser's products.

Rights are the levels of ownership of the story—the pieces of the pie, or shares of future profits, that are bought and sold for money, time, energy, and commitment. Rights determine who owns what and what they can do with what they own.

An example of how right secure financing and access to the networks is the story of the television version of "The Lion, the Witch and the Wardrobe". The Episcopal Radio and Television Foundation purchased the right to produce a film and/or a television program of the seven books in C. S. Lewis's famous series of fantasies *The Chronicles of Narnia*, which retold the story of the Bible from Creation to Revelation in allegorical terms. *The Lion, the Witch and the Wardrobe* was the book in the series that retold the story of the death and resurrection of Jesus.

The foundation made contact with the president of Kraft Foods through the church network of friends, who passed on to Kraft's advertising agency the idea of Kraft sponsoring a television program based on "The Lion, the Witch and the Wardrobe." The agency suggested involving a co-producer with a track record, so the foundation joined forces with the Children's Television Workshop, who produce "Sesame Street," by giving them a share of the television rights for producing the program.

After a year went by, Kraft decided to sponsor the program by financing the production and buying the right to air the program on NBC. The Children's Television Workshop brought Bill Melendez, who animated "Peanuts" for television, on board as the producer of the animation, and the production was under way. When completed, "The Lion, the Witch and the Wardrobe" aired two years in a row during Easter week on NBC.

Some Rules of Thumb for Dividing Television Rights and Future Profits

Note that these are very rough guidelines, which may vary a great deal from the actual rights and percentage of profits a producer gives up, depending on track record, negotiating strength, and nature of the program, time, and the state of the television industry.

You buy the television rights from the author for a fee and, if the author's work is well known, 2–10 percent of your profits as producer. You secure private financing for your production by giving up 50 percent of your profits.

You secure a big-name screenwriter by giving up 2.5–10 percent of your profits plus a fee. Many screenwriters do not require a percentage of your profits. Whether a screenwriter will take a percentage depends on how much you pay and his or her reputation.

You secure a big-name star by giving up 5–10 percent of your profits plus a fee. If you pay enough, you may avoid the percentage.

You secure a big-name director by giving up 5–10 percent of your profits plus a fee. If you pay enough, you may avoid the percentage.

You secure a big-name producer by giving up 25 percent of your profits plus a fee.

You presell a foreign country, such as Italy, Germany, or France, by giving up all rights and profits in that territory for a period of time, such as two years or two air plays, whichever comes first.

You presell a cable movie channel at 30–50 cents per subscriber for a period of time, such as two years or two plays, whichever comes first. If you have a very hot property, or "cover," which will be featured on the cover of the movie channel's magazine, then you may receive as much as $7 million if you give the movie channel the exclusive rights to play your television movie two or three times. If your story demands only a "demi," or half a page, in the channel's magazine, then you might expect $4 million if you give the channel two or three exclusive plays. Of course, by the time you read this, prices will be higher.

If your property could be a movie before airing on television, then you could secure financing from a major motion picture distributor, such as Paramount or Universal, by agreeing to take 10–50 percent of what the distributor receives from the theaters, each of which takes 80–90 percent of the ticket price from their profit and overhead.

An advertiser, in return for financing, will want the right to sponsor your program for two to five air plays on television. After that, the program is yours.

If you go to a network directly, you may receive nothing but a fee and some subsidiary rights to foreign, cable, or merchandising profits.

Remember that there is only 100 percent of producer's profits to give to talent and financing, but the theaters (or cable channels) take their percentage before the distributor (or movie channel) take their percentage, with the producer's profits constituting the remainder. The box office receipts for a movie might end up being divided as follows:

$ 5.00   ticket price
–4.50   90% for the theater

$ 0.50   distributor's gross receipts
–0.40   80% of distributor's gross for the distributor

$ 0.10   to the producer

This 10 cents is what the producer has to divide among those who provide talent and/or financing in return for a percentage of profits.

You may end up giving up all your rights for a small fee that doesn't cover what you spend to buy and develop the property for sale to the network. In most cases, you will not make money on your property (program) until it is in its third rerun (or second sale) to the networks (or to independents). To reach the third rerun, the program must succeed in capturing a large audience in both of its previous airings.

If you are really dedicated to proclaiming the Gospel of Jesus Christ, the amount of money you earn may not make a difference to you, although we are called to be good stewards of the resources he gives us. The most important thing to remember is to retain enough rights maintain control over the production so that it is true to your story, given the changes required by the medium.

If you own the rights to a story you wrote or a story that is not in itself famous, watch out that a similar story is not produced by someone you have shown your story to. You can not copyright an idea, only the way you wrote up the idea. It is common to see the idea of a good but little-known story copied on television with very few changes, and there is practically nothing you can do about it. The best remedy is to buy the rights to a famous story that would attract such a large audience that that title, property, and story are valuable in themselves to a network. The other remedy is to register your story with the Writers Guild. This gives you some leverage, but not much. The best defense is a hot property.

If you do not own the rights to a good story, you can still try to muscle your way onto television by filing a complaint with the FCC charging that the network has been decidedly one-sided in its coverage of a controversial issue of public importance. Even though the FCC is relaxing its regulation of the television gatekeepers, some complaints still work if they are well thought out, legitimate, and important enough.[11] Your complaint will not get you the right to produce and air a network program, but it may get you on the news or cause you to be featured in a commentary. Consult a good entertainment lawyer with a heart for your cause or one of the many books on your rights under the 1934 Communications Act, such as *Talking Back: Public Media Center's Guide to Broadcasting and the Fairness Doctrine for People Who Are Mad as Hell and Aren't Going to Take It Any More*.[12]

Since no individual has an individual right to access and no law can make someone responsible, it may be better to work within the system by making friends with the key gatekeepers at the networks.

Access to any other medium is easier than to network television, but you still have to understand the gatekeepers and persuade them that your communication will be a benefit to them and their audience. Research the medium, prepare your presentation, and then talk to them about it.

Transform your Story into a Script and a Treatment

Once you have secured the rights to a good story, found your financing, and arranged for access to network television, you need to turn your story into a script, or hire a scriptwriter to do so, assuming that you did not start out with a script.

In many cases, a producer will start with a script that he or she will boil down to a one- or two-page treatment to sell the story idea to the networks. If you start with a story, or a book, usually you will want to turn it into a script or a treatment before you can make the sale to a network or interest prominent talent in your production.

The author of a book is not always the best person to transform his or her own work into a script. The author often has trouble sacrificing scenes, devices, or characters to meet the time and space limitations of television. In a book, for instance, you can carry on several complex subplots with many minor characters who come and go. Also, the author of a book can describe characters, feelings, situations, and motivations in great detail, whereas a scriptwriter can't. Television forces you to simplify and condense most books, discarding characters, scenes, and situations, if necessary.

A play is easier to adapt in terms of condensation, but a problem can arise when the original author can't shift his or her thinking from the stage to the television environment. A television audience is not captive, as is an audience in a theater; you have to capture it.

Bringing in a scriptwriter to reformulate a book, play, or short story can save time and money *and* often improve the final teleplay (or film). If you bring in a scriptwriter, you must work to preserve the author's intent, because that is the reason you bought the story in the first place.

These steps of a television production—securing script, rights, financing, access, and talents—often occur simultaneously, with each affecting the other. If you have a script, in most cases the network that picks up your story will want to review and revise it, as will the skilled people you bring on board. They will often defer making a final decision on your story until they know how good your script is, because many great stories defy scripting.

Whether you have a script or just a story, the first step in selling either is often a short treatment. Newtwork executives do not have the time to read every story or script that is submitted, so they will give the property to a reader who will boil it down to one or two pages and give an opinion of how good it is. Rather than leave your story to a reader to turn into a treatment, which may not do justice to it, prepare your own treatment and present it with your story.

A treatment should set forth the premise of your story, your main characters, and a very brief synopsis of the story itself. The more concise, the better. Many television programs have been sold to the networks solely on the basis of a one-sentence synopsis/premise like the descriptions in *TV Guide*. One producer, after failing to sell a complex story idea, said, "How about a Grand Hotel on the water? A love boat?" That brief statement of the story sold the network on the program.

Sometimes you will be required to expand your story into a full-length synopsis of thirty to fifty pages. Do so, keeping in mind the principles you have learned.

If you have not hired a scriptwriter and you are doing your own adaptation, you will find that there are many formats for scripts. For a commercial and public service announcement (psa), the script may look like the example "Love in Action." This commercial was produced for the Episcopal Church. The actual script is much longer. V.O. (voice-over) indicates an unseen person speaking over the picture.

30-SECOND PSA
LOVE IN ACTION

Video	Audio
1. SOUP BEING SERVED TO A STREET PERSON IN A SHELTER	V.O.—For I was hungry, and you fed me . . .
2. A YOUNG BOY HANDING A HOUSE PAINTER A DRINK	V.O.—Thirsty, and you gave me to drink . . .
3. A COUPLE WHOSE CAR BROKE DOWN IN A STORM ARE BEING WEL-COMED INTO A HOME.	V.O.—I was a stranger and you invited me in . . .

News programs, variety programs, game shows, documentaries, teleplays, live-taped teleplays, and Hollywood movies have different script formats and layouts. Before you start writing, research these different formats. Making sure your script is professional-looking will help you sell it to a network.[13]

The degree of detail in a script will vary depending on the scriptwriter, the director, and the producer, as well as on the use of the script within a production. A master script will not have the detail of a shooting script prepared with the director, nor will it include the camera shots and angles that are found in the camera script. The master script is the beginning of a long process. The scriptwriter who prepares the master script may have nothing to do with the final shooting script.

In a film script, you write in terms of shots, whereas in a television script you write in terms of scenes, especially if your production is to be videotaped live. The reason for these different approaches is that television, if taped live, is shot chronologically, that is, as a whole, from beginning to end, whereas film is shot by location, so that once you set up your equipment in a location, you film all shots associated with that location to save money, time, and energy.

"My Palikari" is an example of a master, or "master scene," Hollywood-style script. B.g. means "background"; POV, point of view. Note that there are very few directions, such as "wipe to," "dissolve to," "close shot," or "high-angle shot." The keys to a good television script are in-depth character analysis, the action spelled out, and the dialogue completely realized. Quite often the visual and the action moves the story along as much as the dialogue.

Stage directions, shots, video and audio directions, and other details will be added by the producer, the director, the director of photography, the editor, the actors, and even the scriptwriter as the script is refined during the production planning process. A television program is rarely the product of one man or woman; when it is, it is rarely any good.

"MY PALIKARI"
BY GEORGE KIRGO & LEON CAPETANOS

FADE IN

1. INT. OLYMPIA RESTAURANT—NIGHT—CLOSE ON PHOTO

A large framed panoramic view of Athens, featuring the Acropolis. HEAR recorded Greek music. PULL BACK slowly to REVEAL PETE PANAKOS, wine glass held high. Pete is handsome, powerful, vigorous, full of himself. The toast:

PETE

To the greatest country in the world—after the USA, natch—my Greece! Yiassou!

2. FULL SHOT

His celebrants respond: "Yiassou, to Greece, l'Chayim, salud, bon voyage, Pete!" . . .

***

CUT TO:

9. EXT. SEA—DAY. (Stock or 2nd Unit or 1st Unit)

"My Palikari," starring Telly Savalas and produced by the Center for Television in the Humanities, played on PBS, HBO, Showtime, and the Disney Channel.

As the ship comes toward Piraeus. The Ionian. In the distance: a
large ocean liner. Sound of ship whistle.

10. EXT. SHIP—DAY.

That's Pete on the forward deck, scanning the sea ahead. Passengers pass. Impatient, Pete lights a cigar, a chore in the wind.
He paces a few steps. Stops. Peers out again.

11. POV and ZOOM IN TO ACROPOLIS.

Big rush of emotion.

***

                PETE
Chris, Chris, come here!

                CHRIS
What?

                PETE
              (exasperated)
What? I'll show you what.
Come on!

The passengers sit up to stare at this crazy man. Pete glares as
Chris slowly saunters over. Peter grabs him and LEADS him to
the forward deck.

                PETE
Look, look!

                CHRIS
Where?

                PETE
There, there—

14. POV.

Land. Acropolis, port, hills, etc.

15. PETE AND CHRIS

Pete grins at Chris as his son coolly studies the sight.

                    PETE
        Huh? Huh?

                    CHRIS
        It's nice.

16. ANOTHER ANGLE

    On Pete and Chris with land in b.g.

                    PETE
                  (incredulous)
        Nice?

                    CHRIS
        Yeah. Kind of like . . . Brooklyn.

                    PETE
        Brooklyn—! This is Greece! Alas!

                    ***

    He crosses himself and whispers; as the tears almost fall from
    his eyes—

The script of "My Palikari" is intended for film production,
but it could be shot with video using electronic field production
(EFP). You could also adapt this script to shoot in a studio with
inserted stock shots, as is done with many programs, such as
"Love Boat."

Following are some hints for writing your script, teleplay, or
screen play:

Organize Flow:

Make sure your script flows smoothly and continuously, resulting in a unified, coherent, and entertaining program. If you
prove your premise with rising conflict, then your story will flow.

Organize Pacing:

Make sure that the length of your shots, scenes, and sequences develops the tempo that is required by the story and that enhances the story. Rapid sequences provide excitement and stimulation. Slower cutting slows the pace and induces a feeling of serenity and ease.

Organize Rhythm:

There should be a definite rhythm to a series of cuts, dissolves, and devices that will match the rhythm, mood, and action of your story.

Organize Interrelationships:

Establish motion by a continuous sequence of images.

A sense of action should be suggested at all times. Even when there is no physical motion during a particular scene, action can be suggested through contrast or repetition.

Organize visually:

Visual images should be organized for progression, opposition, and repetition of image size.

Variety is achieved through camera position, lighting, and shading.

Organize Effects:

Dissolves are usually one second to five seconds in length and will establish a smooth transition between scenes.

Fades in and out usually open or close an independent segment and can be considered a curtain that opens on new material and closes at the end of an act.

Lap dissolves, in which one image is faded over another, and match dissolves, in which two items of similar or identical shape are matched in the dissolve, are used to create effects and mood and to promote action.

Superimpositions, frame buffing, and more contemporary

technical effects should be studied before incorporating them into your script so that you are aware of how they affect the audience. New effects and new devices for creating effects are continually being developed. Use any one effect sparingly; overuse will distract from your story.

Remember, your story is the heart of your production. Effects can enhance a good story, but they cannot make a bad story better.

Organize sounds:

It must be established before or during the picture. Avoid sound on cue. If sound comes on at the same time as the picture, it will be unnatural and mechanical. If you are about to have a train come into view, introduce the distant sound of the train first. Or if you have a man walking across the desert, show him and then bring up the sound of walking on sand. Also, avoid music that calls attention to itself, unless that is your purpose.

Dialogue:

Natural-sounding dialogue is best.

Dialogue should consist of short speeches. Long speeches impede action and bore the audience.

Cliches and colloquialisms should be used carefully and sparingly.

Actions:

Actions should be described thoroughly, precisely, yet briefly. Rather than have someone walk over to someone, have them walk fearfully or forcefully.

Use Present Tense Directions.

Be Original. Do Not Fall into the Trite.

Chart the rising tension of your script as a whole. Chart separately each factor that contributes to the rising tension,

OVERALL TENSION

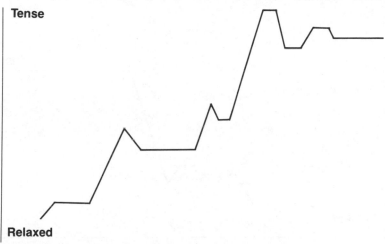

Opens Crisis Exposition Conflict Climax Resolution Close

Tense

Relaxed

such as image, effects, sound, music, and scene lengths. Together these charts will add up to your master chart. The three charts shown here are for overall tension, dialogue, and action.

As production progresses, you should add charts for factors that contribute to dramatic tension and revise the original charts you prepared to keep them current. Eventually, these charts will graphically show the rhythm, flow, and tension of your program. The charts will be useful for analyzing how well your program is going to emotionally grab and entertain your audience.

Budget and Timetable your Production

As soon as you have a story, you should start estimating the cost of producing your television program. The networks, the advertiser, and the financiers will all ask you how much it will cost to produce. Before you go to a network, you turn your

DIALOGUE TENSION

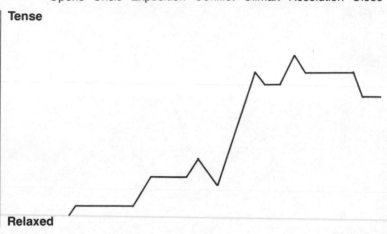

ACTION TENSION

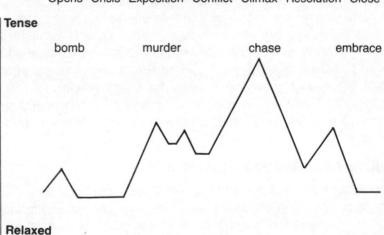

story into a script and prepare a budget based on that script, unless you are seeking development funds to prepare a script, in which case you need to budget the development funds you need.

Next to your script, your budget is the most important tool you have. It helps you determine where you are going, how to get there, and where you have been. The time you spend budgeting and planning will save you a great deal of money in actual production. In preproduction your costs are limited to yourself and one or two others; in production your costs involve a large, paid staff and lots of equipment. In planning your production, you will find ways to hold costs down by minimizing locations, using stock shots, cutting characters, and other devices. Time is money; if you have more time than money, invest it in cutting down your production and postproduction costs.

As a rule of thumb, you will spend 50 percent of your time in preproduction, 20 percent in production, and 30 percent in postproduction. As your skills improve, the time you spend in preproduction will decrease and the time you spend in postproduction will increase until they are 30 percent preproduction and 50 postproduction.

Most budgets are broken down into above-the-line costs and below-the-line costs. Above-the-line costs are the variable and negotiable costs that relate to writing, performing, and the production team, such as the scriptwriter, the star, and the director. Below-the-line costs are the various fixed costs, backup services, and physical elements involved in a production, such as equipment, transportation, and operations personnel, including the cameraperson, soundperson, and technical director.

Budgets consist of a summary top sheet and many pages of details that break down every element of the top sheet. Budget forms are available from many sources, including equipment rental houses like F & B/Ceco. Shown here are a top sheet and detail of account page for account 20, Costumes and Makeup. Please note that rates are only included when necessary.

BUDGET DETAIL
SUMMARY

Project: _____   Date Prepared: _____

Acct.	Description	Rate	Total	Totals	Totals
Above-the-line costs					
1	Story		50,000.00		
2	Continuity & Treatment		6,000.00		
3	Producer		95,000.00		
4	Director		65,000.00		
5	Cast		159,135.00		
6	Bits		38,785.00		
7	Extras		11,123.00		
			Subtotal	375,043.00	
Below-the-line costs					
8	Production Staff Salaries		71,343.00		
9	Technical Operations Crew		49,948.00		
10	Engineering Staff		32,237.00		
11	Set Design & Operation		62,000.00		
12	Video		67,398.00		
13	Editorial		92,000.00		
14	Music & Sound		17,810.00		
15	Studio		130,000.00		
16	Location & Transportation		142,232.00		

18	Titles & Special Effects	58,950.00
19	Art Direction	23,000.00
20	Costumes & Makeup	14,758.00
24	Publicity	19,700.00
25	Misc.	10,000.00
26	General Overhead	140,113.00
	Subtotal 931,498.00	

Grand Total$1,306,541.00

Project: **Date Prepared:** _

Acct.	Description	Rate	Total	Totals	Totals
20	*Costumes & Makeup*				
	A. Wardrobe Dept.				
	1. Wardrobe Designer	*1,400/wk*	*5 wks*	*7,000.00*	
	2. 1st Wardrobe Person		*2 wks*	*1,788.00*	
	3. 2nd Wardrobe Person		*16 days*	*2,063.00*	
	4. Tailor				
	5. Seamstress				*500.00*
	6. Extra Help				
				Subtotal 11,351.00	
	B. Makeup & Hairdressing				
	1. Head Makeup Person		*5 wks*	*1,950.00*	
	2. 2nd Makeup Person				
	3. Head Hairdresser		*4 wks*	*1,457.00*	

4. *Body Makeup*
   Person

5. *Extra Help*

Subtotal 3,407.00

Total $14,758.00

Most accounts on your budget will be broken down into even greater detail than our example, "Costumes & Makeup." Many costs are negotiable or can be lowered through substitution.

At the same time you prepare your budget, you should prepare a production *timetable*. Your master production timetable will be an overview of the entire production and help you to establish the deadlines that will keep your production on course. You will also want to prepare detail timetables for each element in your production, such as personnel. A sample master production timetable is shown.

PRODUCTION TIMETABLE

Task	Month											
	1	2	3	4	5	6	7	8	9	10	11	12
Scripting		xxxxxxxxxxxxxxxxx										
Staffing		xx	xxx				xxx			xx		xx
Preproduction	xxxxxxxxxxxxxxxxxx											
Production							xxxxxx					
Postproduction										xxxxxxxxxxxxx		
Broadcast, Distribution												xxxxx

Storyboard and Plan your Production.

So that you can accurately plan your production, turn your script into a rough storyboard, which you will want to revise and perfect as you proceed. Every key scene should be drawn with the dialogue underneath the drawing (storyboard) so that you will know how the production will look when you film or videotape it. (See the storyboard form illustrated.)

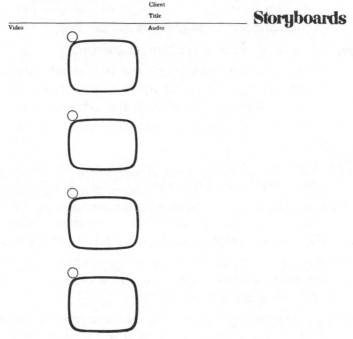

You will want to sketch important scenes and difficult shots from different angles to show required camera treatment.

Analyze all aspects of your production, every step from beginning to end, so that you know exactly where you are going and how you are going to get there. To do this, study your script, storyboard, and sketches. From discussions with your key people determine how you are going to handle every aspect of your production. Remember to consider:

Cast, including costume and makeup requirements.

Preproduction publicity.

Sets and staging designs, including sketches showing lighting, directions, action, and camera shots. Make sure you have enough studio or location space for shots, moves, cable routing, and equipment, such as booms, Given the space you will be working in, make sure there is enough time for moves. Therefore, you must predetermine the facilities, both studio and location, you will use and what permissions and arrangements are needed.

All "on-camera" props and other set dressing

Photography, filming, stock shots, and all material that needs special arrangements, clearances, fees, permissions, permits, insurance, scheduling, and extra staffing

All music and sound needs, including sound effects and pickup problems.

Special effects, graphics, and titles, including artwork, maps, charts, models, and displays.

Video equipment, including video effects equipment. Do you really need a sophisticated video animation system, or would simple graphics and a good effect generator do?

All other necessary and special equipment, including teleprompter, telecine, video disc, slide chain, film chain, monitors, and cueing facilities.

Lighting and atmosphere, making sure that shots will match. Analyze any special lighting that is needed in terms of cost, manpower, equipment, and feasibility.

Videotape, audio tape, and film.

Editing needs.

Publicity.

Distribution.

Keep in mind throughout your production that every technical effect (including camera moves, special effects, inserts, action, and technical moves, such as wipes, fades, and dissolves) acts as a blinking neon light to attract the attention of the viewer. Too many effects, like a busy neon sign, are annoying. Too few, and you may lose your audience. Every technical effect and action must flow organically from and not intrude on the story, unless there is a compelling artistic reason for them to do so. The viewer should be affected by the technical effects, but at not time should he or she be aware of any specific effect, unless you are engaging the viewer as an active character in the action of the story or exposing the mechanism of the story for stylistic reasons.

Bring your Production Team on Board.

Your above-the-line talent, or production team, will be determined to a degree by who you need to make your production bankable. What big names, people with track records, will attract a network or private capital to finance your production? Sometimes all you need is one star like Clint Eastwood or Jessica Lange. Sometimes a director, such as David Lean of *Dr. Zhivago* and *Lawrence of Arabia*, will make your production bankable. Often, you will have to join forces with a co-producer (who may end up with the credit) such as George Lucas of *The Return of the Jedi* and the *Indiana Jones* series.

Besides making your story bankable, the above-the-line talent will affect your budget, because of their fees and percentages; your story, because most of them will want a voice in the final script or you will want to adapt it to fit them; and your production, which they will help you plan and interpret. Be open to their input. You will probably pay them a great deal of money (unless they are donating their time for charitable reasons), so get as much out of them as possible. They can help your production succeed:

The producer is the chief executive and operating officer. He or she is in charge of the production and the production personnel. The producer controls the budget and is ultimately responsible for the success or failure of the production.

The director is responsible for directing the actors and crew. He or she stages the production and is responsible for the visual and audio treatment.

An executive producer may be placed above the producer in the chain of command. If so, the executive producer is either responsible for financing the production or for interfacing with the network or studio, or both. He or she will assume the role of chief executive officer but will delegate budget responsibility to the producer or an associate producer.

A *director of photography* (d.p.) is rare in television production, but a big-budget program like "Shogun" might have one. The director of photography will handle the visual treatment of the film, freeing the director to direct the actors, crew, and stage action.

Finalize your Script and Organize Inserts.

With your key talent, finalize your script. Then working from your final script, obtain or arrange for graphics, photography, film, stock shots, film clips, properties, and everything that needs to be in your production.

Hire Cast and Staff.

Casting is critical. Be selective. Be careful. Cast the right person for the role. Television is an intimate medium that lends itself to close-ups. Make sure that your cast will act naturally in a close-up. Your characters become the cast; therefore, make sure that the actors you choose are your characters. In movies you can have a cast of thousands; in television a small group will suggest a large crowd.

The following staff is typical in a television production:

The *assistant producer* keeps track of the budget.

The *assistant director* lines up all the elements of the production for the director and cues the director during taping.

The *production assistant*, continuity, or script person checks the production against the script and keeps track of time.

The *floor manager* represents the director on the floor of the production and cues the performers and the crew.

The *technical director* oversees all technical and engineering activities and equipment and often operates the video switcher (which switches between cameras and produces special effects) during taping.

The *set designer* designs the sets.

The *art director* determines the look of the production by designing and preparing all graphics and visuals.

The *makeup person*.

The *hair stylist*.

The *costume designer*.

The *lighting director*. The more you know about television the more you will realize how important and difficult lighting is. Achieving the right level of lighting for the camera is difficult, even if it is a low-light camera. Achieving good, attractive, atmospheric, uniform lighting for multiple cameras is an art.

The *video engineer* controls picture quality.

The *audio engineer* controls audio quality and mixes the sound between the several sound sources. In producing a television program, it is very easy to become so wrapped up in the video that you forget about the sound. Good sound quality demands great care and marks the difference between a poor production and a good one.

The *cameraperson*, or camerapeople, operate the camera(s) with the help of the camera crew.

The *soundperson*, or soundpeople, operate the sound booms, microphones, and audio equipment.

The *grips*, or floor crew, are responsible for changing scenes, dressing the sets, and arranging props.

The *gaffers*, or electricians, are responsible for all electrical wiring and for rigging lights.

The *video graphics operator* operates the video graphics equipment.

The *telecine operator*, of film chain operator, runs the film and slide chains that feed film and slides into the video equipment to be stored on videotape or video disc.

The *gofer* "goes for" this and that.

With the new lightweight, compact video equipment, some television journalists and documentary producers have cut personnel down to just themselves and their video camcorder.

However, to be sure you get your shot, a minimum staff is needed for a small production:

Producer/Director

Cameraperson

Soundperson

Lighting

Engineer

Talent

Writer

The writer should be distinct from the producer in most productions to give the production another level of creative control.

Organize Artistic and Technical Services and Facilities.

Prepare for the rental and purchase of all equipment.

Prepare for all artistic services and technical services so that everything is ready and available when you need it.

Prepare all artwork, graphics, special effects, audio effects, music, costumes, props.

Prepare for all location videotaping and filming.

Begin the construction of all sets and scenery.

Reserve all facilities, studios, and locations.

Rehearse

At this point, you will start rehearing your cast and crew. Run through your script to begin blocking out movements of cast, cameras, sound equipment and crew. Have your performers practice their lines, actions, and performances. make sure that the timing is what you want. The sequence of rehearsals is as follows:

A walkthrough, or dry run

A "stagger through" to coordinate technical services

A predress run-through to polish

A dress rehearsal

Production

Note that you will want to hold each type many times to achieve a quality production.

Prepare Camera and Other Scripts.

Prepare breakdown sheets showing the running orders of your videotapings and/or filmings.

BREAKDOWN SHEET
(showing running order)

Page	Scene	Shots	Cameras/Audio	Day/Night	Cast
1	Painting 1		sof cam 1	n	
5	Telly at table	6–8	1,2,3,	n	Telly & bits
			recording break		
10	Car	18	1 dub	n	Telly & bits
13	Street	23	1	n	Chris & girl

Prepare a shooting schedule showing when you are shooting what with what equipment, crew, and cast.

SHOOTING SCHEDULE

Date	Sets-Scenes-Description	Cast	Location
1st day	Set: Restaurant Scene: Going-away party Props: Painting of Athens, Tables and and chairs.	Telly Chris Bits	Studio
2nd day	Set: Scene: Props:		

Prepare a shooting script, reorganizing your script into the order in which you will be videotaping and/or filming.

Prepare a rehearsal script telling people when they will rehearse what where.

Prepare a camera script, and then camera cards for each camera showing them what they are doing when and how. To prepare your camera script you need to familiarize yourself with how a camera works, the distance a camera needs for a shot, and what camera angles will give you an ECU (extra close-up), CU (close-up), an MCU (medium close-up), a BCU (big close-up), a 2-S (two shot), a 3-S (three shot), an MS (medium shot), or a LS (long shot):

CAMERA CARD

Camera: ___3___

Shot	Position	Lens Angle	Scent
1	B	13	Restaurant CU of painting
2	A	35	PULL BACK to LS of Telly in front of painting.
6	C	20	MCU of Telly at table

Prepare scripts for your technical director, video effects operator, audio engineer, soundperson, floor manager, and everybody else who needs to know what they are doing when and how. You will need to familiarize yourself with the working of the respective equipment and with television abbreviations to prepare these scripts. Books on production will take you only so far; you must have some working knowledge of basic television equipment and what it can do to adequately prepare your production, even when you have hired the best talent. Even when you hire the best talent, you must supervise and guide them to realize your vision.

Prepare Studio and Locations.

All too often, studios are rented and the personnel rushed in to produce the program, and the producer and director find that the studio is not prepared to do the type of production work required. You, as executive producer, your producer, and your director should meet with the studio and make sure that you have the space you need, the equipment you need, the backup facilities you need, the crew you need, the storage space, the time to set up, the technical equipment, the dressing rooms, the green room, and everything else essential to your production.

Every production is different, so many studios rent the special equipment they need for each production from an equipment house. You need to prepare them to have on-line, in the system, everything you need before the big day of the production, when you will be spending money by the minute on cast and crew.

Before the day of production, know your way around your studio, know the key personnel, know the equipment, and be prepared for emergencies. Also, have insurance to cover your losses.

Make sure than you have filed the proper requisitions, and prepare contracts for everything. You know what you need at the studio and on location; spell it out in writing.

Some studios have no equipment, just sound stages. This is a holdover from the days of film. Today most television studios have equipment, but you have to rent each piece separately. The basic hookup is one camera and one microphone feeding into one video tape recorder (VTR) (see One-Camera Diagram).

If you add another camera, you will need a switcher, which almost always has a special effects generator built in to it to give you the ability to do wipes, dissolves, fades, chroma key*, and other effects. You also need a sync generator to make sure that the electronic signal from both cameras matches exactly. You will want to have preview monitors so that you can see what you have on each camera and choose your shots. If

---

* Chroma key is the electronic device that allows you to superimpose an actor, or something moving, in front of a map, a scene, a picture, or something else.

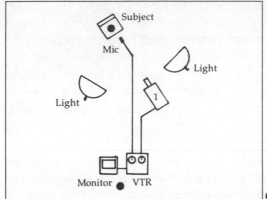

One-Camera Diagram

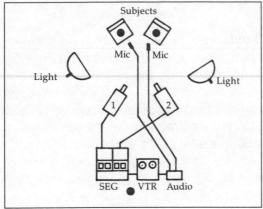

Two-Camera Diagram

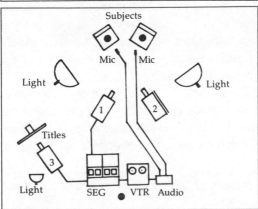

Three-Camera Diagram

at the same time you add another mic (microphone), then you will need an audio mixer to balance the levels and quality of the audio coming from the two mics. This more sophisticated setup would look like the setup in the Two-Camera Diagram. Finally, you will want to add lights and a title camera, which will give you a setup like the one in the Three-Camera diagram. As your production becomes more complex, you will add more equipment. Be aware of how that equipment works and how it interfaces with other equipment.

Line up transportation for your staff and cast. Also, line up catering so that you have food and beverages in the studio or on location to keep your personnel happy.

Do Camera Blocking and Equipment Preparation.

Before your production starts, you need to know what you want your camera, sound, and other equipment to do, and when and how.

Your cameraperson has to act fast. He or she has to compose a good picture in a minimum amount of time, keeping in mind at all times the subject and the light. Help your cameraperson by planning your shots.

Your shot should show what you want it to show and no more.

Each shot should accomplish your purpose. Every camera move has an effect on your audience. You should know what those effects are and use them to tell your story.

Your shot should emphasize what you want it to emphasize. Simplify the elements in a picture. Note that with a zoom there is no parallactic movement, there is only a compression or stretching of perspective. It is not a natural movement. A dolly is better because it actually moves through a scene. The movie *2001*, unlike earlier films, created a feeling of actual movement by dollying through the star field. Zooms in and out on a flat surface, though cheaper, do not create the feeling of movement; therefore, use zooms sparingly and only where appropriate.

Make sure your shot is neither too close or too distant.

Plan your shot so that attention is focused and not diffused or distracted by extraneous objects or lines. Vertical or horizontal lines in the scenery or background should never divide a scene or the subject in two. A change in camera position will solve this problem. You can focus attention by

Exclusion
A visual or audio clue
Color
Camera angle
Composition
Contrast
Movement
Performance

Frame the main subject properly. This is easier said than done. Do not compose your picture for perfect symmetry; it will take away from visual interest. Shoot for an interesting perspective, from a slight angle.

Plan your shot so that you know when action will enter and leave the shot. Movements away and toward a camera are more dramatic than lateral movements across the field of vision.

Your shot should establish the effect you want by revealing, concealing, misleading, or focusing on the central subject. Low shots, shooting up, make subjects look stronger. High shots, looking down, make subjects look weaker. Normal viewpoint is chest high. Note also that verticals at the bottom of a shot cause anxiety and instability; verticals at the top do not.

Avoid lateral reversal effects, which occur because the human eye tends to wander toward frame right. Frame left can support more people, more weight, and more darkness without looking shut-in or crowded.

Plan your shot so that your composition is what you want. Rectangular or square compositions should be avoided. Triangular compositions are pleasing. The right angle suggests opposition and contrast. An S-curve is slow and restful. A Z-curve is fast and exciting. A cross expresses a merging of interests. A circle represents continuity.

The color should be appropriate. Green backgrounds will upset your audience. Blue backgrounds are pleasing. Pink backgrounds establish warmth and love. Be aware of how colors affect people and how to use them properly. In Japan they tend to use more yellow tints in their pictures; in Hollywood, they tend to use more blue; and in New York, photographers tend to use more gray and green.

Plan for a picture with unity, variety, harmony, balance, rhythm, pacing, proportion, and continuity with everything before and after. Use unusual angles or moves only where appropriate. Make sure that the camera will not intrude on your story.

With respect to audio, see Chapter 9. Note that the audio may control the picture's impact, or the picture may control the audio's inmpact, or the impact may be the cumulative effect of both. Plan the relationship between the audio and the visual to create

Contrast (a loud sound in the midst of a peaceful picture)

Uniqueness (sound can establish that the same picture has a different meaning than it had before)

Suspense

Humor

Emphasis

Repetition

Surrealism

Comparison

Foreshadowing

Revelation

Incongruity

Plan your lighting to help establish mood and atmosphere as well as focus attention. Lighting influences your audience by changing their perception of a scene. Lighting can be realistic or atmospheric. It may reveal, hide, enhance, texture, shade, modify, or enlighten. Soft, broad light illuminates without casting shadows. Hard light focuses attention, creates modeling, and casts shadows.

Normally, you will have a direct fill light to light your subject, with a back light to cut down on modeling and harsh shadows and a key light within ten to twenty degrees of a person's nose to give form to your subject. Note that the fill light will reduce wrinkles and unwanted features and the key light will enhance desirable features.

Have the subject of your key light look toward the light.

Avoid steep lighting. A steep back light will spill over onto the face of your subject. A steep front light will cause harsh modeling, give black eyes, long nose, and neck shadows and a haggard appearance. It will also emphasize baldness.

Avoid shallow lighting. A shallow back light will flare into the picture. A shallow front light will make the subject look flat.

Avoid lighting that is too far off the camera axis. Such lighting will create hot spots and strange shadows.

By careful balance of back and front lighting you will give your subject the appropriate three-dimensional look.

You can create realism by imitation or simulation. For example, if you wanted to create the look of a church by imitation, you could shine a light at an angle through a stained glass window on the set. If you wanted to create the same look by simulation, you could use several lights with gels* or use a slide. You can also use stencils, flickerwheels, and patterns to create atmospheric effects.

Your lighting must be planned with the type of camera you will use in mind. Every camera has different light sensitivity, for which your lighting has to adjust.

Analyze your subject to see what features you want to minimize and what features you want to emphasize.

Make sure than any graphics are evenly lit.

Determine how your lighting will be affected by movement.

---

* Gels are transparent colored sheets that go in front of your lights to adjust color temperature and create mood.

Plan your graphics so that they will compose properly within the 4:3 proportions of television. Always provide an adequate border. Make sure that there are no wrinkles or imperfections, because television will magnify any imperfection. Plan your colors and tones to be pleasing, or to achieve the effect you want. Clear tonal and color separation is advisable if you want your graphics to be clear. Keep detail to a minimum and simplify structural forms. Maps should have no more than the essential blocks necessary to indicate the main features. One graphic is better than a succession of graphics; therefore, simplify and combine information.

Do a Run-through and Final Rehearsal

Run through your script to remove any kinks and timing problems. The last run-through is sometimes called a giggle-through because it gives the performers and the personnel a chance to let off any unwanted emotions or feelings prior to production.

Make sure that you have one uninterrupted rehearsal prior to production. This is very important.

Don't repeat a scene unless something needs to be changed, corrected, or improved. Be clear about your directions. Too many revisions will cause hesitation; therefore, be succinct and friendly. Pay close attention to continuity.

Make sure your performers know who they are in terms of the script. Make sure that props are being used properly. Make sure the performers hit their marks and are working to the right camera. Don't let one performer cover another, but don't let them be too far apart. On camera your performers will look farther apart than they are, so bring them in closer than you would think appropriate. Make sure than one performer does not upstage another, or become too prominent because of a lateral reversal effect.

Think in terms of shots and how the shot will look on television. Use a viewfinder, if it helps you to do this. Make sure the performers are framed properly. Make sure that you can see who you want to see. Get rid of excess detail. Make sure that your camera is not shooting off set and that there are no unwanted subjects in the shot.

Check the lights so that there are no lens flares. The new tubeless, chip CCD and CPD cameras do not flare, lag, or bloom, but most cameras do flare (light flames off the subject) lag (residual images trail behind a camera move), and bloom (haloes of light).

Check the boom and mics so that there is no sign of that technology in the picture. Keep an eye out for unwanted shadows and cables in the shot. Make sure that everything is straight, level, and the way you want it to look. Check for any distracting set elements or blemishes.

Check costumes so that the whites don't flare and that nothing has been washed with bleach, which gives a false chroma effect (chromokeyed images fly off the bleach). If you don't have a white peak to control flares, have your cast wear another color. Have the cast stay away from satins or reflective materials unless you intend that effect. Light tones make people look bigger and formless. Dark tones minimize size but also decrease modeling. Colors that are too strong will saturate the picture. Noisy patterns can cause a strobe, flicker, or moire effect that can be very annoying for your audience. Noisy costumes and jewelry can create sound problems. Stay away from colors that will look like skin tones, giving your performers a naked appearance.

Makeup will help your performers to look natural under the lights, but use if sparingly. Less is more. Choose a base that is slightly lighter than the skin tone of the performer. Use powder to prevent shine. Do not choose colors that will read blue or orange on camera unless that is your intent. Highlights and shading will correct for facial faults and define features. Check the makeup on camera to make sure that it works.

Plan your production so that your story is told and none of the technical aspects of the production intrude on and detract from the visual, dramatic telling of the story. If you have decided to pursue a symbolist approach to your material by revealing the technical aspects of your production to your audience, do so, but in such a way that the revelation is part of the fabric of your program and not an obstacle to the audience's enjoyment. The French playwright Maeterlinck, the father of symbolist theater, revealed the stage to his audience by making them a part of the play, not by having effects intrude on their perceptions.

Do Location Production.

On location, your setup might look like:

If you have planned carefully, things should go well. Beware of extraneous noise, weather, crowds, and traffic. Bring everything you need. Double-check all connections, lighting, sound equipment, video equipment, and continuity to make sure that you get what you want. Continuity can be a big problem when you are shooting on location; to help prevent it:

Make sure that color, brightness, contrast, tones, light direction, shots, perspective, and picture quality match from shot to shot.

Make sure that weather conditions match from shot to shot.

248 / HOW TO COMMUNICATE THROUGH THE MEDIA

Don't let your camera cross the line of axis on reverse shots, creating a lateral reversal effect. Move your camera within a 180° arc so that the subjects stay within the arc.

Make sure that costumes match.

Make sure that performances match.

Make sure that action matches.

Make sure that props match and time passes uniformly. (Don't jump from a half-full glass to a full one, for example.)

Avoid jump cutting between unrelated shots or shots which don't match.

Make sure that sound matches

Note: for a video camera focus is established by zooming in on your subject, as tight as possible, focus the lens, and pull back. Your subject is now in focus.

Do Studio Production.

Go in as early as possible. If you can, set up your sets the day before or even before that. Check and double-check all equipment to make sure it works the way you want it to work. Warm up all equipment. Test every part of your camera, audio equipment, VTR, switcher, and any other equipment you have on-line. Clear out all unnecessary cables and all obstacles. Make sure that all equipment is clean. Check audio and video level and quality. Relax. Pray. Enjoy yourself, you are paying for this production. Shoot.

Hold a Cast Party.

Maintain a good rapport with your cast. Plan to work together again. Be supportive.

Edit.

You will want to spend a great deal of time off-line* reviewing your production. Plan your cuts precisely, so that you will save as much money as possible during on-line editing. If your videotape is coded with a S.M.P.T.E.† time code or another code, keep track of all your edit points so that you can go on-line and make your edits without searching for edit points.

Avoid mismatched cutting. Watch for continuity, and make sure your transitions are so smooth they are invisible (unless your story demands otherwise).

Add titles, music, audio effects, graphics, film clips, and whatever you need to make your production work. Take your time.

Feel free to improve on what you have on tape, even if the improvements lead you away from the strict letter of your script. An editor can make or destroy a production. Good editing requires as much creativity as a good script.

Think in visual terms. Advancing your story through pictures is more important than advancing it through words, although both must be there in harmony to fully tell a story through the medium of television.

Review everything up to this point to make sure you are on target and have used the medium to its maximum effectiveness.

Review.

Does your program work? Re-edit if necessary.

---

* Off-line time is time reviewing the videotape on a less expensive VTR, and any time in which you are not on the line of full production, with its heavy expense.
† This is the time code approved by the Society of Motion Picture and Television Engineers.

Distribute.

You are ready to air on the network, and the other avenues of distribution you have set up, such as PBS, theatrical, foreign, and cable movie. Keep track of where your program is going. Make copies, distribute, and keep records.

Your program may have a long life if you keep on top of it. Every new sale is financing for your next production.

Follow Up.

Check the ratings, promotion, advertising, and any payments and billings due. Artists will receive payments every time your program plays. Know when and what you have to pay.

You will receive moneys according to the distribution deals you have set up; know when and how you are to be paid. Trust God, not man.

Survey the reaction to your production so that you can do better next time.

The Life of a Television Program.

Walt Disney established the golden cycle in which he rereleased a movie every five years or so to a new generation of children. Most movies will not stand up to rerelease, however. Television movies generally do not have the life span of theatrical films, but yours could be the exception.

THE LIFE OF A MOVIE

Year	1	2	3	4	5	6	7	8	9	10	11	12	13	14
Theaters	x													
Pay-per-view														
Cable	x													
Pay Cable & STV	xx	xx		x										
Network TV				x	x	x								
Independent TV						xx		xx		xx		xx		xx x
Home Video			xxxxxxxxxxxxxxxxxxxxxxx											
Foreign			xxxxxxxxxxxxxxxxxxxxxxxxxxxxxxxxxxx											

To produce a television program, you have to be creative, self-disciplined, organized, unstructured, persistent, flexible, imaginative, and practical. About half of your energy will be expended on producing your program and the other half fighting for your production. This may seem overwhelming to you, but trust God and you will succeed in producing a powerful program telling the story He has given you to tell.

This overview of the techniques and principles that apply to producing a network television movie is applicable to a television production of any size, but smaller productions will require less of everything. If you are embarking on producing a video on your church, review the steps necessary for a network program and select those perinciples and techniques that are relevant. If you familiarize yourself with the most complex form of production, you will excel in simpler productions, including productions in other audiovisual media.

An excellent exercise is to assemble a group from your church and produce a network movie in miniature with amateur equipment. If you take care to follow all the appropriate steps, you will end up with a successful production. If not, you will know it because of the glaring flaws in your final product.

Having trained many television communicators, I have found that an exercise is the most effective way to learn about the nature of the medium of television. Try it. Have fun, and apply yourself to achieving excellence, in his service.

9. What About Radio and Auditory Media?

Radio is, indeed, the art of the imagination.

ROBERT HILLIARD

Directed at one sense, hearing, radio leaves much to the imagination. Today, the imaginative, dramatic side of radio has been relegated to commercials, with most of the remaining time devoted to music, news, sports, and talk. The golden years of radio drama seem to have passed, never to return, but who knows? A medium flexible enough to feature spots in which Lake Michigan is drained, filled with hot chocolate, and topped by mountains of whipped cream and a gigantic cherry[1] may surprise us by returning to imaginative drama—just as it surprised many pundits by surviving with renewed vigor the onslaught to television.

Today, radio is very successful. Ninety-five percent of all Americans twelve years old or over listen to radio every week.[2] Many communicators overlook radio, however, in spite of the fact that it is an inexpensive way to reach a large audience— often one held captive in cars during the morning and evening rush hours.

Some observers claim that radio has been revitalized by satellite distribution, which gave new strength to the networks by making instant national programming possible, feasible, and attractive to advertisers.* Others see the local nature of most radio stations, which help people plug into their community, as the key to radio's success. Some claim that President

---

* The major radio networks are ABC, NBC, CBS, Mutual, RKO, Sheridan, Satellite Music Network, and Transtar.

Reagan brought radio back as a political tool with his Saturday broadcasts.[3] Because Saturday is a slow day for news, these radio broadcasts influenced newspaper and television news.

All these analysts are right to a degree, but the underlying reason radio is the great survivor is that listening to radio allows people to hear the news, enjoy music, and follow sports wherever they are—thanks to technological improvements in quality and size—while they are doing something else. The absence of sight is a handicap. The advantage is that the radio listener is free to drive, jog, or type. For the listener, radio is portable and unobtrusive. (Note that the same category of media audiocassettes provide listeners with this same freedom, as well as the freedom to choose exactly what they want to hear when they want to hear it.)

The advantages of radio accrue not only to the listener but to the communicator. Radio provides an inexpensive way to reach the local community, the nation, and the world. Radio gives Christian communicators the ability to reach shut-ins who can't make it to church; at the same time, its ability to penetrate hardened political barriers allows Christians to proclaim the Gospel to millions of people in totalitarian countries.

As a Christian communicator, you can use radio for public service announcements, church news, interviews, music, sermons, drama, a magazine program, or many other kinds of programs. Radio gives the communicator complete freedom of time and space. In an instant, with a few sound effects and some narration, you can take your audience back to the Flood, and then jump forward to the Second Coming. There are no visual limits to restrain the human imagination.

However, like every medium, radio demands that one obey the rules in order to communicate effectively. Those who are inexperienced often overdo sound effects; jump to conclusions, forgetting to develop their programs logically; and produce static talk shows because they hesitate to ask their guests tough questions.

To become familiar with the techniques and principles of

radio production, let's examine the steps involved in producing a radio talk show. These principles will also help you produce a good audiocassette. (Almost anyone can produce a bad audio cassette, as many cassette producers have proved.) If you want to produce music, you will want to do research into that area of production.

These principles will touch on radio drama, but before undertaking to produce a drama, you will want to do more research into the nature of sound effects and the principles that apply to presenting drama through an auditory medium. For instance, in an auditory medium, a narrator, as well as the characters' dialogue, takes the place of pictures. The narrator sets the stage, but the narrator who says too much will stop the movement of the story and kill the drama. As always, learning the rules will help you avoid reinventing the wheel.

Producing Your Radio Program

We will examine the steps involved in producing a hypothetical radio program from idea through follow-up. The assumptions made throughout will guide you through the basic principles and techniques of a typical radio interview program.

Review your Choice of Radio

Having asked the appropriate ascertainment questions, discerned your motivational talents, and targeted your audience, you have decided to produce an interview program on a local commercial radio station. This format gives you the opportunity to reach a nonreligious audience through the investigation of current events from a biblical perspective.

You might have considered public service announcements but decided that they would not give you the weekly, in-depth reach of a talk show. You ruled out a preaching program because there were many good preaching programs on the air in your community, and they did not capture the attention of the nonreligious audience you are targeting. Although radio gave you an opportunity to produce some imaginative dramas, you were aware from research that the audience just isn't there for radio drama. Therefore, you have decided to use an interview format that hooks a radio audience through discussion of current events and the presence of a well-known guest.

Obtain Rights, Financing, and Access to Radio

Before you produce your local radio talk show, you need to know if you can finance your program and place it on the air.

Prior to the late 1970s, radio broadcasters were seen as trustees of a scarce public resource, the airwaves, and required to operate "in the public interest." (See the 1934 Communications Act.) Religious programs were one of the most important indicators that a radio broadcaster was doing so and should therefore retain a license to broadcast when that license came up for renewal. Broadcasters sought out mainline religious programs to fill a percentage of their broadcast schedule (usually the Sunday morning "religious ghetto" hours, which were the least attractive to commercial advertisers).

For religious programming, the broadcaster would approach the National Council of Churches (NCC) or the local Association of Regional Religious Communicators (ARRC), the Roman Catholic church, the Board of Rabbis, and sometimes the Southern Baptist church. The NCC, on a national level, or ARRC on a local level, would then coordinate and supply all Protestant programming. The station would divide the time allocated for religious programming among the programs provided by these sources to roughly reflect the demographics of the station's audience.

If you wanted to place a local religious radio program on the air, you would approach your local ARRC, Roman Catholic communications office, Board of Rabbis, Southern Baptist communications office, or mission board with your idea. The group you approached would decide whether or not your program should be included in their radio offering.

Of course, there were exceptions, but in general, the

coordination of religious programming rested in the hands of these representative organizations in close consultation with the broadcasters. The broadcasters were happy because they didn't have to decide what was, or wasn't, legitimate religious programming and by relying on these representatives, could discharge their public interest obligations with a minimum of effort. Also, by selecting programming from this mix of organizations, broadcasters felt that they met the fairness doctrine charge to carry both sides of controversial issues. Secure with this system, broadcasters didn't want to be bothered with other religious groups.

The mainline churches were happy with this arrangement because it gave them some control over the religious programming on radio (and television). Many religious producers were happy with this arrangement because it gave them the opportunity to produce programming for the networks and major stations.

Much of the programming produced was of high quality, often evangelical, but not the type of programming that an advertiser would finance or for which the producer could ask money from the audience. Since time was given without charge to the religious producers, it was clear to everyone that on-air fundraising was inappropriate. Freed from the cost of air time, these mainline religious producers could concentrate on drama, public affairs, and commentary.

The trouble with this system was that it often excluded independent religious program producers, usually evangelical. Some of these independents, such as Billy Graham and Oral Roberts, found ways to buy time on independent stations, but most were denied access to the audiences of the major stations and networks.

After deregulation, stations felt free to sell time to religious producers. Independent producers rushed to buy time. The stations found that they could make money on time they had been giving away. Many mainline programs were dropped or pushed into low-audience time periods.

Today anyone with money has the opportunity to buy air

time. However, the religious programs have to appeal to their audience for support, often at the expense of the nonreligious audience who might be better reached by a program that did not ask for money. Ministry or teaching programs aimed at believers are very important, but there must also be programming aimed at nonbelievers.

If you want to produce a program that will reach those people who will support it, then buy time on a local station (assuming your format is compatible with the identity of the station) and use on-air fund-raising to finance it.

If, however, you want your program to reach a nonreligious audience, then you will have to find an advertiser, underwriter, or off-air support group to finance your program and buy the air time, or you will have to convince a station to carry your program at no cost to you as part of their own program offering. An advertiser will want to air a full complement of commercials selling a product before, after, and during your program.

An underwriter will finance your program as a public service and will probably want credit for it on your program. Underwriters are individuals, companies, and corporations who pay for the production (and sometimes distribution) of a program as part of their public relations activities. Underwriters, unlike advertisers, do not advertise their products on the programs they underwrite. They do, however, receive credit as an underwriter, and they hope to benefit from their association with the program. By law, Public Broadcasting Service (PBS) television and National Public Radio (NPR) cannot carry commercial advertising; therefore, all programs on PBS and NPR are financed by tax dollars, contributions from the viewing public, and/or underwriting. For example, a program like "Masterpiece Theater" might be underwritten by Mobil Oil, which receives credit, as well as the Corporation for Public Broadcasting, which is funded by tax dollars, and viewer contributions, which help the member stations who air the program to do so.

In spite of deregulation, you may be able to convince a station to carry your program at no cost to you. To do so, you will have to convince the station that your program will not only bring them new listeners but also fit in with their program schedule, their rhythm, their psychographics, and their advertising. Every station wants to attract more listeners, if it can do so without losing the listeners it already has. Stations will often contract to carry a loss leader, such as an athletic team, so that the station can attract listeners who will stick with it.

In Atlanta, at the time of this writing, a network affiliate carries my weekly radio program, *Religionwise: A Weekly Look at the News Through the Eyes of Religion*, on Sunday at 6:00 A.M. and 10:00 P.M. The station is fourth in the ratings for the times of my program out of over fifty stations. One of the producers noted that the stations with larger audiences featured preaching programs during those time periods. To compete, it was advisable for the station to carry a religious program that fit in with their format and attracted religious as well as nonreligious listeners who don't want to listen to sermons.

Visit the station you have targeted; meet with the program director, the general manager, the station manager, and others to find out how the station operates and how you can help them to reach a larger audience. Sound them out. Bring goodwill. Know what you're talking about. Be receptive to working with the station to reach the religious or nonreligious audience that they are not reaching but that will be compatible with their present audience.

Be open to finding a sympathetic broadcaster, and be flexible in your format. If you approach a classical music station, be prepared to feature classical church music and to interview musicians and other experts who can discuss the music from a Christian perspective. If you approach a MOR (middle-of-the-road) station, be prepared to feature MOR music with an upbeat interview discussing issues relevant to that audience. If you approach an all-talk station, be prepared to tune your format to the station's personality.

If you are not buying time, the station may ask you to find a co-host from another denomination or faith to give your program a wider reach. Such a co-host, or continuing co-guest, is not a bad idea, because that person can ask the tough questions that will highlight the power of the Gospel of Jesus Christ. As long as you are committed to proclaiming the Gospel without compromise, a co-host can act as a foil for your nonreligious listener and may even help your listener to know Christ, thanks to his Holy Spirit. The truth will out. The important thing is to reach out to the person who would never listen to preaching or a ministry program.

Your format not only must suit the station but must be comfortable for you, considering your motivational talents. If you hate rock music, don't design a program for a rock station. If you are uncomfortable discussing the Gospel with a nonbeliever, don't invite one to be your co-host. Pick out a station by studying and researching the stations in your community, and design your program to fit your talents and the station's characteristics.

Design and Budget your Program

Design your program to give it an identity that is unique, yet fits your station, your audience, your premise, and your genre.

Assuming your station is MOR, you might produce an introductory logo using contemporary Christian music that suggests your program premise, such as Jesus changes lives; Jesus delivers people from the human predicament; or biblical principles affect all of contemporary life. Every program concept, even for a music program, must have a central idea, stated as a premise, to give the program organic continuity and drive.

Once established, the opening music may cross-fade to an announcer, who hooks the audience by introducing your topic, you the host, perhaps another host, and your guest(s). You may want to segue to another piece of music before the interview starts, depending on the nature of the station.

If your station is all-talk, you may open your own program

and introduce your own guests so that your program has the same sound as the other talk/news programs on the station.

Do not include too many guests in the interview segment of your program. Too many voices on radio cause confusion. Two guests, or a co-host and a guest, can enliven the program and make it more interesting by inserting another point of view. Each individual program should have its own premise, which restates your major program premise in terms that apply specifically to your guest(s). To find your guests and topics for each program, read as much as possible, keep up with current events, and discover what matters to your audience.

Design your opening, your close, and all internal entrances, exits, transitions, segues, music cues, announcements, bridges, and effects so that your timing is precise and your program has a distinct personality, mood, theme, and direction on which your audience can rely. If your program is broadcast live, it is even more important that you plan every second that can be planned so that your program goes smoothly. Script your program down to the second.

From your script, budget your program. Amortize the cost of any special opening and closing logos over the run of the series. Include the cost of lining up guests, preparing the music, script, and effects for each program in your initial series, and the cost of your preparation for each interview. Your budget should reflect all in-studio and out-of-studio costs. If your station is not covering all these costs, who is?

Have a good audio producer produce your opening and closing logos, or take great care in producing your logos yourself. The logos will identify your program; in radio, as in most encounters, *you never have a second chance to make a first impression*. Your opening will capture and hook your audience, so make it powerful.

Gather Staff

If the station is producing your program, you may be all the staff necessary, unless you need an assistant to line up guests and/or a secretary to handle correspondence. If your program is not being produced by the station, you will want the following people:

A *producer* who will line up guests and supervise the production of the program.

A *writer*, or *assistant producer* (depending upon the extent of their overall responsibilities), to select all the music, sound, and other materials; script the program, including announcements, week after week; and coordinate all the various elements of the production.

An *announcer* to open and close the program.

A *host* to interview the guests.

Guests who have credentials and a specific reason for coming on your program. These guests should be opinionated, outspoken, rational, interesting, and friendly. Choose guests who have something to say that relates to the premise of your program. An introverted guest who couldn't care less about his or her opinion will kill your program. Your guests should be lined up far in advance of taping (or broadcasting), then reminded a few days before when to be at the studio. Be prepared for your guests not to show up, even though you have done everything in your power to get them there on time.

A *line producer*, or *audio engineer*, to select, balance, and blend the various sound and music sources at the audio control board, or mixer, during the recording of the interview. The interview can be recorded separately and edited in with the other material during an editing session, or the other material can be kept on a reel, or cart, and rolled in to the interview in the recording session.

An *editor* to edit all the program elements together, if necessary.

A *public relations* person to promote your program. Remember, 50 percent of the work is producing the program, and 50 percent is fighting for and promoting it so that it has a reasonable chance to succeed.

You may fill one or more of these roles yourself. If you do, be objective and try to avoid being blinded by your own brilliance.

Prepare Your Program for Production.

Line up all the elements you need for the particular program you will be producing:

Determine the premise for that program.

Select music.

Write announcements.

Prepare all entrances and exits.

Prepare all sound effects.

Line up the guest(s).

Research topic(s).

Research guest(s).

Script everything that can be scripted.

Your host is the key element in your program. The host must have a good voice and be bright, warm, friendly, incisive, driven, concerned, and, most of all, prepared. He or she should have a clear-cut desire to prove the premise. The host should prepare two minutes, or more, for every minute on air. When a host does not prepare and tries to rely on tricks or personality, the audience notices that they are being short-changed. Commitment to the Gospel, interest in the world, and diligent preparation are the minimum.

Record your Program

If you record at the radio station, they should know what they're doing, but don't be surprised if they don't. Studios for speech, popular music, orchestras, choirs, and television are designed with different acoustics. If you station is an MOR music station and records your program in a music studio, it may not have the acoustic liveliness a radio audience expects from a talk program.

If you are building your own recording studio, the following rules will be helpful. Before you build, consult a sound engineer and/or a sound studio architect.

Studios for speech should be spacious enough to give a natural ambiance by allowing a normal reverberation time of approximately 0.4 seconds, without excessive echo. Speech studios that are too dead sound unnatural to your audience. If the room is an irregular shape, there may be selective emphasis of certain frequencies, which will unnaturally color speech. In small studios, the problem will be to achieve a natural sound without excessive resonance and reverberation. In a good studio, a hand clap should die away quickly but not so quickly that it sounds muffled or dead.

Studios for stereo speech should be more dead than for monaural recording.

Studios for popular music should be completely dead, with each microphone placed as close as possible to record each instrument separately and clearly.

Studios for orchestras and in-performance music need to be designed for optimum reverberation to give a natural balance to the instruments and voices.

Studios for television should be as dead as possible.

All studios need to be on solid ground and isolated from outside sound sources like airports, roads, and trains.

If possible, the studio should be floated on rubber.

Sound absorbers, wiring,control room, speakers, monitors, and all equipment and architectural features must be designed with the recording purpose of the studio in mind to give your studio the sound quality you need.

Ventilation should be carefully designed to eliminate outside noises.

Double doors are a must.

Noisy machinery must be isolated and put on antivibration mountings if possible.

Windows to the outside, if absolutely necessary, should be triple-paned and designed to avoid condensation.

Rather than recording your program in a studio, you may want to record on location or over the telephone. Both methods are acceptable, provided your equipment is in good repair and you are careful to obtain good sound quality. Be aware of the acoustics of the area where you record. Natural acoustics can add to a program by making it sound alive. More often than not, however, the area in which you record detracts from your program, especially if there is electrical interference, an air conditioner, or other unwanted sounds undermining your audio quality that go unnoticed until your interview is on tape—or, even worse, on the air.

Recording music in a concert hall or a church is an art. If the recording is done properly, taking into account the echoes and other unique characteristics of the space, it can be very beautiful. If not, it will be a waste of time and money. When in doubt, hire an experienced audio engineer, who will save you money by capturing the sound you want the first time round.

I like to interview people face-to-face to achieve personal rapport. Also, I like to record in a studio so that I know that the sound is of the highest possible quality. You should use the method of recording that works best for you, your station, and your program.

If your program is being broadcast live to allow listeners to call in (or because of station policy), all your logos, music, and sound effects must be rolled in on the spot. Timing is critical. A split second can bring down a curtain of silence that will kill your program. Keep effects to a minimum and rehearse all cues so that your audio engineer or line producer is coordinated with the host, the announcer, and the guests. In most cases, when you are broadcasting live you will be your own announcer and will limit your music to an opening and a close.

If you prerecord your program, you have more latitude to cut in music and sound effects. To keep costs down and spontaneity up, plan your program as carefully as possible.

Do not ask your guest(s) the questions you will ask on the air prior to the actual interview. If you rehearse questions ahead of time, you will find that during the actual interview they will probably tend to condense their answer, since they know you know what they're going to say and they don't want to bore you. Your audience, however, may not follow the logic of the condensed answer. Very few guests can rehearse and then give an answer on mic in a fresh, spontaneous, complete, and logical manner.

Instead of rehearsing the questions you will ask on mic, give your guest(s) the subject area of your questions and tell them to be prepared to answer the toughest questions they can imagine. Usually the questions they imagine will be much more difficult than the ones you pose, so their answers to your questions will be relaxed, complete, and upbeat.

Check your equipment:

Make sure that all microphones have the same impedance.
Low impedance mics usually have a higher audio quality and can have greater cable runs than high impedance mics. Low impedance mics are most often wired as a balanced circuit, and the shield keeps hum and noise at a minimum.
High impedance mics are less expensive in most cases. They are usually wired in an unbalanced fashion; the shield is part of the circuit, so noise and hum can easily enter the circuit.

Make sure that your microphones are polarized properly. Out-of-phase mics will cancel each other. To match the phasing of your mics, connect them one by one to an audio mixer. If the addition of each mic reinforces the total level of audio, then they are in phase. If a mic is out of phase, it will reduce the total audio level. If a mic is out of phase, color code the internal wires to the mic and reverse the two inner conductors in the microphone plug.

Speak to the audio engineer or line producer through each mic to identify the mic, check quality, and set levels.

Check all the connections to make sure they are secure.

Check the mic holder or cradle to make sure it moves freely and is in place.

Check all plugs.

Check all cables for static and other signs of problems.

Check the mixer, or audio control board, to make sure all the pots are clean and the quality is clear and good.

Check the recording deck to see if it is in good working order.

Check the turntable and all input tape decks to make sure they are in good working order.

Equipment does not have to be new to work well; it just has to be maintained, and checked, and double-checked.

These steps may seem trivial, but every producer can tell you horror stories about recording sessions at top studios where some of these steps were neglected and the program did not record or was unusable. Being professional means taking the time to do the job right.

The quality of sound depends on equipment. How you use sound is what affects your audience:

Loud sounds suggest strength and large size.

Soft sounds suggest smallness and weakness.

High-pitched sounds suggest excitement, weakness, brittleness.

Low-pitched sounds suggest power and heaviness.

Major keys suggest vigor.

Minor keys suggest melancholy.

A slow rhythm suggests dignity and seriousness.

A fast rhythm suggests excitement.

Silence can be powerful, but don't pause unless the effect is intended and the pause is very brief. Too long a silence will stop the program dead.

If your guest starts to slow down, you must interrupt. Keep up a good, smooth, fast pace (with some variation) to hold your audience.

Since this is a dialogue/interview, don't allow one person to monopolize the program. Interrupt. Ask questions. Break up any monotony.

Hold applause whenever appropriate so that it does not come in on cue and sound mechanical. In the real world, applause is always delayed by a beat, because it takes time for people to react. Try to make applause sound natural by fading it up quickly a beat or so after the event.

Sudden changes in sound, pitch, intensity, tone, or volume can confuse your audience. They should be used only for a specific effect.

Establish a rhythm that will complement the station on which your program airs.

Direct attention from one speaker to another through sound.

Establish the location of your interview through sound, if that location is not a studio or is not supposed to be a studio.

Never cut voices, music, or other sounds on or off immediately; it will sound unnatural. Allow a beat before and after your program, or a segment of it, ends to establish the ambient noise of the room in which you are recording. Every room has its own sound; if you are prerecording and editing your program, record the room's sound and cut it into your program where necessary. This is not the same as allowing disconcerting pauses, or silences, to drag or stop a program. A beat of ambient noise is a very short period of time. As always, timing is critical.

For drama and dramatic vignettes, sound effects can be produced live or taken from effects records. When broadcasting or recording live, using records can cause delays, so it is often better to have manual, live sound effects on cue. Most sounds sound as you would expect them to when recorded and played back. Someone climbing steps sounds like someone climbing steps when played back. Some real events don't have a distinct sound, so sound effects have been invented for them. A fire usually has no sound, but sound effects people have found that crumpling paper suggests a fire in people's minds. Other real sounds, like a gunshot, for example, do not sound real when recorded and played back, so simulated sound effects are substituted to create a "realistic" sound. If you are going to use sound effects, research and experiment beforehand.

Use segues, cross-fades, fades, cuts, blends, and other devices where appropriate.

Do not let any effect intrude on the program, however. These devices should help move the program along, they should not stand out as effects in the listener's mind. Everything done is intended to bring the program to the listener in an interesting, personal manner. Be restrained in your use of sound, music, and all effects.

Sound can "locate" the speaker for the listener:

If the speaker is on-mic, the listener is located at the same physical spot as the speaker.

A speaker off-mic, at some distance from it, will seem a proportionate distance from the listener, who always sees him- or herself as the center of the scene.

A speaker moving toward the mic seems to be approaching the listener.

A speaker moving away from the mic seems to be moving away from the listener.

Putting the speaker behind a barrier gives the impression that he or she is behind a door or whatever object has been specified in dialogue or by the announcer.

The announcer in radio does what the television picture does, which is to establish setting, tone, topic, mood, locale, time, and place. The host can assume this role.

The host is the protagonist, who initiates the action and who must be relentless in digging for the facts, the stories, and the information that give life to the interview.

If you are the host, relax, trust God, and be yourself. You couldn't be someone else if you tried, so don't try—you will be frustrated and will undermine your own personality.

It is all right for your guests, or you, to preach, proclaim, and ask, briefly and passionately, but avoid dictating to your audience. Telling them to do this and do that will turn them off—unless you are a charismatic personality. (Dictating is appropriate, of course, when you are directing them in an exercise.)

Assume that your listeners are human beings like you, but do not presume that they have had the same experiences you have had and share your perspectives. Explain what you are saying clearly and logically, so your listener can understand. It is said that television programs are aimed at twelve-year-olds, and this is condemned as talking down to the audience. Talking down to your audience is wrong, but visualizing your audience as someone who has no knowledge of your field of expertise but is bright, human, curious, and responsive is an excellent way to make sure that you and your guests explain yourselves on your program in the clearest and most interesting way possible.

Edit

If your program is not broadcast (or recorded) live, then you will want to edit the pieces together. Electronic editing will decrease the sound quality of your prerecorded segments by taking them down a generation. Therefore, editors prefer physical splicing, with effects recorded into the particular segments to be spliced together. With digital audio equipment, sound quality is not affected by electronic editing. Digital audio is the wave of the future.

Editing gives you the freedom to try different combinations of music and sound effects; however, editing is time-consuming and goes beyond the normal approach to producing talk programs. In most cases, programs are recorded (or broadcast) live to save time, money, and energy. If you are concerned with producing a program, with maximum impact and effectiveness, editing may be a must for you so that you can make sure that it works before it goes on the air.

If you are planning to make cassettes from your radio program as a ministry, editing is the place to insert exercises and instructions that will make the cassette more interactive than the program. Also, you will want to reconfigure your program to make it suitable for cassette distribution. A program that is thirty minutes or an hour minus the time allocated for commercials might be condensed to no more than ten to fifteen minutes to hold attention and provide time for discussion. You can edit down your interviews to take out the surplus, or you can eliminate some of the music and announcements. If you want your cassettes to have a useful life of their own as a teaching tool, reconfiguring your program is a necessary step.

Review.

Analyze every aspect of your program and improve what you can. Try not to get stuck in a rut by being defensive about what you have done. There is always room for improvement. Be open to criticism.

Distribute.

Your program may have a much broader reach than you imagine. You have spent time and energy producing your program; make sure that it is distributed as widely as possible to benefit as many people as possible.

To distribute beyond your local station, you can use word of mouth, track down similar stations in other communities through trade magazines, or give your program to a distributor to distribute for you. If you are not soliciting funds on the program or a network, a distributor who packages programs for stations may be interested in the public affairs aspect of your program and may distribute it for a very small fee, much less than perhaps it would cost you to do it yourself. Reconfiguring your program into cassettes is another form of direct distribution.

Follow up.

Survey your audience, ask for comments, seek feedback, and make sure that your program is meeting the goals you have set for it. If it is falling short in any area, revise and improve it.

Respond to your audience, and develop a good working relationship with your radio station.

You are engaged in a ministry. People are the most important part of your work—not things, not equipment, not your program.

Radio is a very powerful communications tool. It is pervasive, convenient, and reasonably inexpensive. Use it properly, and you can communicate powerfully to a large, carefully targeted audience in God's Name. Prayer and Bible study will help you.

As an exercise, try producing your program on audiocassette

using the principles and techniques in this chapter. Have several people review your cassette program so that you can become familiar with the practical aspects of producing an effective program. Feedback is a great teacher.

10. What About Public Speaking?

On the stage he was natural, simple, affecting;
'Twas only when he was off he was acting.

OLIVER GOLDSMITH

It is often said by professors of homiletics (the art of preaching) that a preacher should "preach the sermon the way a good actor speaks his lines."[1] The student about to preach in front of critical classmates may want to ask, How, in fact, does a good actor read his or her lines so that they are natural, unaffected, and poignant?

How indeed? Is the talent that makes a good actor, preacher, lecturer, or public speaker something God gives at birth? Are the rest of us left out in the cold?

Talents can start us off in the right direction, and some of us may have a head start in a specific field of endeavor, but there are many right directions within each field. Study and hard work can perfect the talents we have so that we can perform, write, and even paint well. Although greatness may evade us, being a good actor, public speaker, or preacher is within our grasp if we observe the general rules of effective communication and the rules that apply to whatever genre we have chosen and learn and practice the techniques of performing before a live audience. There are simple keys to speaking before an audience with the same power and effectiveness as a good actor. All of us should be aware of them.

Public speaking, acting, and preaching involve all the senses dramatically. Even without words, a live appearance can say much more than is written. Observe the world around you, and you will see that actions frequently speak louder than words. For example, notice the love communicated when a mother cares for her baby, the frustration exhibited by a person stuck in traffic, or the overwhelming need shown by a hungry child who reaches out to a news cameraperson for help.

Words spoken take on meanings it would take pages of written words to explain. In a book on readable writing, it was noted that: "Spoken language is the primary phenomenon, and writing is only a more or less imperfect reflection of it."[2]

I vividly recall the simple, emotive exercises we were given when I studied at the Strasberg Theater Institute in New York City. The student actor was given a word like *tomorrow* or a simple sentence like *I love you*, and told to speak that word or sentence in as many ways as possible while the other students wrote down the different meanings the actor gave it by varying emotional inflection. Spoken, one word can have fifty different meanings.

William Safire, in his column in the *New York Times Magazine*, pointed out that President Reagan in his Second Inaugural Address used the word *yes* to mean "even" in "and, *yes*, in law"; "lastly," in "and, *yes*, the years when"; and "defiance" in "and, *yes*, the unborn". Safire noted: "Not since Molly Bloom, in James Joyce's *Ulysses*, punctuated her stream of consciousness with *yes* to register passion has this technique been used so variously."[3]

Try this exercise yourself, speaking one word with different emotional inflections to reflect different meanings and asking others to keep track of the different meanings they hear.

Public speaking is important in our society; policy in the executive branch is often set by the president's speeches. What the president says is translated into policy by bureaucrats in the executive branch who comb each speech for references to their field and incorporate the direction indicated in the speech into their policy decisions.

The spoken word contains the meanings the speaker builds

into it, whereas the written word means what it says on the face of it, unless there are words around it to change its meaning. Probably the greatest weakness most speakers have is the tendency to ignore the meaning given to their words by their emotional state and physical actions at the time they deliver those words.

If we look at what critics say about public speaking or oratory during election years, we will find certain recurring terms of praise like these words used to describe Mario Cuomo's rhetorical power during the 1984 election season: *conversational, clear, resonant, eloquent without arrogance, varying inflection, natural, logical, personal,* and *forceful.*[4] All these qualities can be part of our public speaking if we take the time to prepare and practice.

Just as Richard Burton found by observing Elizabeth Taylor in *Cleopatra* that there was a big difference between acting in a theater and acting in a movie, it is important to keep in mind that the setting of a speech will affect how it should be delivered. Actions that powerfully convey emotions on the stage can look quite foolish behind the pulpit.

It is important for a speech to work well in all five of the following ways for it to succeed:

1. The speech must be logical, coherent, and effective, obeying all the rules of good communication.
2. The appropriate oratorical devices, like alliteration, rhetoric, and repetition, must be used properly.
3. The emotions of the speaker must carry the speech.
4. The actions of the speaker must be appropriate for the setting and the subject.
5. The speaker must enunciate and use his or her voice effectively.

These criteria apply whether the speaker is preaching a sermon, delivering a lecture, telling a story, or acting a part in a play.

At the most fundamental level of a speech is the quality of

the material being presented; therefore, before working on presentation, make sure that your material communicates effectively by adhering the general rules of good communication and the specific rules of the genre you've chosen, whether story, commentary, sermon, report, instruction, commercial, song, or comedy. Presentation before an audience is a flexible, powerful medium through which almost every genre can be communicated if the presenter is well prepared.

Of course, we make many speeches throughout our lives to our families, friends, and others that by their very nature need no preparation. We need not concern ourselves here with those, even though there are times when we can do better and some mental preparation would help.

There are many approaches to preparing a good public presentation of a sermon, story, or lecture. If you have a method that works for you, or if you have the God-given talent to be able to speak before a group without preparation, praise God and continue to use your method and talents to his honor and glory.

A friend of mine and a great preacher, the Reverend Everett L. Terry Fullam, came to our studio to record twelve radio sermons and astounded the audio engineer, who had recorded hundreds of preachers over the years, by delivering several sermons, one after the other, without notes, without mistakes, on time. The engineer asked Terry how he could preach so powerfully without notes. Terry said that his mother had been a speech teacher, and from the age of three each child in his family had been required to give logical, coherent talks of a specified length, at a moment's notice, on a subject selected by his mother. Terry is a great preacher, but he has been practicing his craft all his life. The more you practice, the better your public speaking, and the easier it will be for you to prepare. By the way, Terry's sermons led that engineer to the Lord.

At certain times in life, many of us have risen to an occasion and delivered a good, well-received public speech without any preparation. However, most of the time, for most of us, speaking well requires preparation and work. Even though the Holy

Spirit will empower us and witness through us, we are not excused from diligent preparation. We are called to humble ourselves, meditate on his Word, and run the race. Let's not stop short of the goal or fail to do our part.

As a group, Christians, excel at public speaking, especially preaching. Many Christians prepare constantly by studying the Bible, living our faith, studying other Christian speakers, proclaiming the Gospel to others, and participating in Christian education both as students and teachers—and those Christians who don't, should. At the yearly National Religious Broadcasters Convention, the number of good and even excellent speakers is overwhelming and enthralling. Also, as Christians, we have the example of our Lord:

Jesus was an oral communicator. He used the rich register of words, intonations, mnemonic forms (helps for memory), poetry, parables, and gestures which characterize oral communication. He also maintained the learning community of teacher and disciples, in which the communication of a message is embedded in communication between people. Above all, his whole life and teaching were marked by the most important characteristic and test of oral communication, namely the intimate relationship between the message and the messenger.[5]

Those of us who could use help in improving our public presentations can leave aside arguments about which is better preparation, the external, action-oriented English school of acting before an audience or the internal, emotive method approach brought to this country by Lee Strasberg. Instead, let's learn and apply the practical rules and techniques of good public speaking.

Preparing and Delivering your Speech

The following steps will walk you through preparing and delivering an effective speech. As with the previous media, the assumptions will guide you through the complete process of preparing an important public communication.

Review Your Choice.

In most cases, we are asked to speak to such-and-such a group on such-a-such a topic, and we often do so with a minimum of preparation.

Assume you have asked all the appropriate ascertainment questions and have decided that you can best reach your targeted audience through the medium of public speaking. Assume also that your communication is a commentary applying biblical principles to some facet of contemporary life. You have determined that public speaking allows you to work with your audience, helping them through discipling and cognitive development.

Obtain Access and Fund your Public Presentation.

If you have been asked to speak, or have a venue, and are being paid an honorarium, forget this step and go to the next section.

At first glance, it appears that access to auditoriums, churches, and schools does not present the same problems as access to radio and television stations. You have something to say. You have determined through thoughtful analysis that you have the talent and experience to speak on the subject to everyone's benefit. Therefore, it seems that all you have to do is announce your availability, and invitations to speak will pour into your mailbox. You might even call up the local auditorium, book it for a night, advertise, and present your communication to a full house of people who have been waiting for your message. Perhaps. God does work in mysterious and wonderful ways, and he may have an extraordinarily important message for you to deliver.

However, even if the doors open wide and audiences flock to hear you, you will have some important questions to ask:

Will your public speaking be self-supporting from ticket sales or audience donations?

Will your present employer (which might be yourself), church, or denomination finance your speaking engagements to improve public relations, sell a product or concept, or provide employee, institutional, or community education?

Will some person or group send you on the lecture circuit as a ministry or mission?

In most cases, crowds will not be knocking down your door, and invitations will not appear like magic in your mailbox. Rather, platforms and audiences will be available to you to the extent that you meet one or more of the following criteria:

Your reputation as a speaker has gained enough momentum to start opening doors.

An agent, you, or an institution such as your denomination or employer has effectively promoted your public speaking.

The felt needs of your audience, which may or may not be real, are often not those that need to be addressed. The felt needs are often symptoms of deeper, more relevant, spiritual needs. Most audiences feel they need money, financial security, love, better health, and success, when in fact they need God, need to study his Word written, and need to love others as themselves. To reach your audience, you may want to search out their felt need and address it to lean them into a better understanding of what God called you to communicate. Jesus used this method of first addressing a felt need (as in the case of the woman at the well and of Peter fishing) to lead his audience to a better understanding of a more important spiritual need (such as the need for living water and the need to come follow him and become fishers of men). Addressing a felt need to capture your audience's attention is a wise approach—as long as you avoid pandering to temptations.

If you want your public speaking engagements to be sponsored by an institution, the felt needs of that institution should be addressed. Most of my workshops, for instance, were sponsored by one denomination because of their felt need to improve their electronic communications so that they might grow in size and improve internal communications. Because of the perceived success of the so-called electronic church, learning how to use the electronic media was seen as a way to do this. The workshops addressed these needs as well as the deeper needs to learn how to communicate the Gospel and how to develop a deeper relationship with God.

Where your platforms have neither been set up by an institution nor been incorporated into an existing circuit, you or an agent will have to find and develop a speaking circuit. This will take time and require effective communication.

If you are not sponsored, underwritten, or supported by faith partners, you will have to charge for your appearances. Make sure that you take all your costs into consideration, including preparation time between engagements. Don't be hesitant to set a reasonable fee for your appearances, or a reasonable ticket price. If you have properly addressed a felt need of your targeted audience, then they will be willing to cover your cost; and if you are addressing a real spiritual need, then you will be worth your fee.

Prepare your Speech

Your speech must be logical, coherent, and effective, that is, it must obey all the rules of good communication. Thoroughly research the subject of your speech, study the word of God as it applies to your subject, and pray.

Next, taking into consideration the felt needs of your targeted audience and your answers to the relevant ascertainment questions, prepare your speech by consulting and following the fifteen basic steps of effective communicating in conjunction with and modified by the key principles of preparing your genre of communication (in this example, a commentary).

It is preferable to prepare in writing, even though you might like to outline your speeches, until the processes involved are second nature to you.

Your preparation should require at least four times as much time as the spoken length of your speech. If you speaking for one hour, prepare for at least four hours. As an actor, my father,

Robert Allen, invests hours of time to prepare for a thirty-second commercial. Discussing preparation for his role in *Starman*, Jeff Bridges noted:

> I have no trouble abandoning myself to a role. In a sense, I felt you can do whatever you want when you are playing the kind of role I have in "Starman." But at the same time, you should do research and know what you are playing. I mean, if I played a baseball player, I'd hang out with baseball players to find out what they're all about.
>
> Well you can't do that with a spaceman. . . . I had to make certain choices. I observed my children for one thing. I got a lot of ideas from them. They're 16 months and 3 years old. They have innocence and I see them losing it quickly. This was my hook for "Starman." I watched my children observe the world and learned how they react to it.
>
> I also observed some of my stranger friends. . . .
>
> I also did a lot of work with my video machine. . . . I did a lot of work in my living room, taping myself, going through different ways, imaging how it could be. I experimented, going too far in some cases, trying to be a little more subtle in others.
>
> Then I'd show the tape to John Carpenter [the film's director] and we'd talk about it.[6]

Your goal is to present the best speech possible—the more you prepare, the better your speech.

Add Oratorical Devices.

Once you have formulated your written draft in accordance with principles that apply to your genre, thoroughly revise it to conform to your own way of speaking, removing all stylistic traces of a written communication. Do this by reading your speech out loud to an objective audience, or videotape it, if possible. Ask your audience to tell when your speech becomes boring, is stilted, or sounds unnatural. Edit and revise your draft until it sounds like your own natural speech. You don't want to sound like you are reading a manuscript.

Adjust your draft so it sounds spontaneous, fresh, and alive with feeling when you deliver it. To do this, incorporate in it personal reflections, confessions, and references to your own past experiences. We are all sinners saved by God's grace, so let your audience know that you are one of them in as many ways as possible; include your suffering, struggles, and human failings. However, never fail to point out that you have repented and turned over a new leaf, by the grace of God.

Seed the body of your speech with your expressions and rhetoric. If possible, put all your verbs into the present tense. Address your audience directly with the word *you*, and include them with the word *we*. Leave room for off-the-cuff, ad-lib remarks.

Anti-rhetoric rhetoric will help you disarm your audience. Governor Mario Cuomo of New York used this device in the opening of his widely praised speech to the 1984 Democratic Convention: "Please allow me to skip the stories and the poetry and the temptation to deal in nice but vague rhetoric."[7] As G. K. Chesterton wrote: "The aim of a sculptor is to convince us that he is a sculptor; the aim of an orator is to convince us that he is not an orator."[8]

Add appropriate oratorical devices such as rhyme, alliteration, and repetition. These devices will give your speech a lyrical quality and help your audience to remember your key points. The dynamic preacher W. T. Walker developed a great sermon around the lyric "It's me, it's me, of Lord, standing in the need of prayer." With each repetition of this line from an old spiritual, he exposed our need for repentance, salvation, and love for our fellow sinner. The verse imprinted the message indelibly on the listener's mind, so that one left the sermon knowing that "It's me, it's me, or Lord, standing in the need of prayer."

Make sure your speech contains appropriate visual devices such as stories, images, parables, allegories, and metaphors. Like oratorical devices, these visual devices will help carry your message home to your audience by helping them to visualize and remember your key points.

Be sincere, even when you are being humorous. Your audience will know when you are insincere, haughty, or taking them for a ride. Preach to your audience, but don't dictate (unless you are engaging them in a physical or mental exercise). Ask your audience to do something because they want to be involved, but don't demand that they do what you want. Assume that you have many things in common with your audience, but do not presume that they think just the way you do.

Leave your audience with a vision that will stay with them and motivate them in the future. If possible, call upon God and pray for his blessings on you, your audience, and your message, which should be, or agree with, his message.

Learn your Speech.

Memorize your speech—learn it, say it—until it dies and comes to life again with a new freshness that it never had before.

You should be so familiar with your speech that when you speak to your audience it is as if you were composing your speech on the spot for the first time.

Concentration is the key. Concentrate on your speech. Meditate on your speech, the way an actor would concentrate on his or her lines until each word comes alive.

For you as speaker and for your audience:

"What nourishes us is not how much food we eat, but what we actually digest. Similarly, what matters is not how many biblical stories and teachings we hear and read, but how much of the message we remember and reflect on. Often we must live with a saying or story for a long time before it discloses its meaning to us.[9]

Build in your Emotions.

As you concentrate on your speech, translate each word, each line, into the appropriate emotion. If you are talking about Jesus' death, live it, feel it, call up an emotion for each step in his suffering and build in the joy felt by his disciples as he confronted them after his glorious resurrection.

The memory of emotions is the key to the craft of the actor. They associate each line with an appropriate emotion, a real emotion they have felt. It is these emotions that give life to the actor's delivery. The actor's emotions take the audience beyond words to experience the reality of events in the story. You can do the same thing by making a point of observing your own emotions, memorizing them, and recalling them at will. With practice, you will be able to consciously evoke your emotions.

As an exercise, concentrate as you wash your hands. Study every feeling you have. One or two hours later remember and recall exactly what you felt when you washed your hands. Feel the soap. Feel your wet hands. Don't actually wash your hands, but see if you can remember exactly what you felt at each moment.

As you prepare your speech, build in the appropriate emotions. The first emotion you want to feel is a sincere love for your audience. Recall an audience you love, who loved to listen to you—perhaps your family. Feel that exchange of love. Then take each thought, each sentence, in your speech and build into your conscious memory the concrete emotion that sentence brings to you, on top of the feeling of love for your audience.

Sometimes you will build several layers of memories into your speech. Each layer, each concrete emotion, will communicate to your audience exactly what you want your speech to communicate, undergirding the text of your speech. The basic emotion of love for your audience will capture their hearts, and the feelings you build into each line will carry your audience with you on your journey.

Build in your Actions.

Each of your actions during your speech should be appropriate for the setting and the subject. Therefore, just as you did with your emotions, translate your speech into those actions appropriate for each thought in your speech.

If you can practice in front of a videotape camera, do so. Remember to put your camera at a suitable distance to emulate the size of the room in which you will speak. You want your actions to be subtle and natural, yet communicate clearly to the member of your audience who is farthest away from you. Any action that cannot be seen by everyone in your audience is wasted.

Your actions should be restrained and never call attention to themselves. They should punctuate and assist your speech but not intrude on it. Never overact. It is better to do nothing than to do something distracting.

Be totally relaxed. Stand at ease, straight, balanced on both feet, loose, free to deliver your speech. Practice relaxing. Let every part of your body relax and become dead weight, while your mind continues to concentrate on your text. Do not slough, collapse, lean, or tilt your head unless that action is appropriate to illustrate your text.

Practice your Vocal Presentation.

You must enunciate and use your voice effectively. One key is to concentrate on pronouncing your consonants. The consonants define, carry, and propel each word. Try reading through your speech carefully pronouncing each consonant.

Also, visualize each word as you say it. If you are talking about Jesus, see him in the word *Jesus*. If you are talking about the wind, see it in the word *wind*.   Your voice should be clear, resonant, and distinct but not devoid of your own accent. You want to sound alive and real, not artificial. You want to appeal to everyman and everywoman as one of them, yet you need to be uniquely yourself in your speech.

Practice varying your pattern of inflection. There is nothing more deadly than a monotonous speaker. Don't put your audience to sleep; adapt your inflection to the meaning of your text.

Rehearse, Rehearse.

It would be hard to overemphasize rehearsing. Practice as much as you can. If you can practice in the place where you will speak, so much the better. Videotape yourself in action. Watch the tape and criticize yourself. Present your speech in front of a practice audience. Have them criticize you. Practice until your speech says what you want it to say, and more.

Present your Speech.

As you go to speak, pray and relax. Make sure that you have time to yourself before you speak. Remember that Jesus went off by himself as much as possible, given the constant demands of the crowd. Make sure that you are at ease, cared for, and at peace. Know where you are speaking, how you are going to get there, and when you have to leave to go there.

It is advisable not to eat for two or three hours before you speak; a full stomach will make you sluggish. If possible, exercise one or two hours before speaking, so that your body is free from any tension. Scream to let off steam. Let your body go limp. Shake out any tension. Take three deep breaths. Go out to speak with calm assurance that God will give you his peace and empower you. If you are lifting up his Name, the Name of Jesus, he will work through you to communicate to your audience.

Be aware of your audience. Love them. Greet them. Say hello to them. Pray with them. Listen to them. Respond to them. Make them your friends.

If possible, open with an impromptu comment, question, or humorous remark that directly relates you to your audience. Commend them. Mention their community or association. Forge a link between yourself and your audience. Reach out and touch them where they are.

If they begin to look perplexed, rephrase what you have just said and explain to them what you mean. You have prepared for this talk; you will do well, so deal with your audience as if you were in a conversation with a group of close friends. Your friends like you, so will your audience.

Do not talk down to your audience. Respect them enough to disagree with them in love and explain your case to them. Don't hide your point of view. Be yourself. Avoid baiting your audience in an attempt at a Socratic dialogue.

Allow time for questions. Address the questions asked directly. Don't put off any inquirer; it will reflect badly on you. If you can't answer a question, just say so and move on to the next. Don't allow one person to monopolize the time. Politely mention time constraints and the need to allow others time to ask questions. Keep control; you are the speaker.

Be sincere, honest, open, and vulnerable. Have fun and enjoy being with your audience. If possible, close in prayer.

Follow Up.

If you can, survey your audience. Ask them practical questions on how you can best present your material to help them. Find out how you can improve every aspect of your public speaking. If you respect your audience, they will treat you well and give you help improving your speech.

While your speech is fresh in your mind, revise it, and note how you can improve your presentation. Each time you speak you have a chance to build on what you learned the time before.

Speak in the way you speak best, and at the same time work to improve your public speaking.

Public speaking, preaching, acting, lecturing , and teaching are live media of communication. They all require an ability to communicate logically, naturally, and clearly, with feeling. At the most basic level, all live media require relaxation and concentration. These are the most exciting forms of communication because the communicator is face-to-face with his or her audience. With practice and attention to the basic principles of good public speaking, you can excel in these media.

As an exercise, you might prepare a speech following the steps set forth herein. Give that speech to an audience (or videotape it), and analyze how you can improve your public speaking. As Paul wrote to the Ephesians:

And pray also for me, that God will give me a message when I am ready to speak, so that I may speak boldly and make known the gospel's secret. For the sake of this gospel I am an ambassador, though now I am in prison. Pray that I may be bold in speaking about the gospel as I should. (Eph. 6:19–20, GNB)

11. What About the Print Media?

A direct line leads from the book printing activity of the Renaissance to the rise and expansion of the Reformation. When in 1512 the Augustinian monk Martin Luther was appointed as professor of biblical interpretation at Wittenberg, he could work with the printed Latin Bible and the Hebrew edition of the Old Testament. In wrestling for the right understanding and interpretation of the biblical texts he became a reformer

HANS-RUEDI WEBER

It's fun to reflect on the impact of Johann Gutenberg's use of movable type in 1436 or 1437 and his exquisite Mazarin Bible in 1455. It's interesting and unsettling to speculate on the impact of auditory media like radio, which Hitler used so effectively for propaganda, and audiocassettes, which the Ayatollah Khomeini used to help overthrow the shah of Iran. It is intriguing to ponder the impact of television, which exposed the horrors of war in Vietnam and subjects celebrities to microscopic public inspection. Now, articles are beginning to appear that ask the question, Will the Computer Replace God?[1]

No matter how important a particular medium appears in the shaping of history, it is not the medium that reforms or rebels; the medium is only a tool of human beings and the forces they worship. God reforms. Greed, tyranny, and other demons compel and entice people to rebel. The Chinese and the Koreans had movable-type printing two hundred years before Gutenberg, yet that medium did not bring about a spiritual reformation of their societies. Winston Churchill used radio to fire the flames of freedom and repulse Nazi aggression, but radio did not keep him from being voted out of office in July of 1945, mere moments after the victory he helped to engineer.

Print is a respected part of our society, especially among the intelligentsia. Sometimes we long for yesterday when print was the primary medium of communication, and a few of us look with disgust at the "new" media like radio and, of course, television. Yet there was a time when print was seen as a threat to civilization because it helped to disseminate ideas to people who previously had been excluded from the ranks of the learned, as Shakespeare notes in *Henry VI, Part II:*

Thou hast most traitorously corrupted the youth of the realm in erecting a grammar-school: and whereas, before, our forefathers had no other books but the score and the tally, thou hast caused printing to be used; and, contrary to the king, his crown, and dignity, thou hast built a paper-mill. (Act IV, scene 7)

How was the king to control the spread of seditious ideas when they were rapidly being printed in quantity on new printing presses and circulated to a populace being taught to read in grammar schools? He couldn't. Representative democracy grew in power as the king's power waned, and we learned to respect the power of print to educate.

Print is now one of the building blocks of education, our culture, and even our communication through other, nonprint media. The script, printed and distributed to many people from the financier to the technical crew, is fundamental to producing a film or television program and productions in most of the new electronic media. Print is so pervasive and varied in its forms—from a notice duplicated in a copying machine to an embossed special edition—that it would appear impossible to find principles that apply to all its different forms.

In fact, in one sense, there are no principles that apply to all print communications, and if there were, someone would break them. there are, however, broad principles, keys, and hints that apply to most print communications and that can help improve their effectiveness. Watching our children, I am impressed at how easily they learn a new rule of grammar and how quickly they use it. The basic principles of communication, the key principles of a particular genre, and typographic principles will all help you improve, even if you decide for good reason not to follow them. Learn those principles, make them your own, and modify them to suit your own work.

There are many forms of print, and once you have decided on the one you will use, study it to see what unique principles of typography and usage pertain. For illustrative purposes, we will focus here on a common form of Christian print communication, the newsletter or bulletin. Newsletters have been called "the fastest growing area of journalism."[2] Recently at a religious convention I observed two people wrestling over where to put a picture on a newsletter. Newsletters appear everywhere, especially in my mailbox, from all types of organizations—most seeking money—in all imaginable styles. I have spent thousands of dollars for art work to produce a sophisticated newsletter, and I have sent out a simple letter on letterhead, but principles such as neatness, composition, and clarity pertain to both.

If you are reporting, follow the basic principles of communication and the principles that govern the genre of the report. If you want a commentary in your newsletter, write one, observing the relevant rules. Whatever genre you use, keep your writing simple, clear, concise, and in your own voice. As David Lambuth said so clearly in *The Golden Book on Writing*:

Good writing . . . comes only from clear thinking, set down in simple and natural speech, and *afterwards* revised in accordance with good usage. . . .
Use your eyes and ears. Think. Read . . . read . . . and still read. And then, when you have found your idea, don't be afraid of it . . . ; write it down as nearly as possible as you would express it in speech; swiftly, un-selfconsciously, without stopping to think about the form of it at all. Revise it afterwards—but only afterwards. To stop and think about the form in mid-career, while the idea is in motion, is like throwing out your clutch half-way up a hill and having to start in low again. You never get back your old momentum.

After all, good writing is like good social usage. It is learned by constant association with those who practice it, and it must be instinctive and un-selfconscious before it is of the slightest value. That is why you can learn to write well only by reading well.[3]

Professor Lambuth's book is a must for anyone who wants to write well. After thoroughly disparaging the notion that one can write by rules, he sets forth clearly and briefly the principles of good writing. Read it if you haven't done so, for it will become one of your most treasured books.

Even though you must write in your own voice, you will want to observe the basic rules of grammar and spelling; if you don't, you won't have an audience. Struggle to read a letter written by a small child, and you will appreciate the rules of grammar, spelling, and style. Observe and learn the appropriate principles so well that they become part of you— serviceable tools. Here are the steps for publishing a newsletter, illustrating some of the principles relevant to the print media:

Publishing your Newsletter

The following steps will walk you through preparing a successful newsletter. If you know everything you need to know about print, and about newsletters, then you may want to skip ahead to the next chapter. If your newsletters accomplish what you want them to accomplish, you may not need this advice. However, if you want to improve the effectiveness of your communication, then these steps should prove helpful to you.

Review your Choice.

Like public speaking, publishing a newsletter often seems to just happen. Sometimes newsletters are inherited from previous administrations. Sometimes we start writing letters and they turn into newsletters. Often these unplanned newsletters get the better of us by stealing our time, not achieving our goals, or locking us into a "look" and/or direction we don't like but perpetuate because of simple inertia. Perhaps the printer is not doing a good job, but it is hard to break off relations. Maybe the art director has fallen into an old-fashioned style but is donating time so it's hard to discuss the problem with him or her. Perhaps the editor is charging too much but is a close friend. Maybe new technology would cut costs and improve appearance, but you feel trapped in the old technology.

If you publish a newsletter that seems out of control, the sooner you stop, step back, and review why are you publishing it, the better. If you are not publishing a newsletter, but are considering it, take the time to ask all the appropriate ascertainment questions so that you start off on the right foot.

Your target audience is one of the key indicators. If your audience is small, a slick newsletter may be overkill. The minimum for bulk mail is two hundred addressees. If you have fewer than two hundred people in your audience, a simple letter might do the job.

Too many people in your audience can also be a problem. At the Episcopal Radio-TV Foundation, we mailed the newsletter to supporters, friends, and all the clergy in the denomination, about thirty-five thousand people, as a part of our ministry. Each mailing cost us around six thousand dollars and required several days of time from an art director, an artist, an editor, writers, two secretaries, and myself, as president, as well as the typographer, photographer, printer, and mailing service. Because of the size of the mailing list and the cost, we sent the newsletter out quarterly. Responding donors barely covered the newsletter's costs.

To raise money effectively, a newsletter should go out once a month, with some extra, special editions scattered throughout the year. The total number of newsletters per year should be between twelve and seventeen. This frequency considerably increases the number of donors and the size of their donations. (Not only do mailing services attest to this, but it is our company's [Good News Communications, Inc.] experience as well.)

The Episcopal Radio-TV Foundation's newsletter was trying to cover so many bases, from reporting the news to selling audiocassettes, that it was less effective than if it had been targeted on one area. The correct approach would have been to analyze our mailing list and divide it into different audience groups, each to receive its own newsletter. Perhaps an annual or semiannual mailing to all the audiences would report the full range of offerings and services of the foundation. Supporters would receive a monthly letter reporting the news and setting forth the vision. The audience for audiovisual materials would receive a quarterly update on new offerings. Those clergy who neither bought nor gave would receive the semiannual or annual overview of activities and offerings.

On the other hand, in the case of the Episcopal Radio-TV Foundation's newsletter, the motivation to minister to the entire mailing list far outweighed any financial considerations that would have suggested targeted mailings. It is important, however, to ask the right questions so that your decisions are informed and rational, rather than haphazard and wasteful.

To the questions stated in the previous chapters, you may want to add the following questions to shape the premise and form of your newsletter:

Who will fund your newsletter?

You? Your organization? Your audience?

Where does your mailing list come from?

Your friends and supporters will be most responsive to your mission, ministry, and appeals. If you use lists from a mailing list service, or from other organizations, you will have to make those lists your own over time. A rule of thumb is that from 2 to 4 percent of the people on the list will respond. Once you have located givers, they will continue to give if you care for them.

Unlike the media previously discussed, direct mail newsletters have no access problem—except the cost of mailing, acquiring of the appropriate lists, and the fact the some of your closest friends might tell you to stop sending them your newsletter.

Never use a list without permission to do so: Thou shall not steal.

Remember to purge your list frequently to remove people who are not interested. Also, keep constant track of address changes. This will be easy if you have a list of several hundred names, but when you get to several thousand names purging and correcting becomes a considerable task.

Assume that you have asked the right ascertainment questions, targeted your audience and determined that a monthly newsletter is the most appropriate and effective way for you to communicate what you need to communicate.

Recruit your Staff.

If you have a small mailing list and a simple newsletter, you may want to publish it yourself without the expense of a staff. Even volunteers cost money, time, energy, and space. The financial cost of volunteers is often buried in other costs; if you review the economic realities, you will discover that your volunteers do cost you money.

Of course, if you have a sizable mailing list, you will need help, and volunteers can save you money if trained, supervised, and nourished. Most newsletters require a core staff of two or three people:

An *editor/writer* prepares the written content of the newsletter.

An *art director* lays out the newsletter, including any art work.

An *assistant* or secretary may duplicate, sort, fold, and/or handle mailing of the newsletter.

As the format of your newsletter becomes more polished and your mailing list grows, you may want to add the following:

A *printer* and his or staff print the newsletter.

A *mailing service* mails the newsletter.

A *writer*, or writers, may supply articles and/or columns.

An *assistant art-director* handles mechanicals (the artwork laid out on a board, ready for the printer) and pasteup.

A *typographic house* or typesetter sets type.

A *photographer* takes pictures and develops them.

An *artist* prepares special art work, such as drawings.

A *computer operator* keeps track of the mailing list.

Many printers, even "quick copy" printers, have pasteup people who can help you with your layout and do the mechanicals. They charge an hourly rate or by the job.

Many positions can be filled by volunteers. In each case, count the cost of hiring someone to perform the necessary job, the quality required, and the cost savings of using a volunteer.

You may be well advised to hire a top-quality professional art director to lay out just your first newsletter and then use that layout as a model. If so, tell the art director what you intend; as a servant of our Lord, you do not want to take advantage of anyone.

Research and Solicit Articles.

To produce a weekly, monthly, quartely, or yearly publication, you need to do research, locate stories, study the word of God, and ask associates and friends to contribute stories and articles that relate to the purpose and premise of your newsletter. All research needs parameters and guidelines. Your statement of purpose, formulated as a premise, will guide your research and solicitation of articles. Without an overall purpose, your newsletter will be aimless.

The more focused your newsletter is, the more successful it will be in communicating with its audience. Research has shown that newsletters with clearly defined, precise, limited purposes are more effective in generating donor response than those that try to cover all bases. Even if you are not seeking donations, your newsletter is a chance to reach each person on your mailing list—formulate your purpose with each person in mind: Ask, What do I want my newsletter to do?

Do I want to discipline my audience?

Do I want to lift up Jesus?

Do I want to communicate good news?

Do I want to strengthen relationships?

Do I want to enhance knowledge?

Do I want to call my audience to repent?

The purpose of your newsletter should complement the purpose of your organization, ministry, or mission. It may be that you first need to refine and clarify the purpose of your organization, ministry, or mission. If so, do so, after seeking the will of God through prayer and Bible study.

When you have a premise, let your premise guide you in researching material and soliciting articles. Don't get sidetracked by every good idea that comes along. Be selective, by letting your purpose select for you. If your purpose is to make known what your church is doing, let it help you decide not to accept a great article on Sino-Soviet relations just written by your best friend.

You can use a wide range of genres in your newsletter: reports, perhaps a book review; commentaries; interviews; stories; instructions; commercial/advertisements; and even contests and games. However, each article should flow from your premise. Also, each article should have its own premise, which flows, in turn, from the premise of your newsletter.

Research is one of the keys to turning out an effective newsletter. If you are producing the newsletter for your parish, research stories about members of the congregation, look at the church calendar and find out what is going on, find out who needs prayers and who needs help, discover ways in which your church relates to and helps your community, and check, check, check, so that your newsletter is informative and accurate.

Prepare a Draft of your Newsletter.

To prepare your articles, you must know why and what you are writing. Plan each article by writing down your premise, collecting your research, listing your main points, outlining the proof of your premise, and drafting your article in accordance with the appropriate principles of good communication and the genre you have chosen.

Your audience needs to know where you are going, so tell them—up front. Also, tell them when you have arrived. Your audience will want a beginning, a middle, and an end; give it to them.

If you have others write stories, make sure they are clear about the purpose of your newsletter and the guidelines you have set for articles. If you ask a friend or an influential individual to write an article and you do not provide guidelines, you may find yourself embarrassed with an article that you can't use. To make sure that an article about someone is what you want, do the interview and write the article yourself or use a writer whose work is known to you.   Since stories are the most powerful genre, where possible, write stories. You may use stories to illustrate your work, mission, and ministry. You may want to write stories about your staff, helpers, or associates. Perhaps the telling of uplifting miracles and signs of God's presence in your life will further your premise. If you look and ask, there are more than enough stories to keep your newsletter going for a lifetime.

Use your own style, but be clear, concise, concrete, complete, convincing, and courteous. Be consistent in time and point of view. Try to use active verbs and common words whenever you can.

Sentences that lack the appropriate causal connections can say too little and destroy the logic of an article. This problem is now confronting many textbooks, which have been so simplified to reach poor readers that they have lost their internal logic.

Where possible, keep sentences and paragraphs short. Don't

use too many adjectives and adverbs, but remember that prepositional phrases make your writing specific. Adjectives often pronounce your judgment that so-and-so is beautiful, intelligent, kind, or whatever adjective you have used. Such judgments can alienate your audience, so it is often preferable to describe rather than proclaim. When you use modifiers, remember to put them in their proper place.

Establish common ground with your reader. Using everyday language (not slang) and underlining your humanity and failings are two techniques that can help you do this.

Illustrate your article verbally with quotes, vignettes, and the other devices mentioned in the chapter on genres. However, use all such devices carefully and sparingly; you want your newsletter to be brief.

Set forth your needs in a positive, straightforward manner. Repeat key points, but don't be verbose. Most of your audience will prefer short, succinct newsletters. Give them what they want, as long as you are not compromising the Gospel.

One of the most important things you can do is to allow time to set your draft aside long enough to gain a fresh perspective toward it.

Design and Lay Out your Newsletter.

The look of your newsletter is important even if it is a simple letter on letterhead. Make sure that your newsletter is readable and attractive.

Your masthead identifies you, your organization, and/or your work. On your letter, make sure that your organization's name, address, telephone number, corporate officers, trustees, and/or staff box are clear and distinctive. Do not include too much information in your masthead; you don't want your newsletter to be cluttered. Some experts say that your masthead should occupy one fourth to one third of your top page. It should look neat and clean when your newsletter is open. Your name, the newsletter's name, your logo, and/or your organization's name should be prominent.

Headings carry the titles for different sections of your newsletter. If typeset, they are usually set boldface, or larger. Keep your minor headings simple and well separated from the text of your articles by white space.

Be as conscious of white space as you are of the copy. White space divides and clarifies your text.

Don't hesitate to underline key words and thoughts, using italics or highlighting with boldface type. Readers like to be directed to the key ideas and points.

Using more than two type styles, however, can cause clutter and confusion. Also, try not to use too many colors; two are enough, and colors cost money.

Use visuals carefully and selectively in proportion to the type. Make sure that your visuals look good, are balanced, and are oriented properly when you fold the newsletter.

Symbols, drawings, and photographs can enhance a newsletter if used in moderations. All artwork must be sharp to reproduce well. You may want to start a file of artwork and photographs to use in future newsletters.

Lateral reversal effects, which I mentioned with regard to television, also affect the format and layout of a newsletter (although not to the same degree because the television viewer's eyes followthe scan line of the electron beam, exaggerating normal eye movement from left top to bottom right). Because of our eye movement, pictures and artwork look bigger and heavier in the bottom right corner of your paper. Solid visuals at the bottom of a page look less stable than solid visuals at the top because the viewer sees the bottom visual as something he or she is leaning over.

Make sure that bulk mailing and other necessary statements appear in the appropriate places and are easy to read. Segregate any schedule of events and lay it out with the convenience of the reader in mind.

Put the point that you want to emphasize most in a postscript (p.s.). After looking at the heading, your reader will next look at the postscript.

Experts say that there is a minimum and a maximum line length for optimum readability: a line of type should not exceed five or six inches or be less than three inches. The smaller the type you use, the shorter the line, as long as the line is not too short for the type.

Edit and Revise

After doing an initial layout of your newsletter, take time to look over both layout and copy very carefully for inconsistencies, inaccuracies, obscurity, damaging comments, negativism, typographical errors, spelling, grammar, composition, style, clutter, confusion, logic—every tiny detail. Your newsletter represents you; make sure it is exactly what you want. Strike any dead language, excess artwork, superfluous material, and anything that detracts from your premise. Negative and ambivalent language like "could have," "if we had," and "might be able to" should be deleted in most cases.

Decide on the Final Layout and Paste Up your Newsletter.

This is your chance to get it right, so make sure your newsletter works before printing or duplicating it.

Print.

Give the printer, duplicator, or copier exactly what they need to give you the final product you want. If you mimeograph your newsletter, you need to type it on special stencils. The usual "quick copy" process uses paper plates made from your camera-ready originals. For the best resolution, use a printer who prepares metal pates and strips-in photographs and line drawings.

For an inexpensive two-color newsletter, you can have your masthead printed in one color and then run each newsletter on that printed masthead paper.

There is an economy of scale with regard to printing: the larger the run, the less the cost per copy, because the costs of preparation, making the plates, and mixing the ink.

You will want to use good quality paper with good texture and weight. If your paper is too thin, the ink may bleed through the paper. If your paper is too thick, the ink may smear. Make sure that your ink and paper marry well. Of course, how your newsletter is printed will make a difference.

If you are making a self-mailer, you will need a heavier paper stock so that it can go through the mail.

Your printer, paper company, or art director will help you choose paper. Tests have shown that people react differently to different paper texture and color. According to one study:

white textured stock used for fund-raising mail produced more donations (in numbers and actual dollars) than fund-raising mail printed on *white offset stock*.

Ivory text and cover used for an entire lead-produced mailing package produced more responses than the package printed on *white offset and index stock*.

Gray textured cover used for order forms produced more sales than order forms printed on *white index stock.*

The use of *blue textured cover stock* for the questionnaire portion of a survey directed to the health care market produced a higher percentage of answers per thousand questionnaires mailed than did the same questionnaire printed on *white index stock.*[4]

Mail your Newsletter.

Mail it yourself if you have a small mailing list. Or employ volunteers or use a mailing service. But be careful that your newsletter goes out to the right people with the right postage in the right configuration. Be sure to follow post office bulk mail regulations carefully. If your newsletter needs to be packaged with return envelopes, make sure the right envelopes go out with the right letter. Anyone who has done a newsletter has stories about letters that didn't make it or didn't include the right envelope. These are learning experiences that, with more care, could have been avoided.

Solicit Feedback.

Feedback from your readers is your key to the future. Seek their advice and follow it when appropriate.

If you are not now publishing a newsletter, try a test run to some acquaintances and see how all the pieces fit together. Direct mail is a very powerful means of communication. Some people claim that it is responsibile for the rebirth of the evangelical movement in the United States. Be that as it may, use direct mail wisely, and it will help you further your mission and ministry.

Conclusion: What Does God Want Me to Say?

He who listens to you listens to me; he who rejects you rejects me; but he who rejects me rejects him who sent me.

LUKE 10:16

Knowing God, knowing his presence and power, standing face-to-face in awe of him, if only for an instant, fills us with the need and the desire to communicate what he wants us to communicate. That experience of him through faith, through his word written, through his Holy Spirit, makes us his ambassadors, destined to communicate him in word and deed. From the moment we accept his salvation and his lordship over our lives, we are his official messengers, sent to officially represent his Truth to all the kingdoms of the world. As Jesus said before his ascension, "But you will receive power when the Holy Spirit comes on you; and you will be my witnesses in Jerusalem, and in all Judea and Sumaria, and to the ends of the earth" (Acts 1:8).

We "will be" his witnesses; it is a necessary consequence of our being his people, filled with his power by his Holy Spirit. Like all witnesses, we attest to a fact and an event of which we have personal knowledge, the great news of the resurrection and lordship of Jesus Christ. According to Jesus, testifying to him is not a choice, an alternative, or a probability. It is a joyous aspect of our enthusiastic love for him, exceeding in intensity our desire to tell others about our other loves: our families, our friends, or our favorite pastime. There is no alternative: you and I "will be" his witnesses. As Jesus says to his disciples after washing their feet, "When the Counselor comes, whom I will send to you from the Father, the Spirit of truth who goes out from the Father, he will testify about me; but you also must testify, for you have been with me from the beginning" (John 15:26–27). Then, after praying for himself and his disciples, Jesus prays to his Father for all believers: "I pray also for those who will believe in me through their message, that all of them may be one, Father, just as you are in me and I am in you. May they also be in us so that the world may believe that you have sent me" (John 17:20–21). Believing and being united with him, we want the world to believe and share in his blessings. What is the message? To what or whom are we to testify? What does God want us to communicate?

He wants us to communicate him, God—Father, Son, and Holy Spirit—his lordship, his Salvation, his Son, Jesus Christ:

For this reason God raised him to the highest place above and gave him the name which is greater than any other name.

And so, in honor of the name of Jesus all beings in heaven, on earth, and in the world below will fall on their knees, and will openly proclaim Jesus Christ is Lord.

[And, in conclusion, Paul tells why God wants us to communicate Jesus:] to the glory of God the Father. (Phil. 2:9–11, GNB)

The simple, straightforward reason for history, for our creation in his image, for our salvation effected for us by Christ, and for our communication of his Gospel, is to glorify God:

If anyone speaks, he should do it as one speaking the very words of God. If anyone serves, he should do it with the strength God provides, so that in all things God may be praised through Jesus Christ. To him be the glory and the power for ever and ever. Amen. (1 Pet. 4:11)

His plan for our lives and his reason for rescuing us from righteous judgment, death, and eternal damnation derives from his pleasure and purpose, which is simply to be with us, walk with us, talk with us, and give us life eternal so that he may be praised and glorified:

Let us give thanks to the God and Father of our Lord Jesus Christ! For in union with Christ he has blessed us by giving us every spiritual blessing in the heavenly world. Even before the world was made, God had already chosen us to be his through our union with Christ, so that we would be holy and without fault before him.

Because of his love God had already decided that through Jesus Christ he would make us his sons—this was his pleasure and purpose. Let us praise God for his glorious grace, for the free gift he gave us in his dear Son! For by the death of Christ we are set free, that is, our sins are forgiven. How great is the grace of God, which he gave to us in such large measure!

In all his wisdom and insight God did what he purposed, and made known to us the secret plan he had already decided to complete by means of Christ. This plan, which God will complete when the time is right, is to bring all creation together, everything in heaven and on earth, with Christ as head.

All things are done according to God's plan and decision; and God chose us to be his own people in union with Christ because of his own purpose, based on what he had decided from the very beginning. Let us then who were the first to hope in Christ, praise God's glory.

And you also became God's people when you heard the true message, the Good News that brought you salvation. You believed in Christ, and God put his stamp of ownership on you by giving you the Holy Spirit he had promised. The Spirit is the guarantee that we shall receive what God has promised his people, and this assures us that God will give complete freedom to those who are his. Let us praise his glory! (Eph. 1:3–14, GNB)

Sometimes it is hard for us to completely appreciate the fact that the Gospel is God-centered, not self-centered. Often, we first look at what God can do for *me* as an individual to get *me* out of the mess *I* am in or to improve *my* life, by redeeming *me*, blessing *me*, and providing for *me*—all of which God promises and gives *me* in Christ, for he is the answer. Then, when it becomes clear that there is a larger problem, the fallen state of our world, we look to God to change others so our lives will improve and we will be able to live together in his kingdom here and now. Finally, as he sanctifies and glorifies us, we realize that the focal point of the Good News is God himself, that the problem is sin, just estrangement from our Creator, with whom we were created to be in community, and that turning our attention to him, by the power of his grace, brings life eternal.

One can see this process of spiritual maturation in rearing children. At first, our eldest son would condescend to say *please* when it was made perfectly clear to him by his parents that he was not going to get what he wanted until he did so and showed some consideration for the giver rather than just demanding what he wanted. Next he moved on to using *please* to manipulate, reasoning that it would make his parents change their response, and often it did. This *please*, and the subsequent *thank you*, sounded nicer but still fell far short of respect for the rights of the giver, since this *please* manifested the unmistakable tone of manipulative self-interest. Finally, *please* and *thank you* started to become expressions of appreciation and love—love that transformed his character from selfishness to gracefulness of a maturing young person. Our will for him is that he becomes what he has the potential to become: a loving, caring, and giving person. His maturation glorifies us as parents and blesses him by making him a blessing to others.

Just as my wife and I ask our son to say *please* and *thank you*, God calls us to glorify and appreciate him: "Be joyful always; pray continually; give thanks in all circumstances, for this is God's will for you in Christ Jesus" (1 Thess. 5:16–18). In thanking, praising, and glorifying him, we ourselves are transformed into what he meant us to be, co-heirs of his kingdom, in communion with him, expressing love toward him and our neighbors, worthy communicators of his truth.

When we communicate, thank, and praise him, we are called to be transparent, so clearly focused on him by the power of his Spirit that those around us see him in us. In this way, we become truly ourselves, truly what he meant us to be, his heirs. As we love, respect, and appreciate the Giver, we grow by leaps and bounds. When we focus instead on his gift of new life and our rights as heirs, we stop growing spiritually.

The appropriate word here is *agape*, one of the many words for love in Greek.* *Agape* is selfless giving, love so oriented toward others that the lover takes no thought for self. *Agape* is Jesus' death on the cross to save you and me—and even his worst enemies—from the wrath of judgment.

To communicate what God wants us to, Jesus and his salvation, we must allow him to reconstruct us in his image. When a building is being rebuilt and improved, there are times when the dust, the materials, and the exposed guts of what needs to be replaced look worse than before reconstruction started. At those moments, when decay is being stripped away, it may appear better to tear the building down and start from scratch. However, when the reconstruction is finished, it becomes clear that the temporary state of disrepair was absolutely necessary and worthwhile.

The same holds true for our lives. While God is stripping away the rotten materials, we often question the process. But when we perceive the new person that he is making each of us, we rejoice in his grace. As we glimpse the new self, we see that the cost to us is temporary, whereas the cost to God was the life of his son, whom he raised to new life to reconstruct us. In the same way, the cost to a child of being brought up well is the acceptance of discipline in the midst of having all their needs met; the cost to the parents is hard work and selfless giving, preparing the child to leave home as an independent person.

Because of our new life in him, we joyously communicate him and his salvation. Because he is reconstructing us in his

---

* There are many words in Greek that stand for "love" or "to love"; however, there are four primary words, which form the basis of studies such as C. S. Lewis's excellent book, *The Four Loves* (New York: Harcourt, Brace, Jovanovich, 1960).

image, we will witness to him in word and deed. Because he is the Lord of our life and we are his ambassadors, we must strive to proclaim him and his gospel more effectively. It is as his ambassadors, under his lordship, that we are called to excellence in our communications. As Paul said, each of us must strive

to win the prize for which Christ Jesus has already won me to himself. Of course, my brothers, I really do not think that I have already won it; the one thing I do, however, is to forget what is behind me and do my best to reach what is ahead. So I run straight toward the goal in order to win the prize, which is God's call through Christ Jesus to the life above. (Phil. 3:12–14, GNB)

A few years ago a runner in the New York City marathon slipped from the pack and took the subway to the station nearest the finish. At first, it appeared that she had won in record time; then someone recognized her as having been on the subway. How often we deceive ourselves into thinking that we can take a shortcut, only to be caught and lose the prize! Quality in our communication of him and his truth means that we dedicate ourselves to running to the finish line and avoiding shortcuts on the way.

Our communications, no matter what genre or medium, must be as carefully executed as the best nonreligious communication. Because he is our standard of excellence, what we create should reflect the highest quality of work, Christian or otherwise. Yet how often do we look at Christian films and television programs and wince at the lack of quality, or get bored but excuse the mediocrity because it adheres to our theological perspective?

Do we think that we can step out of the pack and ride the Holy Spirit to the finish? In a way, we can, but not by impatiently jumping the gun or by cutting corners. To win the prize, we must follow the rules and run the race, and by the very act of doing so, we "shall run, and not be weary" (Isa. 40:31) because his Spirit will empower us.

The very first step in running the race is for us to wait upon the Lord for the gun to sound. Not only should we wait, going over the course in our minds, counting the cost and reviewing our strategy, like any good runner, but we also wait for God to give us the opportunity, the message, and the boldness to communicate, as Paul notes in his Letter to Ephesians (6:19–20). In our waiting, the Lord shall renew our strength by filling us with his Spirit, so when he gives us the signal to run, we "shall mount up with wings as eagles" (Isa. 40:31), soar ahead of the pack, and ride the power of the Holy Spirit to the finish.

Waiting for the Lord is an active process in which we allow him by faith to rebuild and spiritually circumcise us, cutting away the excess spiritual flesh around our hearts so that we are personally and privately marked as his people, capable of proclaiming his truth. This spiritual circumcision is not our doing but his, as Paul notes: "In union with Christ you were circumcised, not with the circumcision that is made by men, but with the circumcision made by Christ, which consists of being freed from the power of this sinful self" (Col. 2:11, GNB). This circumcision of our hearts "is the work of God's Spirit, not of the written Law" so that we receive "praise from God, not from man" (Rom. 2:29, GNB).

We can be the best communicators in the world, but until we allow his Spirit to work in our hearts, cutting away our sinful selves and filling us with him, our work will be empty, hollow, and spiritually dead. Allowing God to operate on us brings pain, but it ends in glory: "And the God of all grace, who called you to his eternal glory in Christ, after you have suffered a little while, will himself restore you and make you strong firm and steadfast" (1 Pet. 5:10). Therefore, we rejoice that he shapes us and disciplines us "because the Lord disciplines those he loves, as a Father the son he delights in" (Prov. 3:12). Furthermore, God "comforts us in all our troubles, so that we can comfort those in any trouble with the comfort we ourselves have received from God. For just as the suffering of Christ flows over into our lives, so also through Christ our comfort overflows" (2 Cor. 1:4–5).

Waiting for God does not mean ignoring his mandate to preach the Gospel, informing our fellow Christians that we can't witness until the gun goes off. For the starting gun sounds the instant we are filled by faith with his Spirit and are presented with the opportunity to make him known to someone who does not know him. Just as we must not jump the gun, so we must not miss it by lingering at the starting line. We must always be on watch, actively aware of the opportunities he gives us: "Do you not say, 'Four months more and then the harvest'? I tell you, open your eyes and look at the fields! They are ripe for the harvest" (John 4:35).

Some of these opportunities demand only that we "gossip" the Gospel, telling others in conversation about our faith and experience of his presence. Other opportunities arise because we are actively involved in following him, praying, and seeking his opportunities to witness through the appropriate medium and genre. As Paul tells us, "Make good use of every opportunity you have, because these are evil days. Don't be fools then, but try to find out what the Lord wants you to do" (Eph. 5:16–17, GNB).

Sometimes we do not even linger at the starting line but hide in the parish hall amongst our friends. As the writer of Hebrews says:

There is much we have to say about this matter, but it is hard to explain to you, because you are so slow to understand. There has been enough time for you to be teachers—yet you still need someone to teach you the first lessons of God's message. . . .
    Let us go forward! And this is what we will do if God allows. (Heb. 5:11–12; 6:3, GNB)

The problem with hanging around the parish hall with our Christian friends is that God just might kick us out. Jesus told his followers to go to Judea, Samaria, and the ends of the earth once they were filled with power by the Holy Spirit (Acts 1:8); they were filled with power on Pentecost but did not go to Judea and Samaria. They stayed in Jerusalem and went daily to the Temple. Then Stephen was stoned, and "that very day the church in Jerusalem began to suffer cruel persecution. All the believers, except the apostles, were scattered throughout the provinces of Judea and Samaria" (Acts 8:2, GNB). Soon thereafter, Saul was miraculously converted on his way to Damascus to persecute believers. Saul's conversion is a dramatic act of God, but why didn't God convert Saul before Stephen was stoned? or before the persecution of the believers started?

If Saul had been converted sooner, he might have been able to stop the persecution, the stoning, and the scattering of the believers. However, if he had stopped the persecution, would the believers have left the Temple (which was defunct anyway because the believers were now the Temple of God's Holy Spirit)? Would the believers have lingered in Jerusalem, ignoring Jesus' command?

Of course, as the Reverend John Howe, who first postulated this hypothesis, notes, this line of reasoning is pure speculation. Jesus had told the believers to testify first in Jerusalem, and they were doing his work when the persecution broke out. Furthermore, God disciplines us, but he is not the author of the evil desires that tempt us to sin, although God can and will bring good out of our disobedience, so that his will, will be done. Being forced out of Jerusalem, the believers fulfilled God's call to testify in Judea, Samaria, and to the ends of the earth. However, God may decide not to bring faithfulness out of our disobedience; rather, he may make us take another lap around the Sinai, or we may find ourselves wrestling with him, until our hip is thrown out of joint and we limp away, living testimonies to his power.

In any event, God calls to us, whether we are hiding in the fellowship hall, or in our garden: "You who dwell in the gardens with friends in attendance, let me hear your voice" (Song of Songs 8:11). He wants to hear our voices outside of our own gardens. He calls to us to speak up. He calls us out of hiding to the starting line, where he fires the gun and we are off running to win the prize of eternal life with him in his garden in his kingdom.

This is not to say that we do not need fellowship, we do. God has called us "into fellowship with his Son Jesus Christ" (1 Cor. 1:9). We are called to be the church of God, "holy, together with all those everywhere who call on the name of our Lord Jesus Christ" (1 Cor. 1:2). We are one body, the body of Christ, and cannot function apart from the Body, which is all the believers. It is in the Body that we are nourished, supported, and sustained during the grueling race he calls us to run.

Not only does the local church provide essential fellowship, but also professional groups, Bible study groups, and others nourish and sustain Christian communicators. In New York City there is the New York Arts Group (NYAG), which gives Christians in the arts and communication refuge and support. Broadway actors and actresses, dancers, singers, writers, artists, and others in NYAG subgroups can discuss the problems they face, vent frustrations, confess failings, and work through the decisions confronting them with other believers who are sensitive to the unique forces in their professions and committed to a biblical faith. The fellowship of believers in NYAG can relate to problems facing those in these professions that quite often the local parish cannot. Furthermore, NYAG has proved to be a vehicle for evangelism, strengthening the faith of the members and giving them courage to witness to the people with whom they work. There are many other fellowship groups around the country that have a similar purpose and ministry, such as the Fellowship of Christians in the Arts, Media, and Entertainment on the West Coast and the Fellowship of Companies for Christ that ministers to corporate chief executive officers.

The fellowship of his Church provides us with rest stops along the route of the race and between laps, for Jesus continues to send us out into the world to testify to him, just as he sent the Twelve, the seventy-two, and all the believers with these words:

All authority in heaven and on earth has been given to me. Therefore go and make disciples of all nations, baptizing them in the name of the Father and of the Son and of the Holy Spirit, and teaching them to obey everything I have commanded you. And surely I will be with you always, to the very end of the age. (Matt. 28:18 ff)

Of course, as part of his Body, we never leave the fellowship of the Church even in the farthest mission field, for he is with us. However, throughout the Book of Acts God is uprooting believers, scattering churches, and even splitting up teams of itinerant evangelists, so that his word can be proclaimed to the ends of the earth. Often, three years is mentioned as the maximum time for an evangelist in the Book of Acts to stay in one particular local church. We should not be surprised if we ourselves are uprooted from the comforts of our communities.

We need to learn and obey the rules of the race that can be found in his Bible. If we submit to him, he will write these rules on our hearts by the power of his Spirit. As God told the prophet Jeremiah: "I will put my law within them and write it on their hearts. I will be their God, and they will be my people" (Jer. 31:33, GNB). Submission to his authority is the key to running the race successfully. As James tells us, "So then, submit yourselves to God. Resist the Devil and he will run away from you. Come near to God, and he will come near to you. . . . Humble yourselves before the lord and he will lift you up" (James 4:7–8, 10, GNB).

It must not be forgotten, however, that running the race is often exhilarating. When we do well, we can be overcome by pride in our accomplishments and end up running toward the wrong goal. It is at these moments we must "beware the yeast of the Pharisees" (Matt. 16:5), those false doctrines that cause us to put our faith in ourselves. When our presentations are well received, when we are being courted by politicians and prospering as communicators of his truth, we must humble ourselves and give credit to him before we are swept along by the crowd and turned from proclaiming him to selling a watered-down version of his Gospel for our own self-aggrandizement. As Peter says, "In their greed, these teachers will exploit you with stories they have made up. Their condemnation has long been hanging over them" (2 Pet. 2:3).

The problem is the strong appeal of recognition and approval, which can lead to us being taken "captive through hollow and deceptive philosophy, which depends on human tradition and the basic principles of this world rather than on Christ" (Col. 2:8). However, "whoever wants to be the world's friend makes himself God's enemy" (James 4:4).

The longer we run the race, the more we understand how easy it is to fall into hypocrisy by taking too seriously the approval of the crowd. Often, it is when the crowd is least enamored of our work for his sake that we are best succeeding. As Jesus has told us,

If the world hates you, keep in mind that it hated me first. If you belonged to the world, it would love you as its own. As it is, you do not belong to the world, but I have chosen you out of the world. That is why the world hates you. (John 15:18–19)

If we are not careful to keep him in focus, our striving for excellence can turn us from our goal of proclaiming him, but if we love him, he will keep us on course. For example, several years ago, our company produced a nationwide teleconference on aging that was broadcast by satellite to over four thousand people at fifty-nine locations around the United States. We worked very hard to make sure that the quality of the program was excellent. With our client, we asked the right ascertainment questions and applied the answers and the principles of the genre and medium we chose. We produced the teleconference at the most modern video production studio in New York City. The teleconference was scheduled so that one hour of satellite-casting of the views of experts from the New York City studio would alternate with one hour of local disussion for a period of six hours. We were in production and on the satellite for a total of three hours, with local discussion bracketing the on-air time.

After the first hour of telecasting, the engineers and the studio personnel praised the high quality of the production. I was proud because it was beautiful. However, as I was basking in self-satisfaction, a Christian friend of mine in television production said that she loved beautiful productions, but asked where the heart was, Jesus, since this production was for the Church.

I was convicted. Stepping to the side, I prayed to God to stop the production if it was not honoring him (thinking while I prayed that the production was for a church agency, $120,000 was being spent, and there was no way the production would stop).

Immediately, the power went off in the control room. The power in the studio stayed on, the circuits were okay. Con Edison was still in service, but the power in the control room, the brain, went off. All the computers, which had taken hours to program, were out. All the camera control units were dead. No power, no explanation. The engineers were desperate. The second airtime was fast approaching. I took our production team aside and prayed, "God, forgive me for the impertinent prayer. This is your production. Glorify your Name. Amen."

Ten minute had passed. Suddenly, the power came back on. Only thirty seconds of satellite time was lost. Color was perfect. Miraculously, the computer programs were intact. The next speaker preached Jesus and his Gospel. We thank him.

As we run, the good news we are called to preach to those along the way is that Jesus is Lord and Savior and his good news of "repentance and the forgiveness of sins" (Luke 24:47, GNB)—the great news that the drug addict, who has been told that he is trapped, can turn from drugs to Christ through the power of his Spirit; the good news that the malcontent can turn from a life of unhappiness to a new life in Christ; and the news that even the most self-centered among us can enter into a relationship of love and giving with the Son of God. This is good news, that we who stand condemned by our disobedience are set free by the Judge, if we accept his Love. Jesus' first message is, "Repent, for the kingdom of heaven is near" (matt. 4:17).

Repentance and forgiveness is Good News because it offers us a new opportunity at being who God created us to be, but we often preach repentance as if it were bad news and we, not God, stand in judgment. Paul puts it bluntly: "Or do you show contempt for the riches of his kindness, tolerance and patience, not realizing that God's kindness leads you to repentance?" (Rom. 2:4). Preaching repentance as if it were bad news rather than Good News often predisposes us to combative relationships that undermine the effectiveness of our message. To be able to turn from a life of alcoholism, a life of fear, or a life of greed, which can only lead to eternal damnation, to a life of freedom from the bonds of sin and self is great news that offers help to the helpless and hope to the hopeless. Unlike Jonah, we should long for the joyful repentance of the lost, tell them the Good News, and pray for God's patience and forgiveness for even the worst of our acquaintances, which just may be ourselves. As Jesus tells us, "There will be more joy in heaven over one sinner who repents than over ninety-nine respectable people who do not need to repent" (Luke 15:7).

One evening, as I was discussing the Gospel with a few followers of a Tibetan Buddhist monk, they informed me that according to their teacher, life was a cesspool and the best thing to do was to give up and drown in the filth to reach a state of nonbeing. As a Christian, I agreed that we lived in a fallen, sinful world, but the good news is that Jesus is offering us his hand to pull us out of the cesspool into a new world of light and life. There is no need to drown in hopelessness, for we have the opportunity to live in hope. The call to repentance is simply a call to turn around from looking at the filth, so that we can see his outstretched hand and grab hold of his offer of life eternal.

As we run the race, we exercise our commission to communicate him and thereby develop our spiritual stamina and strength, which is our ability to trust in him. The more we trust in him, the more courage we have to tell others about him, and the more we have to tell others. As Paul says:

God in his mercy has given us this work to do, and so we do not become discouraged. We put aside all secret and shameful deeds; we do not act with deceit, nor do we falsify the word of God. . . . For it is not ourselves we preach; we preach Jesus Christ as lord, and ourselves as servants for Jesus' sake. . . .

We are often troubled, but not crushed; sometimes in doubt, but never in despair; there are many enemies, but we are never without a friend; and though badly hurt at times, we are not destroyed. At all times we carry in our mortal bodies the death of Jesus, so that his life may also be seen in our bodies. . . .

The scripture says, "I spoke because I believed." In the same spirit of faith we also speak because we believe. We know that God who raised up the Lord Jesus to life, will also raise us up with Jesus and take us, together with you, into his presence. . . .

For this reason we never become discouraged. Even though our physical being is gradually decaying, yet our spiritual being is being renewed every day. (2 Cor. 4:1–2, 5, 8–10, 13–14, 16, GNB)

With every step we take in faith, we find that God is faithful, our faith grows, and we become better communicators of his Gospel. Not only does our growing strength, which is a gift from him, help us to deal with the blows of the Adversary and forgive the sins of others against us, but it also gives us the ability to repeat and refine our presentation of the Gospel. Robert Price, a political communicator commenting on how he would run the 1985 re-election campaign of New York City's Mayor Koch, notes: "I would promote that theme by repetition. I've always gone on the theory that only after you repeat it a hundred times will the public first begin to hear the message."[1] Paul concurs: "It is no trouble for me to write the same things to you again, and it is a safeguard for you" (Phil. 3:1).

However, no matter how well we communicate the Gospel, nor how many times we repeat it, it is his Holy Spirit who converts, not us. As the Reverend Michael Youssef is fond of pointing out, Christianity is not like Islam, in which the believer has to convert the nonbeliever in any way possible, including bribery, and, if unsuccessful, deal death to the nonbeliever. As Christians, we are blessed that the Holy Spirit teaches us what to say, convicts the world of sin, converts, and baptizes. But we also must testify, for we are his fellow workers.

Running the race to fulfill his call does not always mean to take off around the world looking for opportunities to proclaim the Gospel; rather, as we have discussed, he often calls us to witness where we are and tells us to "Occupy til I come" (Luke 19:13, KJV). In fact, we are called to occupy all areas of life, all professions, and all nations, and to make disciples of him everywhere. We are not to abandon the lost or the institutions of the world to the Adversary. Instead, we are to occupy and help him to redeem all of humanity.

We are not the only people with a mission. Many excellent communicators are proclaiming false gods, including sex, money, and even the forces of darkness. For example, George Lucas, talking about his successful films, notes: "*Raiders [of the Lost Ark]* will be the most action-oriented of the Indiana Jones movies—the others should deal more with the occult."[2] Ever since a miraculous recovery from a childhood injury, Lucas has had a mission to proclaim an occult Force. We have a mission to proclaim the Author of all creation, who entered his creation to give us the gift of eternal life in fellowship with him through the death and resurrection of his only begotten Son, Jesus the Christ. We should make movies and other communications at least as successful as, if not better than, the ones made by those who follow false gods.

We must wait upon him, pay for his guidance, seek the message he has for us to deliver to the audience of his choice, and when he sounds the gun to start, we must run the race to the finish line, victoriously celebrating with shouts of thanksgiving his victory over death.

We are his communicators. Let us glorify his Holy Name.

As the scripture says, "Everyone who calls out to the Lord for help will be saved."

But how can they call to him for help if they have not believed? And how can they believe if they have not heard the message? And how can they hear if the message is not proclaimed? And how can the message be proclaimed if the messengers are not sent out? As the scripture says, "How wonderful is the coming of messengers who bring good news!" But not all have accepted the Good News. Isaiah himself said, "Lord, who believed our message?" So then, faith comes from hearing the message, and the message comes through preaching Christ. (Rom. 10:13–17, GNB)

So whoever believes in the Son of God has this testimony in his own heart; but whosoever does not believe God, has made a liar of him, because he has not believed what God has said about his Son. The testimony is this: God has given us eternal life, and this life has its source in his Son. Whoever has the Son has this life; whoever does not have the Son of God does not have life. (I John 5:10–12, GNB)

Notes

CHAPTER 1

1. C. E. Swann, "The Electric Church," *Presbyterian Survey* (May 1980), pp. 9–16.
2. J. Pierce, "Don't Blame TV for Poor Attendance," *The Episcopalian*, vol. 149, no. 6 (June 1984), p. 1.
3. David Puttnam, "Chariots Begins at Home," *Hard Cash: How to Finance Independent Feature Films* (Los Angeles: Independent Feature Project, 1982), p. 1.
4. Johannes Heinrichs, "Theory of Practical Communication: A Christian Approach," *Journal of the World Association for Christian Communication*, vol. 28 (1981), p. 6.

CHAPTER 2

1. Stephan Minot, *Three Genres: The Writing of Fiction, Poetry, and Drama* (Englewood Cliffs, N.J.: Prentice-Hall, 1965), p. 11.
2. Examples abound throughout Church history, from Peter in Acts 2 through Dwight L. Moody to some of our contemporary television evangelists such as Oral Roberts. See Jeffrey K. Hadden and Charles E. Swann, *Prime Time Preachers* (Reading, Mass.: Addison-Wesley, 1981), esp. the chapter "The Video Vicarage."
3. John R. W. Scott, *Between Two Worlds: The Art of Preaching in the Twentieth Century* (Grand Rapids, Mich.: Eerdmans, 1982), p. 103.
4. Frank E. Gaebelein, "The Creator and Creativity," *Christianity Today*, October 1984, p. 38.
5. Michael Aeschliman, "Malcolm Muggeridge: A Comedian in the Circus of God's Grace," *The University Bookman*, Summer 1984, p. 108.
6. George Gerbner, "Television as Religion," *Media and Values*, no. 17 (Fall 1981), p. 1.
7. See Michael Sragow, "Raiders of the Lost Ark," *Rolling Stone*, June 25, 1981; and Woodrow Nichols, "Celluloid Prometheus: The Transcendentalism of George Lucas," *SCP Newsletter*, Winter 1984–85, pp. 9–10.
8. Norman Stone, "A Writer Pitched Headfirst into Hell,' " *New York Times Book Review*, October 28, 1984, p. 1.
9. Haing S. Ngor, quoted by Samuel G. Freedman, "In The Killing Fields,' a Cambodian Actor Relives His Nation's Ordeal," *New York Times*, October 28, 1984.

10. Umberto Eco, "How I Wrote The Name of the Rose,' " *New York Times Book Review*, October 14, 1984, p. 37.
11. Vincent Canby, "Truffaut: The Man Was Revealed Through His Art," *New York Times*, November 4, 1984, p. 37.
12. Les Brown, *Keeping Your Eye on Television* (New York: Pilgrim Press, 1979), pp. 7–8.
13. Ibid., p. 8.
14. Ibid., p. 16.
15. Joel Chaseman, in a speech at the Town Hall of California, Los Angeles, January 27, 1981.
16. "Fairness Struggle Taking Shape," *Broadcasting*, October 26, 1981, p. 42.
17. John Carman, "Violence on TV: A Network Survival Ploy?" *Atlanta Journal*, October 28, 1984.
18. W. Somerset Maugham, *Of Human Bondage* (London: Heineman, 1915; New York: Penguin Books, 1984), p. 248.
19. Canby, "Truffaut."
20. "Study: Determination More Vital Than Talent," *Atlanta Journal and Constitution*, February 17, 1985.

CHAPTER 3

1. Henrik Ibsen, quoted by Lajos Egri, *The Art of Dramatic Writing*, rev. ed. (New York: Simon & Shuster, 1960), p. 32.
2. The Marketing and Research Corporation of Princeton, New Jersey.
3. See Richard Nelson Bolles, Margaret Broadley, Doc Frohock, and Bernard Haldane.
4. I have drawn on the work of Doc Frohock and many other sources for these sample exercises.
5. Bernard Haldane, one of the pioneers in career counseling, in his book *Career Satisfaction and Success: A Guide to Job Freedom*, and Richard Bolles, in his book *What Color Is Your Parachute?* have set forth some very simple do-it-yourself guides, charts, and other tools to help you discern your motivational talents. I highly recommend these books if you are interested in in-depth career counseling or self-discovery.
6. Richard Bolles, *What Color Is Your Parachute?* (Berkeley, CA: Ten Speed Press, 1981.), p. 83.
7. Hal Lancaster, "Hey Fans! It Was Some Kinda Action, Real Barnburner!" *Wall Street Journal*, December 3, 1984.
8. The Reverend Robert D. Noble, *Spiritual Gifts* (St. John's Episcopal Church, 270 North Placer Avenue, Idaho Falls, Idaho 83401).

CHAPTER 4

1. George Gallup, "New Emphasis Needed in Religious TV," *Religious Broadcasting*, June 1984, p. 24.

2. See Harold Hostetler's article, "A Major Study Vindicates Religious Television," *Religious Broadcasting*, June 1984, p. 18.
3. *Wall Street Journal*, November 1, 1984.
4. "CBS Drops Movie Evaluation Plan After Leak," *Broadcasting*, August 9, 1982, p. 61.
5. Arthur Unger, "Television's Search for the Last Taboo," *Television Quarterly*, vol. 21, no. 2 (1984), p. 7.
6. John Koten, "To Grab Viewer's Attention, TV Ads Aim for the Eardrum," *Wall Street Journal*, January 26, 1984.
7. Julie Salamon, "Sex and Hollywood: Doing It More, Enjoying It Less," *Wall Street Journal*, December 11, 1984.
8. See "If God Held a Press Conference," *Christianity Today*, May 21, 1982, p. 12.
9. "Americans Taking More Interest in Religion, Poll Shows," Associated Press, September 19, 1983.
10. George W. Cornell, "Outer Space Movies: The Gospel According to Hollywood," *Atlanta Journal*, May 28, 1983. Note that *E.T.*, the *Star Wars* trilogy, and *Ghandi* do not have Christian themes.
12. " 'Highway to Heaven' Upholds Values," *NFD Journal* (November–December 1984).
13. Bill Abrams, "TV Advertisers Are No Longer Shunning Movies with Controversial Social Themes," *Wall Street Journal*, October 30, 1984.
14. Brown, *Keeping Your Eye on Television*, p. 23.
15. Walter Karp, "The Networks from Left to Right," *Channels* (April–May 1982), pp. 23–27, 56.
16. George Gallup, The Gallup Youth Survey," (Princeton, N.J.: December 17, 1980).
17. Janet Farrell and Michael Morgan, "Adolescent Program Preferences and Cultivation Patterns" (Paper delivered at the Conference on Culture and Communications, Temple University, Philadelphia, Penn., by the Annenberg School of Communications, University of Pennsylvania, 1981).

CHAPTER 5

1. Martha Bayles, ""A Passage Through India," *Wall Street Journal*, December 17, 1984.
2. John T. Malloy, *Dress for Success* (New York: Warner Books, 1976).
3. John Phelan, "Surfaces in the Mediaworld of Political Fashion," *Media Development*, vol. 31, (April 1984), p. 12.
4. Stewart M. Hoover, "Television and Viewer Attitudes About Work," (Annenberg School of Communications: April 19, 1981).
5. "Teaching the ABC's," *Channels*, April–May 1981, p. 10.
6. Mark Edmunson, "McLuhan: It's All Going According to Marshall's Plan," *Channels*, May–June 1984, p. 49.
7. Robert Coles, "What Harm to the Children?" *Channels*, June–July 1981, p. 31.
8. M. Megee, "Notes on the Significance of Crime Statistics: On Television:

(paper written at City University of New York, Hunter College, New York, 1980).

9. Reuven Frank, quoted by Alex S. Jones in "Sometimes, It Seems, the Camera Does Lie. Here's How," *New York Times*, February 17, 1985.
10. The Rober Organization, *Evolving Public Attitudes Toward Television and Other Mass Media 1959–1980* (New York: Television Information Office), pp. 4, 13–14.
11. Jerry Mander, *Four Arguments for Elimination of Television* (New York: William Morrow, 1970), pp. 250–54.
12. Granville Toogood Associates, 5 Salem Straits, Darien, Conn.
13. Egri, *Art of Dramatic Writing*, p. 263.
14. Ibid., p. 6.
15. The November 30, 1981, meeting of the North American Broadcast Section of the World Association for Christian Communication.
16. Charles F. Mullewtt, "From Dialects of Language, Rhetoric to Grammar: The Case for Coherence," *The University Bookman*, Winter 1984, pp. 45–54.
17. Mario Vargas Llosa, "Is Fiction the Art of Lying?" *New York Times Book Review*, October 7, 1984, p. 1, 40.

CHAPTER 6

1. George Gerbner, "Television as Religion," *Media & Values*, no. 17 (Fall 1981).
2. See Rene Wellek and Austin Warren, *Theory of Literature* (New York: Harcourt, Brace & World, 1956), pp. 226–37.
3. See Northrop Frye, *Anatomy of Criticism* (New York: Atheneum, 1968). From one point of view, our civilization's stories have gone from mythic to demonic.
4. Schopenhauer, quoted by Rudolf Flesch in *The Art of Readable Writing* (New York: Harper & Row, 1949), p. 46.
5. Jack Finney, *Time and Again*, (New York: Simon & Schuster, 1970).
6. *Isogesis* is from the Reverend Canon Dr. William A. Johnson at the Institute of Theology, New York City.
7. "Cronkite Calls for 'Truth in Packaging' for TV Journalism," *Broadcasting*, September 21, 1981.
8. According to a 1984 survey conducted by Frank N. Magid Associates, reported in "Magid Study Stirs Things Up," *Broadcasting*, October 29, 1984.
9. Ben Wattenberg, *The Good News Is the Bad News Is Wrong* (New York: Simon and Schuster, 1984).
10. Robert L. Hilliard, *Writing for Television and Radio* (New York: Hastings House, 1976), p. 134.
11. Charles Ruas, quoted in Jonathan Cott, "A Few Words with Norman, Truman, and Gore," *New York Times Book Review*, January 13, 1985, p. 14.
12. See "What's on a 6-Year-Old's Mind? TV Shows, TV Ads, TV Stars," *Wall*

Street Journal, January 16, 1985, where it notes that children are ignornant of civil government, but keenly aware of television.

13. Sidney Smith, quoted in Flesch, *Art of Readable Writing*, p. 139.

CHAPTER 7

1. Robert W. Morse, *The TV Report* (New York: Regional Religious Educational Coordinators of the Episcopal Church, 1978). See Jean Piaget, *The Origins of Intelligence in Children*, trans. Margaret Cook. (New York: W. W. Norton, 1963); and David Elkind, *Children and Adolescents: Interpretive Essays on Jean Piaget* (New York: Oxford University Press, 1970).
2. Ibid., p. 8.
3. David Littlejohn, "Communicating Ideas by Television," in *Television as a Social Force* (Praeger, 1975), p. 72.
4. Jerry Mander, quoted in Morse, *TV Report*, "TV's Capture of the Mind," *Mother Jones*, January 1978, p. 60.
5. Ibid.
6. Morse, *TV Report*, p. 82.
7. Ibid., p. 100.
8. See Lawrence Kohlberg, "Stage and Sequence: The Cognitive-Development Approach to Socialization," *Handbook of Socialization and Research* (New York: Rand McNally, 1969), p. 391.
9. Morse, *TV Report*, p. 107.
10. John Rosemond, "Pre-schoolers Who Watch TV Show Symptoms of Learning Disabilities," *Atlanta Constitution*, November 16, 1983.
11. Ibid., p. 114, 116.
12. See Laurel Leff, "TV Comes to Town; Fads and New Wants Come Along with It," *Wall Street Journal*, October 2, 1979.

CHAPTER 8

Paul Klein is a television producer and former vice president at NBC who frequently holds forth on the power of television. This quote comes from his talk with Focus (Fellowship of Christians in Universities and Schools) students on March 17, 1980.

1. A. C. Neilsen Company.
2. A. E. Siegel, "Television Violence: Recent Research on its Effects," *Television Awareness Training: The Viewer's Guide* (New York, 1980).
3. David Pearl, chief of the Behavioral Sciences Branch of Extramural Research Programs at the National Institute of Mental Health (NIMH), quoted in "Under the Gun: Hill Examines TV Violence," *Broadcasting*, October 29, 1984, p. 33.
4. See "Violent Films Linked to Sexual Assault," Sentinel Wire Service, Madison, Wisc. (1984).

326 / NOTES

5. Mary Magee, "Notes on the Significance of Crime Statistics," in *On Television* (New York, 1980).
6. Charlotte Johnson, "Reel-Life Mayhem vs. Real-Life Madmen," *Atlanta Journal*, April 2, 1981.
7. Gerbner, "Television as Religion".
8. Ibid.
9. Robert E. A. Lee, "Why Don't People in Movies Ever Pray?" *Media & Values*, Fall 1981, p. 4.
10. Benjamin J. Stein, "TV: A Religious Wasteland," *Wall Street Journal*, January 9, 1985, p. 24.
11. See "FCC Finds First Fairness Violation Since Fowler," *Broadcasting*, October 29, 1984, p. 34.
12. *Talking Back: Public Media Center's Guide to Broadcasting and the Fairness Doctrine for People Who Are Mad as Hell and Aren't Going to Take It Any More* (San Francisco: The Public Media Center, 1983). Note that this book is not Christian and has some references and perspectives that may shock you; it is a good guide to your rights, however.
13. A great introduction to scripting is Robert L. Hilliard's *Writing for Television and Radio* (New York: Hastings House, 1976).

CHAPTER 9

1. Hilliard, *Writing for Television and Radio*, pp. 14, 15.
2. *Broadcasting*, December 17, 1984, p. 94.
3. "Reagan Bringing Radio Back as a Political Tool," *Broadcasting*, October 29, 1984, p. 62.

CHAPTER 10

1. Rt. Rev. John Seville Higgens, "Ten Commandments for Preachers," *The Living Church*, January 13, 1985, p. 11.
2. E. H. Sturtevant, quoted in Flesch, *Art of Readable Writing*, p. 81.
3. William Safire, "On Language," *New York Times Magazine*, February 10, 1985, p. 10.
4. John Tagg, "Understanding Mario Cuomo," *National Review* February 8, 1985, pp. 15 ff.
5. Hans-Ruedi Weber, "Liberating the Bible from Print," *Media Development*, March 1982, p. 6.
6. Joe Baltake, "Jeff Bridges Had No Models to Follow for 'Starman' Role," *Atlanta Journal & Atlanta Constitution*, February 10, 1985.
7. William Safire, "Ringing Rhetoric: The Return of Political Oratory," *New York Times Magazine*, August 19, 1984, p. 15.
8. John Tagg, "Understanding Mario Cuomo," *National Review*, February 8, 1985, p. 85.
9. Weber, *Liberating the Bible from Print*, p. 7.

CHAPTER 11

1. Richard Kirby, "Will the Computer Replace God?" *St. Andrew's Cross*, Winter 1983, p. 3.
2. *New York Times*, according to the National Sisters Communications Service notice entitled "A Major New Resource on Newsletters."
3. David Lambuth, The Golden Book on Writing (New York: Viking, 1964), pp. 4–5.
4. *Direct Response Mail Research Reports* tested under the supervision of Intermarket Marketing & Development, P.O. Box 225, Dayton, OH 45401, in cooperation with Cover & Text Paper Group, American Paper Institute.

CHAPTER 12

1. Robert Price,"Running on the Record," *New York Times*, February 17, 1985.
2. Michael Sragrow, "Raiders of the Lost Ark," *Rolling Stone*, June 25, 1981, p. 22.

Index

DATE DUE			
DEC 14 '88			

DEMCO 38-297